ROBERT PINGET

Robert Pinget
COURTESY PHOTO PIC, PARIS

ROBERT PINGET

THE NOVEL AS QUEST

Robert M. Henkels, Jr.

331539

THE UNIVERSITY OF ALABAMA PRESS
University, Alabama

This book is dedicated to Professor Reinhard Kuhn, who cajoled it into being through his Pingetian talent for asking leading questions.

Permission to quote from Pinget's published works, as cited specifically in the Notes and the Bibliography, has been granted by Les Editions de Minuit, Calder & Boyars, The Red Dust Press, and Grove Press, and is herewith gratefully acknowledged. (See note 5, pages 228–29.) Permission to quote from Tony Duvert's brilliant essay "La Parole et la fiction," *Critique*, 252 (May, 1968), is also gratefully acknowledged.

Thanks are also extended to Emory University for a Faculty Research Grant covering final bibliographical work in the preparation of the manuscript; to Dr. Esteban R. Egea for his collaboration in establishing a computerized concordance of *Fable;* to M. Jérôme Lindon of Les Editions de Minuit for giving me access to the files of his publishing house; to Sydney L. Eaton and F. P. Squibb for their able editorial assistance; to Professor Richard Kinkade for his helpful advice in diverse matters both arcane and pragmatic; to my wife for her invaluable patience and support; and finally to Robert Pinget himself for his generous cooperation and encouragement.

Illustrations not otherwise credited are by Robert Pinget.

Library of Congress Cataloging in Publication Data

Henkels, Robert M
   Robert Pinget.

   Bibliography: p.
   Includes index.
   1. Pinget, Robert—Criticism and interpretation.
PQ2631.I638Z67   843'.9'14   74–2815
ISBN 0–8173–7233–3

Copyright © 1979 by
The University of Alabama Press
ALL RIGHTS RESERVED
Manufactured in the United States of America

CONTENTS

ANTIPREFACE vii

INTRODUCTION 1

PART ONE: SURREALISTIC HOUSE-RAZING 9

1. AN INVENTORY OF INVENTION. *Between Fantoine and Agapa (Entre Fantoine et Agapa,* 1951), *Mahu or the Material (Mahu ou le matériau,* 1952), *The Fox and the Compass (Le Renard et la boussole,* 1955). 11

2. OUTER LIMITS—INNER LIMITS. *Graal Flibuste* (1956) and *Baga* (1958). 36

PART TWO: TWISTING MYSTERY'S TALE 65

3. FROM QUEST TO INQUEST. *Monsieur Levert (Le Fiston,* 1959) and *Clope to the Dossier (Clope au dossier,* 1961). 67

4. THE LUMBER ROOM OF MEMORY. *The Inquisitory (L'Inquisitoire,* 1962) and *Someone (Quelqu'un,* 1965). 98

PART THREE: APPROACHING SILENCE 121

5. WORDS ON STAGE. *Pinget's Theater.* 123

6. LIVING VOICES. *The Libera Me Domine (Le Libera,* 1967) and *Recurring Melody (Passacaille,* 1969). 143

7. FABULAE FABULARUM. *Fable* (1971) and *This Voice (Cette Voix,* 1975). 172

PART FOUR: TAKING STOCK 191

8. PINGET, BECKETT, ROBBE-GRILLET. 193

9. CONCLUSION 219

AFTERWORD. *Dictation (La Dictée), The Month of August (Le Mois d'Août), The Man Who Got Away (Le Réscapé).* 224

NOTES 227

BIBLIOGRAPHY 248

INDEX 268

ANTIPREFACE

For good cause, critics have labelled Robert Pinget an "antinovelist." He delights in popping the many strings of clichés about writers and writing that hang in the air like so many limp balloons. His harlequinesque narrators turn the conventions of the traditional novel inside out and cavort in them, to the readers' amusement and alarm. Pinget refused politely when first asked to contribute a preface to this introduction to his novels. Later, he suggested that the letter of refusal itself might give a more informative commentary on his attitude toward his work than a commonplace preface. Here, then, is an antipreface, written by an antinovelist, a statement that sets in bold relief some of the author's subconscious sources and his desire to let his work speak for itself.

Paris
February 25, 1974

Dear Rip:

    Congratulations on your success. . . . You must be very happy that so much work is rewarded at last. I admire your tenacity and hope the busy summer you foresee doesn't tire you too much. You've got to take it a little easy, after all.

    As regards a preface to your work by me, it does not seem to me to be a good idea. Perhaps for the principle of the thing, but especially since I am very awkward at that kind of exercise. What is there to say, anyway, that you shouldn't say yourself? You have already paid me an unexpected honor in grappling with my work, which I do not always understand very well, as you know. That kind of psychoanalysis, in the long run, which I undertook unwillingly to end up with *Passacaille*, gives me reason today not to be proud of myself, I assure you. No desire to pour myself out over my lucubrations . . .

    No travel plans at this point. So we will get together in Europe next January. Take care.

Cordially, *Robert Pinget*

ROBERT PINGET

Introduction

> I have births to burn. There's no other way I can explain these ideas coming to me pell-mell about my first years. I have millions of them, all contradictory and about the origins in general of things known and unknown, that is poetry.
>
> —PINGET, *The Fox and the Compass*

> When you begin a story, the best thing to do is to say I was born, it's the best way to set out, for the older you get the more numerous your childhoods become, they multiply and there you already have a cause of confusion.
>
> —PINGET, *Mahu or the Material*

> I am a King. Yes a King. I am the King of me.
>
> —PINGET, *Baga*

One fine morning King Architruc, the narrator-hero of Pinget's *Baga*, awakens in the bedchamber of his shabby castle. He yawns, clambers out of bed, and makes his way to the mirror. What he sees looking back at him is less than awe-inspiring.

> I have a large, pimply head. Some bumps, a little acne. My lashes fall into my eyes, my nose is like a potato, and my ears like two cabbage leaves. The hair is light reddish. The teeth two in number. The neck fat and white, the breasts droopy, held up under the arms by yellow unkempt hair. I have three hairs on my sternum, which I shave on Saturday. My abdomen is swollen from the stomach on down. Formerly I used to pull it in like everyone else. I don't anymore. I can only see my sex if I lean over. The surprise isn't exactly overpowering.[1]

After running through a somewhat perfunctory toilette, Architruc ("Mr. Thingamajig") pads off to water his house plants, to listen to a wheezing performance of chamber music by the court ensemble, and eventually to set down for posterity a series of outrageous adventures featuring himself as their hero.

So much for serious autobiography in Robert Pinget's novels! In Architruc's self-denigrating observations we hardly have a faithfully realistic portrait of the artist. The clear-eyed novelist and the woebegotten "king" of shreds and patches do not resemble each other physically or intellectually. The association between them remains as tenuous as Architruc's "royalty." For Architruc is a self-proclaimed monarch and the reader never learns whether or not he is merely a pretender. His nameless kingdom encompasses a rat-infested valley somewhere within the imaginary province of Pinget's fiction bounded by the towns of Fantoine and Agapa. As Olivier de Magny wondered, rhetorically:

> What does this snotty king . . . incarnate except the parody of all royalty? Does he not pulverize [everything] joyously right down to his own credibility? Does he assert himself in any other way than in asserting, in the same motion, the impossibility of his being, thus joining willy-nilly the terrible creatures of Samuel Beckett?[2]

By the same token, in comparing the faces of the author and his character, the features of each cancel out the other, leaving only the words. Here and elsewhere, Pinget casts netlike hypotheses at elusive targets in his quest for certainty. The past, the self, death, all slip from the loops of words intended to encircle them. The novelist's quest continues nonetheless, and the landscape of Pinget's imaginary domain becomes increasingly familiar from one book to the next. But his kingdom remains explicitly and self-consciously fictional, severed from the illusion of autobiographical verisimilitude by extensive use of fantasy and whimsy. The key to the kingdom of this writer's writer will therefore be found not in Pinget's biography but in his work, in the record of the joy and anguish of a novelist filling the blank page in a frustrated search for unity. Even so, a few selected pieces of biographical data may help to establish a line of demarcation between the author and the characters he has created, and to clarify the purpose of this introductory study of his fiction to date.

Robert Pinget was born in Geneva, Switzerland, in 1919, and was educated there in the law. After receiving his degree, he moved to Paris in 1946, where he studied painting and had a one-man show that was well received by the critics. However, Pinget proved to be as little committed to painting as a career as he was to the law. Gradually he discovered that his real interest was in writing. Pinget did not make the transition from one form of self expression to another overnight. His drawing talent spilled over as doodles and designs in the margins of his manuscripts displayed at the French pavillion of the Montreal World's Fair in 1967, and in due course he would make use of his legal training, giving his longest novel (to date) the format of a preliminary hearing. The frequency with which artist characters appear in his first books reveals the writer's interest in the painter he might have become. Furthermore, he came to writing only after trying his hand at a number of professions. He tried journalism for a time, but soon abandoned it. Working as an interior decorator, he developed the sensitivity to detail in the arrangement of rooms that would subsequently flourish in descriptive passages in his writings. He visited Yugoslavia and Israel, gathering impressions that would surface in *The Fox and the Compass (Le Renard et la boussole)*. He taught a variety of subjects at a secondary school near London, learning English while keeping a chapter ahead of his students. All this time, he was accumulating material that he would later juggle adroitly in his restless, kaleidoscopic narratives.

The first book that Pinget wrote was also the first to appear in print: no manuscripts lay mouldering in drawers for *this* author (in striking contrast to the manuscripts of his narrator-protagonists). *Between Fantoine and Agapa (Entre Fantoine et Agapa)* appeared in 1953 under the imprint of a provincial press. Its publication came about through a combination of chance and authorial enterprise. No established house being willing to take a risk on an unknown name, Pinget sent the manuscript of *Between Fantoine and Agapa* to *Les Editions du Feu*, a provincial literary review at Jarnac. The editorial board liked the work, and when the author agreed to finance publication costs himself, arrangements were made forthwith to bring out the collection of stories as a separate volume.

Albert Camus read Pinget's second book in manuscript when *The Fox and the Compass (Le Renard et la boussole)* was submitted to Gallimard for consideration. Camus' reaction was enthusiastic to the point of his suggesting that the book be entered for one of France's prestigious annual literary awards. Pinget had difficulty finding a publisher. His prankish stylistic tricks and surrealistic stance made editors leery and readers uneasy. Fortunately, Alain Robbe-Grillet was less cautious. He spoke favorably of *The Fox and the Compass (Le Renard et la Boussole)*, brought out by Gallimard, to his editor. And Pinget's next novel was accepted by Les Editions de Minuit. That same publishing house has handled all of Pinget's subsequent output, and has also reprinted and reissued Pinget's first three books, with a certain number of textual variations. The reprinted version of *Between Fantoine and Agapa*, for example, has been cut somewhat. The changes in the text of *Graal Flibuste* in the definitive 1966 edition restore short segments of this work that Pinget had reluctantly deleted before its first publication. The acceptance of *Graal Flibuste* by Jérôme Lindon of Les Editions de Minuit established a fruitful and continuing working relationship between an experimental novelist and an editor unafraid of innovation. Indeed, it is entirely appropriate that Pinget's work should bear the colors of Les Editions de Minuit, the underground press, founded during the Resistance, that befriended the most daring avant-garde novelists after World War II. Pinget is unstintingly grateful for the encouragement he has received from his editor, Jérôme Lindon (as am I for the assistance of his staff in making material available to me for this study), and the first small but provocative volume has been followed by twelve novels or *"récits"* and eight dramatic works in the years from 1951 through 1975.[3]

Despite the prolific, innovative flow of fiction from Pinget's pen, his work has been slow to capture the attention of a large reading public and even now is unlikely to make best-seller charts. In retrospect, the reasons for this cool reception seem obvious. The brevity and the fanciful tone of *Between Fantoine and Agapa* and *The Fox and the Compass* put some readers off. An atmosphere of practical jokery lingered over Pinget's world and the public was reluctant to be taken in. Strangely enough, British readers seemed to like the early experiments of Pinget and his fellow innovators better than most French critics, a flattering but frustrating experience for a beginning novelist. Pinget remains popular in the British Isles today and almost all of his books are available in translation in Great Britain.[4] Several editions or translations of Pinget's work have already been made available in America, and more are on the way. For those who can read him in his native language, Pinget's one act play *L'Hy-*

pothèse is included with a short introduction, notes and discussion questions in volume two of the *Panorama du Théâtre*, edited by Professors Kuhn and Benay. As for English translations, *Monsieur Levert (Le Fiston)*, *The Inquisitory (L'Inquisitoire)* and a volume containing three plays have already appeared in the United States, and *The Libera Me Domine (Le Libera)* was slated for publication in 1977.[5] The Ford Foundation sponsored a visit by Pinget to the United States. The British Broadcasting System and Radio Stuttgart have performed his radio plays. And the novels have been translated into eleven languages (German, English, Danish, Hungarian, Italian, Dutch, Portuguese, Rumanian, Swedish, Czechoslovakian, and Serbo-Croatian). Nevertheless, piqued by the paradox of his popularity abroad and the reserve shown his work at home, Pinget once exlaimed in understandable annoyance:

> In France we don't count, we're just useless bores. But who represents French literature abroad today? Why do radio and television stations and theaters produce our work in Frankfort, Stuttgart, and London? Why are we received like poets in Argentina or America and shunted aside here?[6]

Happily, the disproportion between the responses of French and foreign critics subsequently diminished. Two of Pinget's later works, *The Inquisitory (L'Inquisitoire)* and *Someone (Quelqu'un)*, received, respectively, the Prix des Critiques (1963) and the Prix Femina (1965), and these awards stirred up a considerable interest in the narratives that had preceded them. The French government, through the Centre National des Lettres, honored Pinget by awarding him a one-year sabbatical stipend for 1975-76. Only three or four such national awards are granted each year for the purpose of encouraging the most promising French novelists, poets, and critics to advance their work free of financial worry.

Obviously, it is too early to predict what contours Pinget's *"oeuvre"* will ultimately assume; the man is very much alive and is probably at his desk writing feverishly at this very moment. But it is evident, based on what Pinget has published so far, that his fiction has evolved from book to book, as an elaborate, tongue-in-cheek saga, as a mock-chronicle that thumbs its nose at chronology and relates the helterskelter life of an imaginary *world*—albeit one whose elements are, as yet, only loosely interconnected, so far as one can tell.

Unfortunately, most of what has been written about Pinget and his work to date has been of a fragmentary nature. This is quite understandable, especially as it applies to reviews of his earlier works as they appeared. There is now a serious need, however, for a somewhat more comprehensive approach to all of Pinget's published work to date. The present study, which takes as its point of departure not only Pinget's works but also perceptive articles about them by such critics as Olivier de Magny, Jean-Luc Seylaz, Stephan Bann, Tony Duvert, Jean Roudaut, Jean-Claude Lieber, Jacques Lanotte, Philippe Boyer, and others, is offered as a general introduction to Pinget's writings from 1953 through 1975. It is designed to encourage the reader to pluck up his or her courage and to set out on a double voyage of discovery—to stow the baggage of preconceived ideas and push on in a search for something unavailable in one's daily life and one's normal surroundings.

The voyage that Pinget proposes has nothing in common with an escapist drug "trip"—except, perhaps, the whiff of danger, the pleasure or the pain (and maybe both) of the experience itself, and the distinct possibility that one may never see the world in quite the same way as before. Pinget makes his companions painfully aware of the evolving quest of the writer seeking suitable forms and techniques with which to express his changing vision of things. The present study will concentrate on the novel as a continuing "quest," one that both destroys and creates itself, because Pinget himself repeats that figure most frequently. But any far-ranging study of this author must also explore his growing interest in the sonorities of spoken language, for Pinget has clearly moved further and further in that direction. In a 1962 interview Pinget replied to the impossible question "What are you trying to do?" as follows:

> What am I trying to do? To translate into the language of today the problems of today. The thought of man is in his language.

In the final analysis, words—their sound associations and nuances

—are the very stuff of which Pinget's *world* is made. However imperfect as a vehicle for discovery language may be, man becomes conscious of himself and his surroundings through it, filtering his sense impressions through language as light is filtered through a lens. In this sense we are all deeply involved in and bound by language. Like Pinget's "characters" (if one can so designate them), all men are seekers in an endless quest—beings in a state of becoming, voices seeking the precise tones that will express their essence. In Pinget's fiction, the link between the creation of personality and the continuous verbal process in which words encircle and envelop without defining anything precisely takes on a hilarious and unsettling reality.

Taking literally Pinget's statement that the thought of man is in his language, we will begin by examining how the theme and configuration of the quest shape his fiction's forms. The attempt to see Pinget's work as a whole will include a chronological account of the stages in the continuing quest that strings itself out as a long, unresolved inquiry. The novels can be divided into periods, or stages, if one accepts a certain arbitrariness for the sake of clarity. Seen from the point of view of the evolution of narrative form, Pinget's fiction moves from surrealistic parodies, to the format of open-ended investigation, and finally to verbal arabesques of permutation and combination. From the point of view of rhetorical devices and content, his fiction falls into three cycles, the first mystical, the second realistic, and the third mythological.[7] Nomenclature aside, the books can also be grouped by affinities, and that is why they can be perceived as episodes in an ongoing search.

Finally, our tour of Pinget's maze will conclude with a brief comparison of his "quest" and the works of two of his fellow experimenters, Alain Robbe-Grillet and Samuel Beckett.

As I have said, this work is "introductory" in nature, and it will have served its principal purpose only if it leads its readers to become friends of its subject: the bewitching writings of Robert Pinget *in their entirety*. And the more intimate the friendships that may develop, the better.

part one

Surrealistic House-Razing

1 An Inventory of Invention

Between Fantoine and Agapa (Entre Fantoine et Agapa), Mahu or the Material (Mahu ou le Matériau), The Fox and the Compass (Le Renard et la Boussole)

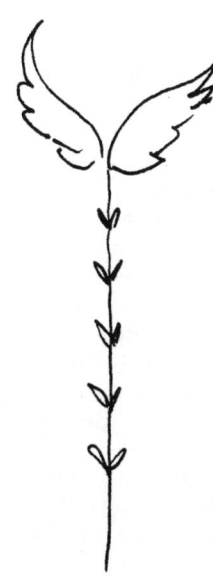

> One of McLuhan's insistent themes has been that the electric age has heightened our perception of structure by disrupting what he calls the lineality of information flow. We are not so ABCDE-minded as before, not so sequential and compartmentalized. As McLuhan puts it, contemporary forms of communication require very little story line. The films of Fellini, Resnais, and Bergman are largely devoid of "plots." . . .
>
> McLuhan contends that, without the distraction of a story line, we get a very high degree of participation and involvement in the forms of communication, which is another way of saying the processes of learning. One has to work hard, and one wants to, at discovering patterns and assigning meanings to one's experiences. The focus of intellectual energy becomes the active investigation of structures and relationships, rather than the passive reception of someone else's story.—Postman and Weingartner, *Teaching as a Subversive Activity*.

When Pinget's first books slipped into the stream of French letters in 1952 they caused hardly a ripple. The young apprentice teacher, writing feverishly near London, may have been disconcerted by the lack of popular recognition, but the initially guarded reaction to his work is understandable, given the preoccupations and literary fashions of the day. Sartrean existentialism was all the rage and political "engagement" was expected of budding novelists. Pinget's work was unfashionably and stubbornly apolitical. He refused then, as he has refused since, to preach, to teach, or to campaign for any alleged commonweal. Nor has he altered his early Merry Andrew manner to please sober-sided editors or to follow fashion. Yet, though Pinget's stance as a private man was out of authorial fashion, like the existentialists he, too, was aiming to unsettle his readers' complacent acceptance of outmoded reflexes of thought and expression. Actually, for all their "revolutionary" ideas, existentialist writers tampered precious little (if at all) with literary conventions per se. Pinget struck out in an entirely different direction by concerning himself with words and the void behind them, rather than with conventional themes or plots. Like the early surrealists, Pinget proceeds on the assumption that the most radical change in human behavior comes about through altering patterns of perception, not ideologies or institutions. As Tony Duvert pointed out in his masterful study of Pinget's basic approach:

> A theme, a meaning, animates this voyage into uncertainty. A simple thesis, repeated and constant in Pinget's work, it is stated flatly, a "moral" not to be discussed, along the lines that, life begins, plays itself out and ends badly, to which one can add a strong feeling that nothing is sayable. The interesting aspect of this theme is certainly not philosophical, but aesthetic. It participates, with the bitterness it gives rise to, in the narrative "tone." It is the fundamental source of the metamorphic word, of the sweet and sour humor, of the brief outburst of violence; it designates the point of view of the narrator who is tossed about in the absurd, not an existentialist absurd, but that aggressively funny absurd, near nonsense, which seeks him out, accuses him, and makes him ridiculous. So what I [have] called a "thesis" in the loosest sense of the word, is not the core of the book, but the ground from which it grows.[1]

Pinget began by writing feathery, moonstruck, verbal fantasies as different from the muscular prose of Sartre as Rabelais is different from John Calvin. In the fifties, Pinget may have seemed a light-fingered Harlequin, but his desire to blow conventionalized wisdom sky-high was nonetheless genuine. His preliminary romps through the dictionary follow a carefully thought-out plan for upsetting the expected. For Pinget centers on language as the prime candidate for radical change, realizing from the beginning that the avenue between speech and perception works both ways and that, as Berill remarked in *Man's Emerging Mind*:

> Every language conceals within its structure a vast array of unconscious assumptions about life and the universe, all that you take for granted and everything that seems to make common sense—the long forgotten history of thought itself, still coercing the living to

think along the old established ways. Speech itself imprisons us, although in different ways, and each kind expresses a different view. What is sense to you may be nonsense to another, or the other way round. Each sees but a part, yet it is our natural purpose to see the whole . . . [2]

Pinget's early books make stimulating, if difficult, fare because of the originality of both what he says and the way in which he says it. Both his substance and his style reflect, in terms of the narrative, the atmosphere of discovery and doubt that Einstein's relativity theory has left as a legacy. In Pinget's world, nothing is nailed down. Everything and everybody is in an endless process of becoming. The rationalistic assumption that man understands reality and can communicate his knowledge in comprehensible language is therefore systematically called into question. For Pinget, the anchors that kept the craft of the novel in calm waters, such as belief in an anthropomorphic Creator, the power of reason, and the validity of aesthetic standards, no longer hold. He expresses the skepticism and disarray of the times through the content of his novels by accumulating mutually exclusive options between which the reader is forced to choose. The relativistic chaos of Pinget's world resembles the fluidic models of reality proposed by contemporary physicists and linguists.[3]

Pinget experiments with dislocated narrative forms in order to set his narrators' words in collision. The novels' bizarre structures run contrary to the reader's expectations so that both content and form express the kaleidoscopic mental world of the times in arresting and ingenious ways. His first published book, written when he was thirty-four, *Entre Fantoine et Agapa* (1953), is a colorful addition to the literature of imagination and nonsense. As in Cyrano de Bergerac's fantastic voyages and the experiments of André Breton, the author revels in parody and invention, ridiculing constraint and enlarging the scope of verbal expression. The text, divided into two parts, freewheels through some twenty surrealistic flights of fancy and an enigmatic journal. On first reading, the parts of the book seem to be related neither to each other nor to the whole. Because of the lack of narrative connection, the author appears to be writing to and for himself, chuckling over a particularly intricate play on words, or perhaps trying to exorcise fears inexpressible any other way. The disturbing initial impression of chaos gradually gives way, however, to an appreciation of the book's underlying unity. Pinget uses the fanciful fragments of part one as verbal setting-up exercises. The non sequitur entries in the journal (part two), form nonlinear episodes in a continuing quest, the writer's continuing adventures with words, their relation to him and the world.

With malicious gusto, Pinget assumes the role of both judge and defendant in this rollicking verbal trial. The title refers to the description of two small towns, so he first poses as a Balzacian omniscient author, scuttling about, presenting an imaginary world. The matter-of-fact opening sentences sound flat at first, recalling the tired spiel of a tourist guide, but within half a paragraph the jaded cicerone turns into a circus barker, and the circus barker, a spangled word-juggler, daring a translator to take him on.[4]

> Le curé de Fantoine est un amateur. Il n'a pas la bosse de Dieu. Il s'ennuie. Il est abonné à des revues de théâtre. Il lisote les auteurs à la mode. Il grapille dans les vignes savantes. Il passe pour un érudit mais il est un faquin.[5]

> The curate of Fantoine is an amateur. He's not very good at God. He's bored. He subscribes to theater magazines. He glances through authors in vogue. He gleans in erudite vineyards. He passes for a scholar, but he is a fraud.

In this passage, as throughout the book, Pinget's simple syntax builds a platform for acrobatic leaps from the real to the imaginary, the everyday to the unexpected. In transition from eye to mind, and from mind to page, the "*curé*" somehow becomes confused with the steeple of his church, "*le clocher.*"

> Le clocher est du neuvième siècle. Il a beaucoup d'allure. Dommage qu'il se promène la nuit. Il ne sait pas lire. Il visite l'église, le village, les alentours. On s'habitue à son humeur.[6]

> The belfry is from the ninth century. It is most attractive. Too bad he walks about at night. He can't read. He visits the church, the village, the surrounding area. You get used to his moods.

AN INVENTORY OF INVENTION

As in most of the overlapping identities in *Between Fantoine and Agapa (Entre Fantoine et Agapa)*, a thread of traceable association lurks below the surface. The text shifts from the subject of a modern priest's reading habits to an allusion to illiteracy in the ninth century. Perhaps the substitution of a building for a man is remotely explainable. Priests are in short supply in rural France and a curate is often obliged to serve several parishes in the diocese, giving rise to much movement to and fro.

But it is soon obvious that the author's imaginary province, like his prose, runs on a jerry-built illogic all its own—that Pinget contrasts the freedom of association of his images and the linear thrust of his sentence rhythms, juxtaposing and scrambling levels of language in fresh and unexpected combinations. Like Lewis Carroll's Humpty Dumpty, Pinget elects to profit from the suggestive power of language and syntax to the fullest.

> "When I use a word," Humpty Dumpty said, in a rather scornful tone, "it means just what I choose it to mean—neither more nor less."
> "The question is," said Alice, "whether you *can* make words mean so many different things."
> "The question is," said Humpty Dumpty, "which is to be master—that's all."[7]

There is no question of who is master in *Between Fantoine and Agapa*. In a flash, figures of speech become characters. People turn into animals and things turn into people. Our companion in this eccentric adjunct to the expected guides us with increasing arbitrariness. Pinget continues to jolt habitual patterns of perception and disorients the reader to the point where it becomes necessary for him to try to get his bearings. He finds that Pinget has placed him in a zone where the real and the fanciful mingle. Lost between two imaginary towns, the reader is at No Place, in the kingdom of Nonsense, in a realm into which he has been led with gentle authority and one that acquires a unique vitality and identity.

Pinget provides no conventional narrative framework. As he comments indirectly on his aims, the method of his verbal madness comes to the fore. A passage from the fragment *"Le Perroquet"* (*"The Parrot"*), is particularly revealing:

> A magazine was pursuing an investigation on the birth of dialogue. The author of the articles showed tendentiously that dialogue was a bastardized form of monologue. He insisted on the degenerate character [of it]. "Doesn't a monologue, under its most abstract aspect of 'reflexion to oneself' have all the creative power of spontaneity?" he said. "When you talk to yourself affirmations and rejoinders have the very freedom and vigor that the intrusion of an interlocutor makes immediately anemic."[8]

The prose of *Between Fantoine and Agapa* is marked by a complete freedom of association. It simply enumerates, suggests, and describes; there is no attempt to explain anything or to convince the reader of anything.

Pinget delights in multiplying ambiguous effects and in twisting phrases into unexpected shapes. In the passage describing the steeple at Fantoine, for example, the reader is inclined to substitute *"cocher"* ("coachman") for *"clocher"* ("steeple"), thinking that there has perhaps been a misprint. But the resulting sentence is no more satisfying than the original. The author plays with both words in order to create a polyvalent context in which neither of them makes conventional sense. *Between Fantoine and Agapa* revives the long-dormant tradition of polysemous writing, and Pinget is clearly a polysemous writer, drawn to verbal signs with multiple meanings. Indeed, a thorough stylistic study of the author of *Between Fantoine and Agapa* would require the talents of a scribe both learned in the art of glossing complex tropes and willing to smudge the end of his nose on pages of black ink in order to get to the level where the real action is taking place. Yet, as Pinget writes, "Language is what you have to take as is." Naming things and forming sentences are acts of exploration. The narrators use words to sort out a multilayered reality that bewilders and frightens them, to discover a unity in it. The attempt is never, and can never be, completely successful. Such apparently innocuous verbal vices as jargon and circumlocution shatter the illusion that words form an adequate pattern for ordering reality. Words simply fail to play dead. Bursting out of any frame that attempts to limit them to a single value, they let in chaotic diversity and pratfall surprises.

When a husband and wife spread their picnic provisions under a sign reading *"Interdiction d'impétrer l'alopécie"* ("Interdiction to Penetrate the Alyopecia"), the man rushes to their dictionary to decipher the warning:

> *Interdiction*, on sait ce que ça veut dire. *Impétrer*, c'est mis: "Obtenir des pouvoirs publics." *Alopécie:* "Chute ou absence totale ou partielle des cheveux, des sourcils etc." C'est déjà plus compliqué. Je suis un peu chauve mais pas tout à fait. Ça me concerne-t-il? Ma femme a redemandé à l'aubergiste si elle connaissait l'interdiction. L'aubergiste a fait "chut" avec son doigt. On n'a pas insisté parce qu'on se rendait compte qu'on gênait. Il y avait du remue-ménage dans l'auberge. La grand'mère s'était intoxiquée. La veille, elle avait uriné dans le pot de confitures sur sa table de nuit en croyant que c'était l'autre. A l'heure du goûter on lui avait donné le pot de confitures sans faire attention et elle avait tout avalé.[9]

> *Interdiction*, we know what that means. *To Impetrate*, it says "to obtain from civil authorities." *Aleopecia*, "shedding or absence, total or partial, of hair, eyebrows etc." That only makes things more confusing. I'm a little bald, but not completely. Does that mean me? My wife asked the innkeeper again if she knew about the interdiction. The innkeeper made a sign to "shhh" with her finger. We didn't insist since we realized we were causing embarrassment. There was quite a stir in the inn. The grandmother had gotten intoxicated. The night before, she had urinated in the jam pot on the night table thinking it was the other one. They had given her the jam pot at tea-time without noticing and she had gulped it down.

Puzzled, the travelers return home with their child.

> Au milieu de la nuit, le gosse s'est réveillé et il a vomi de la confiture. Ma femme n'y comprenait rien. Elle se faisait des cheveux. Mais pas longtemps parce qu'une demi-heure après, elle était chauve comme un genou.[10]

> In the middle of the night, the kid woke up and he spit up jam. My wife couldn't figure it out. She started getting gray hairs over it. But not for long because a half-hour later, she was bald as a billiard ball.

Through his satire of officialese, Pinget suggests that the public domain of speech provides treacherous terrain for sleeping. The use of two popular expressions, *"se faire des cheveux"* ("to get gray hairs") and *"être chauve comme un genou"* ("to go as bald as a billiard ball"), the first metaphorically, and the second as a simile, produces a sentence that is illogical at the functional level and absurd on the analytical level. So language thumbs its rubbery clown's nose at the restrictive ideal of dictionary definitions.

Experimenting with the suggestive sonorities of language need not be disagreeably disturbing. In Pinget's hands it gives the sensation of expanding perspectives, as well as sounding the void that words fail to cover. In the following excerpt, liberating laughter is aroused when Pinget combines the slang meaning of *"concombre,"* often used to describe a fool, and the cucumber's suggestively protuberant appearance.

> Once there was a young cucumber, but was he ever unlikeable! He used to tan himself. He turned orange-colored; first one on the beach, last to leave. He would distend his provocative peduncule with his eyes half closed. The cucumbresses were crazy about him. . . .

The cucumber's popular success triggers a cucumber fad. Children play vulgar games with them. The curate preaches on the word's origins. The forces of righteousness arise in wrath.

> But do you think the guilty one, the first one on the beach, was bothered? Not at all. They let him do his lewd tricks in the sun the whole season. It is therefore probable that he will start all over again next summer.[11]

Throughout these fragments, openness of expression and freedom of association sustain several images and interpretations. Pinget keeps operative the notions of the cucumber as a vegetable, as a sex organ, and, as the suggestive slang expression, *"un con tout court"* ("an ass"). He uses the nonsense tale to open the lens of language to simultaneous, ambiguous, and unexpected impressions. What Pinget is actually describing remains confusing and disjointed. Each element runs to a fanciful blind-alley or reveals a fresh configuration in a dazzling kaleidoscope. The diary with which the book ends heightens the impression of incompleteness to the point of oppressiveness. Its terse, disconnected entries, covering a span in time from November to September, are evenly spaced and in chronological order. Pinget sustains the surrealistic tone, adding a pseudosociological element by means of descriptions of the sports, weather, landscape, vegetation, music, burial customs, and health practices of the host country.

Skipping from subject to subject, the narrator refrains from either drawing conclusions from his observations or synthesizing them. The language wanders off on digressions in which technical terms stammer and slip into gibberish and eventually lapse into silence, an equation of silence and death that will eventually become a major theme.

> Lose a contour, or a segment, or a whole side of the body, and the hachured surface diminishes by as much, the armpits are no longer included in it. You stroll about with holes, carrying your charcoal silhouette in your satchel. The cheek frees itself from control. The jaw, conspicuous, is not sitting in session between the neck and the glottis; the nostril's wings break out in pharyngeal edemas; nauseating liquors leak out along the apophyses. The truncated sphincters surge back toward the nerve centers, the epigastrium subdivides itself. The satchel finally falls too, your hand invaginates itself and the sketch elaborated the night before is stained with liquid excrement . . .[12]

Here Pinget parodies medical jargon with an almost Rabelaisian verve and energy. As technical terms accumulate, their meaning becomes more and more obscure. The passage's chopped-up logic disintegrates, following the blurring sketch and the physical description's dislocation. Pinget transcends parody, challenging the validity of so-called natural relationships between words and things, much as Sartre's Roquentin does when describing his face in *Nausea*.

Robert Pinget's word juggling, though often amusing, is very much in earnest.

The diary and the book end as unexpectedly and unpredictably as they began. (Pinget wisely eliminated a fanciful film scenario from the final draft, realizing that fantasy works best in smallish doses.) Thus *Between Fantoine and Agapa* strikes one as deliberately inconclusive and baffling. Disordered and fanciful fragments trip up the reader throughout. Any attempt to discover a coherent story by advancing hypotheses in series is systematically frustrated. But through that frustration Pinget draws attention to the very effort to understand. The open quality of the prose mirrors the multiplicity and variety of experience conveyed without reducing it. The mode of nonsense portrays a creating mind where the "story"

> is all about several people, each of whom was several people, in different places at the same time.[13]

In short, *Between Fantoine and Agapa*, in addition to its being a witty tour de force in its own right, is a spirited prelude to the novels that will follow. The fragmented narrative and the zany, elliptic prose combine to produce an elusive, dreamlike effect. In this book Pinget formulates his own rationale for artistic creation, in addition to stretching the reader's imagination:

> Incapable of being a man who walks, smokes, sees friends, my natural reaction is to invent in potter's clay or on canvas or on paper a gait, a taste of smoke, a visit where my arteries palpitate.
>
> I am therefore convinced today, that you don't try, in a work of art, to bring forth the true or the beautiful at all. You have recourse to art—as to a subterfuge—to keep breathing.[14]

Writing fiction is, then, an exercise of discovery—without beginning, without end, and without culmination. In this vaguely alarming, light-hearted introduction to Pinget's later work, fiction involves a constantly repeated stock-taking.

MAHU OR THE MATERIAL (MAHU OU LE MATÉRIAU)

In his next book, Pinget extends the themes and techniques presented through the nonsense tale to another genre and continues to flout the conventions of linear exposition. Like the short pieces of *Between Fantoine and Agapa*, the narrative seems to invent itself as it goes along. This time, however, the satiric target is more specific. *Mahu or the Material* (1952), with tongue-in-cheek, probes the condition and potential of the novel. In the first part, Pinget questions traditional structures and themes from within, simply sweeping them away or else brushing them aside through parody and pastiche. In the second part, he shakes the genre from paralysis by scrutinizing the validity of expressions and accepted modes of communication. Since the act of questioning builds upon the very conventions that it has laid low, the cacophony of questions and answers indicates a possible way to renew the novel. Before making that tentative affirmation, however, Pinget rejects both the notion of the novel as an all-inclusive synthesis of reality and the idea that the genre should take the successfully completed voyage as its model.

Pinget communicates his complex, introspective themes by exposing the reader to three works-in-progress presented simultaneously. In the author's bizarre imaginary community, novel writing has become all the rage, and his characters all write feverishly to beat their neighbors to press and onto the public library's shelves. The first narrative strand describes the life of Mahu, one of fourteen (!) brothers of the same age, who decides to go to work. He finds the job of more than usual difficulty because, among other eccentricities, his employer, Juan Simon, often hides letters in packages to avoid using the postal service. This bizarre subterfuge prevents Sinture, the snooping postmaster, from tampering with incoming and outgoing mail. Mahu's account proceeds coherently up to an event that is left open to opposing interpretations. While passing by the school of Petite Fiente ("Little Bird Dropping"), Juan Simon's daughter, it first appears that Mahu slapped the little girl. When the same scene recurs in another version, Mahu only pretends to strike the child, to tease her. Finally, Pinget reverses roles, claiming that Petite Fiente slapped Mahu. Which account is correct? It is impossible to tell, and from this point on Mahu's story, like the tales in *Between Fantoine and Agapa*, plays on several possible interpretations, each against the others.

The inclusion of manuscripts by Latirail and Mlle. Lorpailleur scrambles matters still further. While Mahu writes for pleasure, his rivals strive to reduce the disorder of objective reality to a representative, manipulative pattern. It is their frustrated desire to extract a finality or compose a unity from experience that compels them to write. Their literary efforts also gratify certain aggressive personal needs, and pseudo-creative activity also gives them the illusion that their lives have a purpose. Gide's would-be writer-protagonist in *Paludes* hides behind the same pretext of impending creative activity in order to avoid emerging from his boggy inertia. The project of writing a novel enables Pinget's characters to assume an authority that they do not have. Since the omniscient novelist relegates others to supporting roles, and since both Latirail and Mlle. Lorpailleur know Mahu, both try to establish him as a satellite in fictional worlds orbiting around themselves. A comical war of the novelists breaks out, with each would-be narrator trying to impose his story on those around him, and in the struggle, these pseudo-"serious" writers slip on the banana peel of Pinget's satire. The explanatory note on the novel's dust jacket, probably written by the author himself, describes the result:

> The story quickly becomes rather complicated. Not content to create themselves continually, the characters soon create each other. Events go around in circles, come apart, go backwards, turn off into two or parallel series that immediately react upon each other, destroy each other, or combine in a synthesis that is bold, indefinable, and always unexpected.

Alain Robbe-Grillet described the novel's forward progress as a "permanent sabotage," pointing to the crucial contrast between the intentions and the results achieved by Pinget's aspiring novelist characters:

> The characters of this novel do not belong to the domain of psychology, or sociology, or even to that of symbolism, and even less to the

domain of history or manners. They are *pure creatures* who take their form only from the spirit of creativity. Their existence . . . is only a planless process of becoming subjected from sentence to sentence to the most extravagant mutations, at the mercy of the slightest thought which crosses the mind, of the most random phrase or of the most fleeting suspicion. Nevertheless, they *make* each other, but instead of each of them creating its own reality, a whole is made. Like a living fabric whose every call blossoms and shapes its neighbors, these characters form each other endlessly. The world around them is only at the stage of being a secretion; one could almost say the *waste product* of their lies, and their delirium.[15]

As Robbe-Grillet suggested, the impish independence of words in *Mahu ou le matériau* makes a mockery of the over-confident novelist's drafts and outlines. Latirail believes fatuously that his scheme of structuring plot around a quest is a conscious decision; in fact, it springs from a subconscious association with gold-rush days that the name "Lorpailleur" ("gold scrabbler") sets in motion. He wants to entitle his novel *Les Chercheurs de poux (The Louse Hunters)*, an ironic allusion to Rimbaud's poem of the same name, which explores the association of sounds and subconscious daydreams. Latirail changes the title to *Les Chercheurs de clous (The Nail Hunters)*. Why? Alain Bosquet has suggested that the change

> . . . is born from the word that the hand has put on the paper subconsciously. The plot will develop from that word; it is not the writer's job to get mixed up in the process or to intervene with his bumbling logic. Why choose the word "pou"? The mind which revolts against itself chooses a paronym, *"clou."* Perhaps . . . because of the memory of a rule of grammar learned long ago: Words ending in *ou*, like *"clou,"* add *s* in the plural. There are seven exceptions that take an *x*, like *"poux."*[16]

Pinget keeps exposing the superficiality of Latirail's simplistic, ludicrous efforts to base his narrative on "real" events. Poor Latirail hopes to ground his story in facts or objects and to illuminate their symbolic meanings later. As he says to Mahu:

> I'm simply going to get into the skin of one of the seekers and have him find symbolic things. Things which will be my life. A large

porcelain vase is Ninette, for example. A railroad timetable is my travels. A vial of sleeping pills, my dreams.[17]

Latirail's method fails for several obvious reasons. Any person who lives so unobservingly and unimaginatively would find it difficult even to start to imagine being somebody else. Like Flaubert and Dos Passos, the two recognized, professional novelists squeeze real-life occurrences into their manuscripts. But these unassimilated lumps only serve to make the text all the more far-fetched and confusing. The deliberately clumsy neorealistic attempt to hold up a mirror image of a clearly ordered life backfires. Both Latirail and Mlle. Lorpailleur would like to proceed in a linear fashion, step by step, linking strands of narrative together logically. But the texts connecting objective reality and subconscious fantasy send their projects down a spiral of ever-narrowing concentric circles ending in frustration and silence.

Pinget's challenge of narrative conventions goes beyond rejection of the novel as an ordering of experience, a voyage of discovery, or realistic experiment. Through the caricature character, Sinture, Pinget questions both the validity of the omniscient author's very existence and his relationship to his material. The postmaster is aware of everything going on in Fantoine and Agapa. Every letter, every thought in every consciousness, passes through his consciousness. He has established the kind of control and understanding that Latirail seeks in vain. Sinture sees himself as the puppet master of a *"comédie humaine,"* as the spider at the center of a web of local intrigue. (Even his name suggests a *"ceinture,"* "a belt," a restricting force that shapes the smallest details of the lives that are developing within his sphere.) Pinget might have made Sinture the center of consciousness of his novel. Had he done so, *Mahu or the Material* might have had the tight coherence, the controlled plot, the clearly defined characters, and the reassuring impression of harmony of a "well-made" novel. But he deliberately rejected that option. Why should Sinture go to the trouble of writing? What would he learn? He would know the end of a book while telling the beginning. A novel with Sinture as its narrator would fall as flat as a well-rehearsed joke told once too often.

The reader expecting a novel of that kind from Robert Pinget would be justified if he exclaimed, in a pun on the central character's name, "*On m'a eu*," "I've been had!" For the narrator of the second part of the novel is not Latirail, Mlle. Lorpailleur, or Sinture, but Mahu, the woolgatherer who rambles through life as if he were a character in a shaggy-dog story. Sinture knows and he keeps silent. Mahu lacks knowledge and he stammers. In the second part, Mahu addresses his interlocutor with thirty-five monologues that are not answers but so many inquiries, hypotheses, and questions. He defends the helter-skelter nature of the prose as a necessary condition for exploration. The rambling monologues fly in the face of Latirail's threadbare homilies on style. Yet Mahu's technique and its justifications, in addition to opening possibilities, set limits for the novel. Mahu writes in the present tense and in the interrogative mood, keeping to a conversational style as much as possible—a diffuse manner that suits his conception of fiction. He uses the present tense because to him the division of time into past, present, and future seems arbitrarily rigid. As he puts it:

> You think you're progressing from one precision to the next, when, in fact, you are regressing. The only precision is the one you have in your hands.[18]

The novel's second half contains more than one hundred thirty questions, each reflecting Mahu's active imagination as it shies away from definitive answers. The insistence and whimsicality of the queries recalls the litany of "what-if" questions of a child. "When you walk, do you pay attention?" "Do you think you are responsible for other people's legs?" The urgent need for flexibility in the spoken word becomes obvious when Mahu tries to express the complexity of his reactions:

> I find that many people know how to tell stories, even everybody, writing ruins it, the voice is no longer in it, the eyes either, there's nothing you can do about it, when you talk you are more true than what you have seen since you explain yourself, you are at the same time the ear and the brain of the person listening, but above all you are his eyes, you look with him, and he doesn't do anything, the story is alive because I am alive next to him. Understand? I don't write for fun, but just to invent people around me to listen to me. Otherwise, what good would I be?[19]

But Mahu cannot buttonhole his listener or reader indefinitely, and in any case the reactions that he wants to express would soon outpace his capacity to put them into words:

> But you see, as I tell the story it gets further and further away. Soon it will be yesterday or before yesterday. Soon, the more precisely I tell you things, the further away they will be. If I told you everything without skipping, it would have happened last year.[20]

Obviously, therefore, Mahu will never be able to bring his narrative to an end, if one means by this extracting a definitive conclusion or synthesis from the raw material of life swirling over, around, and under him. Realizing dimly that his task becomes more difficult with passing time, he lets the narrative become even more freewheeling instead of moving toward a conclusion until, abruptly, just as one is getting used to these soaring or one-winged flights of fancy, the reader turns the last page. The lack of a climactic ending does not indicate failure, however, for in the last chapter, in a sort of exiting whinny of laughter, Mahu affirms his success despite its nonconformity to narrative norms or rules.

> Don't need to lie anymore. I lied a lot at the beginning to get to this point, for truth. It shows that truth extricates itself from an inextricable muddle . . .
>
> Between you and me, the first part is a novel that didn't work out. But there's no harm. It was useful to me as warm-up scales. The important thing for me is not to sing well but to hear my voice without bronchitis. You know, there are lots of little whistles with a case of bronchitis. There we are. I have nothing more to say except that everything remains mine. I have won.[21]

Pinget has also won, for he has begun both to clear the ground of what he considers to be outmoded conventions and to reshape the novel to suit his own purposes. The complexity of his material makes Mahu's goal of a minute-by-minute account impossible of achievement, but the act of coordinating impressions without omitting their random, helter-skelter confusion rings truer than composing a tightly constructed story whose all-inclusiveness and finished quality would be illusory. Instead of presenting a closed work susceptible only to narrowly defined interpretations, Pinget dramatizes the continuity of the creative impulse itself and the frustrations it encounters. Gide achieved a similar effect in *The Counterfeiters* by switching back and forth between the unfulfilled potential of projected narrative and the actuality of the accompanying story. Pinget moves in the same direction by superimposing the narratives flowing through *Mahu or the Material* in a complex verbal montage. Having rejected traditional structures, he constructs a narrative that takes form as a breathless catalog of material. Against all odds, a story somehow emerges from Mahu's probing of possibilities, the story of composition itself. The protagonist's dazzling, sometimes incomprehensible verbal associations in Part Two gather the narrative threads together in madcap, unpredictable ways. After the opening note of *Between Fantoine and Agapa*, with *Mahu or the Material* Pinget gives notice that he will try to revive the novel through a wide-eyed vision of protean "material," and Mahu's mutterings give a high-spirited preview of Pinget's future experiments.

THE FOX AND THE COMPASS (LE RENARD ET LA BOUSSOLE)

If Mahu is a teacher, he instructs sheerly through example. His acrobatic verbal virtuosity does not prescribe a series of precise remedies for the tired blood of the narrative because Mahu does not initiate a system but, rather, represents an attitude. Pinget's next work follows another emerging *récit*'s wild birth pangs, ending in an aborted manuscript. *The Fox and the Compass* hurtles along the roller coaster of loopy literary creativity at the same breakneck speed and with the same uproarious, unsettling results. Although the book continues to develop the theories and practices of Pinget's earlier work, it has a distinct tone and impact all its own. The basic narrative structure is familiar. Once again Pinget tells a story-within-a-story through the device of a writer-narrator's diary. The resulting structural ambiguity enables him to play with the chinese boxes of three simultaneous inquiries, each frustrated to some degree. Pinget tries to shape the muddled contents of a work-in-progress into a coherent, conclusive conventional narrative, while his protagonist hopes to sort out his chaotic thoughts through fiction, and the reader struggles to follow a thread of continuity clarifying the text as a whole. The three efforts parallel Pinget's characteristically circular questioning as he tries to integrate the material of all his books into a ramblingly consistent cycle.

Although the off-hand tone, the predilection for the present tense, the theme of the voyage, and the delectation in ambiguity in *The Fox and the Compass* recall the earlier works, this novel marks a new stage in the writer's challenge to, and changing of, our habitual processes of thought and expression. Elements of satire and pastiche that were previously of major importance now play a secondary role. Pinget turns away from merely spoofing the "well-made" nineteenth-century narrative and expands Mahu's stammering to a full-length novel by eliminating the divisions that separate *Mahu or the Material* into short fragments. Pinget's previously scant use of punctuation becomes even more skimpy, resulting in telescoped phrases and clauses and obscured transitions. The novelist seems to have cleared his throat in his first two books, or, like Mahu, to have run through his warming-up scales. Now the tone of voice changes and the prose deals more directly with serious questions of writing and what writing means. The following passage, addressed to the reader, shows that the change is by design:

> What madness this uncut conversation with you is, I don't have time to catch my breath but that's the way I wanted it, a breath is a change of air and I am too willing to change air, I wanted just once to have no recourse to subterfuge. The subterfuge of breathing? Yes, vital, but the exercise of holding their breath that some people do makes them live more intensely, and think of divers, they wouldn't go very deep without this asceticism, careful, I'm not an ascetic. I chose my examples poorly. I desire nothing else but an approximative way of speaking, you should have picked that up I've been repeating it long enough, what I mean by what madness is this: having decided to break silence I risk boredom for you by these eternal contemplations of my navel on purpose, instead of keeping them for myself I offer them generously to you.[22]

Pinget fashions a continuous monologue whose non sequiturs and ambiguities express and produce powerful feelings of frustration and disorientation. He develops this sensation carefully to the point that the narrator seems to lose control of his material and to be lost in it, transforming the carnivalesque celebration of the gratuitous, the far-fetched, and the bizarre into a nightmare of anguish and despair. The narrator of *The Fox and the Compass* never finds a way to close the work on a "logical" note. Pinget does not give him the last laugh. Instead, unlike Mahu, the joke is on him. Porridge's journal moves in a circle, starting with the suggestion of the novel's potential, moving along to unsuccessful attempts to bring it to life, and ending with hysterical laughter as he decides to start over.

The book begins with John Tintouin Porridge puzzling over the form, subject, motifs, and beginning of the story he is planning to write. Should his plot be autobiographical and easy to follow? Or should it reflect the haphazard quality of impressions flitting through his consciousness as he sits at his desk, pen in hand? Scoffing at "books that tell simple stories," Porridge leans toward the second alternative and envisages a flexible form suitable to his subject: birth. Organizing his novel around that theme makes sense for several reasons. Birth symbolizes the culmination of unknown causes—the release of unmeasured potential. By extension, birth suggests painting and poetry, and Porridge plans to deal with both. Yet, the central problem remains unresolved: how should he actually begin? Why not with his own birth, he wonders—not to provide a social or historical reference point, but to cover origins with confusion and shroud them with portentious mystery. But Porridge simply lacks the energy to start with his own birth. Furthermore, he admits that he cannot imagine an ending and complains that his powers are limited. At the beginning of the book, his story is at the creative zero point and the novel follows the narrative as it develops from the varied associations of ideas and themes. In other words, his narrator's fruitless search for a starting point serves Pinget as an introduction to *The Fox and the Compass* "in the middle of things" *(in medias res.)*

Addressing an unidentified party, probably the reader, in the familiar *"tu"* form, Porridge leaves aside his musings about the novel and woolgathers about the characteristics of spiders and about two giraffe figures that he drew on the envelope of a letter sent to his nephews. He wakes up the next morning with the Old Testament phrase "beware of the little foxes" running through his mind. As he muses about the origins of this animal's suspicious nature, its "foxiness," the image of a particular fox comes into focus. The nomadic life of the fox reminds Porridge of the legend of the Wandering Jew, and both, the fox and the Wandering Jew, suggest themselves as likely characters for Porridge's story, in which he hopes to express a sense of rootlessness.

Porridge's mind shifts next to a gigantic fresco that he plans to paint. Raising a theme that will recur at the novel's end, Porridge plans to make The Creation, the birth of the Universe, the subject of his massive, and somewhat bizarre, work of art. He waxes rhapsodic about all the animals to be included and describes at great length the various foods that will fill the canvas into its smallest corners. Then there is an abrupt shift of subject without any transition or preparation. All of a sudden the description of the canvas is scrapped and Porridge starts rambling on with facts and figures about Israel and a discursive account of a visit there. Since the book swings frequently from asides about Porridge's "real" life to the imagined story that he plans to tell in his novel, the transition can be explained in several ways, none of them logically satisfactory. Is the reader to suppose that Porridge has dropped his novel in progress and taken a trip to Israel? Or is the voyage episode simply another draft of the novel that is having such trouble being born? Both answers are equally plausible but neither explains the confusion completely.

Owing to frequent gyrations from first-person reminiscences to third-person narration, the real nature of the voyage to Israel remains sketchy. Nonetheless, the journey theme dramatizes the attempt to tell a coherent tale. Like any wanderer, the fox seeks a home. The Jew searches for security and national identity in the Promised Land. Porridge tries not to *"perdre la boussole,"* "lose his bearings," in complex narrative devices and autobiographical material.

The text's focus changes back and forth from observations of life on board a steamer full of Jews from different countries and stopovers in various Mediterranean ports as the ship nears Israel. Memories of previous voyages accumulate, and frequent shifts in chronology break continuity. The image of the unfinished sketch recurs when Porridge dwells on the character of an artist who deliberately leaves his drawings incomplete. The momentary identification of the narrator and this character underscores Pinget's method of interrupting each scene before it stands as a detachable coherent unit. The physical displacement necessary for any voyage parallels Porridge's search for identity and his doubts that he will ever be able to hit upon a conclusion for his narrative.

When the steamer lands at Haifa, the novel centers on another search for identity, this time a historical one. By blurring the time focus through flashbacks to the Biblical past, Porridge recalls centuries of wandering and exile prior to the founding of Israel. Descriptions of the twentieth-century port lie side by side with verses from the Psalms, an account of the establishment of the Covenant, fragments of the Saul-David story, and a tour guide's lyrical praise of modern Israel. Porridge considers scrapping the manuscript and starting over, but the plight of that tireless seeker, the Jew, suggests an analogue for his own anguished search for identity and control of the projected novel that keeps slipping away from him. The long reprise of the tour guide's glib monologue does not dissipate the agonizing feeling that, for all its pain, the search for the Promised Land has been more satisfying than the voyage's end. The fullness of the quest and the relative emptiness of the accomplishment become the more pronounced when Don Quixote and Sancho Panza are added to the cast of characters.

On a superficial level, David's reckless idealism and Renard's common sense link *The Fox and the Compass* and *Don Quixote*. The allusion to Cervantes serves, moreover, to bring the nature of the quest of Pinget's narrator into sharper focus. Don Quixote lives and dies trying to "live by the book." He never stops striving to impose the way of life learned by reading about chivalry onto the far more complex and unpredictable flow of human behavior. Porridge's attempts to bring his manuscript to a conventional conclusion is quixotic in the broadest sense of the word. He has chosen as his model the linear pattern of traditional nineteenth-century travel literature. But at every turn his chaotic imagination breaks out of its constraints. The life he experiences will not fit into the forms that literary heritage has provided to give it shape, and the chosen model creaks and finally collapses under the strain. As his despair over the manuscript's lack of order becomes more severe, Porridge interjects unrelated memories and alternate possibilities. The work-in-progress falls apart in the telling, yet the narrator refuses to stop writing, since the very act of keeping a journal has become more important to him than what he writes in it.

The increasingly episodic nature of the "narrative" and the fanciful associations of sound and image linking one projected plot and the next remind the reader that he is following not a novel but the evolution of a novel being created. The project becomes a failed novel in the protagonist's mind after he rejects building the story around David and Renard or the trip to Palestine. Now he writes more frequently in the first person, and his imaginary voyage turns inward upon itself, ending with the frustrated would-be author, alone in his room, staring at the four walls.

Accelerating shifts in perspective of the presentation of the trip to Israel end in a climactic, chaotic blur as Porridge is gradually disoriented by the complexities of his chosen material and structure. The conclusion butts up against an impasse, confirming that the David/Renard narrative is a failure. Pinget does not close the novel on a dejected note, however, and Porridge doggedly continues keeping his diary of the activities at Fantoine. Although the David/Renard experiment is unsuccessful, the attempt to write the narrative goes on. For Porridge, as for Mahu, the constantly thwarted desire to find a pattern is the very essence of his task. The constant quest for form in disorder is more significant for him than the failure of the quest. The David/Renard experiment is, then, just another episode in a continuing struggle.

In the diary that follows the David/Renard narrative, the notes that Porridge has accumulated eventually expand beyond his control. The very language that Porridge uses breaks through the restrictions of logical discourse, exploding into words as sound. The introduction of new possibilities of interpretation only serves to complete the narrative's breakdown. The reappearance of characters from Pinget's first two books makes possible a number of tentative connections to the corpus of information accumulating about Fantoine, Agapa, and their inhabitants. Porridge's errands around town and his frequent visits to cafés and bars put him in contact with Petite Fiente, Mahu, Juan Simon, Sophie Narre, Latirail, and

Mlle. Lorpailleur, all recurring characters, a technique that will become more significant in later novels.

Porridge then begins to write his diary, for a short time, from the point of view of old Chinze, the local shoemaker. Can it be that Porridge has never left the village at all? Perhaps the novel is an elaborate transposition of village life. The text becomes increasingly surrealistic after the suggestion of such possible interpretations, and the scene shifts to a medical amphitheatre where a surgeon is calmly dissecting the cadaver of Joan of Arc. To the horror of curious onlookers, the doctor discovers male organs, and the spectators' choppy commentary sputters into verbal fireworks similar to Ionesco's early dialogues:

> — Miséricorde, dit l'abbé. — Juste ciel, dit l'institutrice. — Mein Gott, dit le bilan. — Diantre, dit la générale. — Les vaches, disent Cécile et Michonne. — Superbe, dit Poppie. — Vice de forme, disent les jurés. — A croquer, dit le rat d'égout. — Guignolesque, dit le tailleur . . . — Sauteuse. — Fumier. — Crotte de bique. — Arbousier. — Coloquinte. — Faisan. — Faisandée. — Pebroque. — Parapluie, madame. — Instigateur. — Souricière. — Chapardeur. — Oiseleuse. — Trou du cul. — Fesses-cuites. — Bitte de singe. — Plume d'oie. — Couille d'asperge. — Verge d'arsouille. — Souille la vierge. — Perce-la-nouille . . .²³

— Mercy on us, says the priest. — Heavens Above, says the schoolmistress. — Mein Gott, says the Balance-sheet. — What the Hell, says the general's wife. — The dirty rats, says Cecile and Michonne. — Superb, says Poppie, — Faulty drafting, say the jurors. — Good enough to eat, says the sewer rat. — Outlandish, says the tailor . . . — Bed-hopper. — Horse's Ass. — Aspen. — Crab Apple. — Poppycock. — Fricasseed . . . — Instigator. — Mouse-trap. — Scrounger. — Fowler. — Asshole. — Cooked-butt. — Monkey prick. — Feather of goose. — One balled asparagus. — Hot cock. — Soil the Virgin. — Pierce the Noodle.

As if to regain its balance after this exhausting verbal jag, the journal continues with a detailed description of a room, assumedly Porridge's, until the narrator abruptly cuts the description short. Conscious that he is getting nowhere, Porridge calls on Mlle. Lorpailleur for advice. She finds that his maxims and aphorisms show talent, but that they would have more impact if Porridge extracted them from his diary and put them into the mouths of the characters of a novel. Does he in fact have any characters, she asks? Porridge replies with a list that starts with

> ... Renard, David, Benjamin, Lazarus, Traiko, Mary-Magdalen, Cervantes ... Sancho, innkeepers, children ... the emperor, the queen of Sheba, the Soudanese, the Samaritans, the prophets ...[24]

and goes on to mention Pharaoh, dogs, cats, birds, Lake Tiberias, the river Jordan—a list that, not surprisingly, astonishes Mlle. Lorpailleur. When she asks him about the *subject* of his novel, Porridge replies:

> [It's about] origins ... You see, I had begun in a certain way, then it branched off, and it happens that the most important part is in the branching off, it is purely original, it is the very source [of the work].[25]

At last Porridge states openly the importance of ambiguity in his work and faces the question of why he refuses to compose a coherent story. To do so would be to destroy the constant "branching out" that lies at the heart of what he is trying to express. For Mlle. Lorpailleur, whose literary sensitivity is as sharp as a butter knife, the solution is simple. Porridge should fix his story firmly in a geographical and historical context by beginning: "I was born." But none of her suggestions pleases Porridge, and his harridan colleague exits raving:

> Je suis née à brûle-pourpoint. (Rire d'hystérique). Autant dire que j'étais brûlée à l'avance. A qui la faute? Première-née, nouveau-née, dernière-née, mort-née, ivre-morte, aigre-doux, vert-de-grisée, trotte-menu, tire-bouchonne, tragi-comique, sous-cutanée, pseudo-feuillue, quasi-contrate, neo-sexy, post-natatoire, avant-coureuse, semi-lunaire, intra-veineuse ... tue-mouche, mezzo-soprano, pituite, mouline-à-vente, caf'conce, froufrouteuse, verveine, calligraphe, cacophone, chattière, rattière, belle-manière, maniabelluaire, bagnolanière, mille-banière, mer, mer, mer, mer ...[26]

I was born in white heat. (Hysterical laugh). Might say burned early. Whose the fault? [I was] First born, new born, last born,

born-dead, dead drunk, sweet and sour, copper-tanked, pitter-patter, tiddle-toddle, tidly-opener, tragi-comic, subcutaneous, pseudo-foliaged . . . neo-sexy, post-natatory, fore-runner, semi-lunary, intravenous, . . . fly-swatter, mezzo-soprano, gastric-catarrh, wind bag, jazz joint, crinolined, verbena, calligrapher, cacaphone, catly, ratly, mannerly, managiberly, carlanyardly, thousand-bannerdly, shi, shi, shi . . .

After Mlle. Lorpailleur's departure, Porridge admits that he is unable to finish, but instead of simply giving up he makes a breathless summary lapsing into incoherence. The book ends then where it began, as Porridge doggedly reintroduces himself before starting yet another story. Will he follow Mlle. Lorpailleur's advice after all? The pages at the end of the book do not answer that (or any other) question and suggest only unfulfilled possibilities.

In *The Fox and the Compass*, Pinget develops many themes and techniques that he has used before. He wonders whether, after parodying the straightforward narrative in the first two books, it is possible to tell any story completely. He continues to treat art as a continuing voyage of discovery, and Porridge would certainly subscribe to Mahu's notion that writing is an inevitably inconclusive attempt to shoehorn experience into a form where the relationship of word to object could be one to one. Pinget also achieves a new, obsessive effect by winding his narrative more tightly upon itself and looping its convolutions around preceding works.

The reappearance in *Mahu or the Material* of characters and places mentioned in *Between Fantoine and Agapa* may at first pass unnoticed or may seem to be coincidental. But by the third book the inhabitants of Fantoine and Agapa start to be vaguely recognizable, strangely familiar, like actors in a repertory company changing roles from week to week. Porridge's narrative eventually swallows itself with its circular construction calling attention to the elliptical shape of his fiction where two contrary movements cancel each other. Porridge carefully delineates the author's imaginary province, yet his assertions contradict and undermine versions given earlier. This process of doing and undoing raises the question of the paradoxical interplay of pattern and disorder, of parody and its original, of the aleatory linkage of words, all major concerns in the works of the surrealistic stage of Pinget's development.

2 Outer Limits—Inner Limits
Graal Filibuste and *Baga*

Lièvre de vase

They order, said I, this matter [of journeys] much better in France.—Sterne, *A Sentimental Journey*

First, I considered myself as having a face, hands, and all that machine composed of flesh and bones such as appears in a cadaver, which mechanism I designated by the name, body.—Descartes, *Meditations*

The title of Pinget's next novel, *Graal Flibuste* (1955), is deliberately equivocal and hence untranslatable. The words of the title carry several suggestive values in French (the Grail Quest; pirate adventures; the mystery of an archaic or learned word; the hint of an obscure pun or neologism) without limiting themselves to any one. The title also stems from the name of the deity of the strange territory that the protagonist explores, an Oz-like land in comparison to which life in Fantoine and Agapa seems almost humdrum.

Describing a journey to a fantasy land opens up several possibilities to the novelist. If he chooses satire, he can recount with tongue in cheek a foreigner's reactions to an alien culture in the manner of a Swift, Voltaire, or Montesquieu. If he wants to exercise his imagination, he may scamper off along the path of Lewis Carroll or that of Alain Fournier. If he chooses to rock literary conventions to their foundations, he can give his narrative a mock-heroic twist in the tradition of a Cervantes, Fielding, Sterne, Gide, or Joyce. In *Graal Flibuste,* Pinget broadens the parody of conventions associated with the voyage motif and thus extends the experimentation in *The Fox and the Compass* by using the last two of the three alternatives simultaneously. Contact with the imaginary in *Graal Flibuste* calls the rationality of the "real" world into question. The flight from the senseless tangle of everyday experience to an artificial realm where every act has meaning comes full circle as Pinget distorts or violates the most fundamental assumptions and conventions of the travel *récit* in order to expose as illusory the fiction that life "makes sense" or "adds up." His peripatetic characters have no point of departure, no itinerary, and no destination. His bumbling explorer never sets out. He moves in a world as strange as Alice's Wonderland, but Alice will awaken from her dream, whereas Pinget provides his explorer with no such convenient means of escape. Alice's incongruous adventures have the bizarre but consistent underpinnings of a special "behind-the-looking-glass" logic, whereas Pinget's nameless character wanders aimlessly in a domain that is devoid of *any* sort of logic. True, he puts one foot carefully in front of the other, like the forward-striding travellers in epics, but he will never return to Penelope in Ithaca. He is shipwrecked because conventional, sequential logic does not operate in the kingdom where he flounders. No rescue such as that of Giraudoux's heroine in *Suzanne and the Pacific* awaits him. His is a dream from which there is no waking, a dream in which forward movement is illusory. He will never find his way, and eventually Pinget will abandon him abruptly as, nameless to the end, he gazes at an arch framing new uncertainties. The author provides no clearly defined points of reference by which to connect the voyage, or the experience of reading about it, to past or future activity. Each stage of the traveller's journey is an independent episode in his quest to discover himself and the kingdom around him. In *Graal Flibuste*, travelling sets in motion an endless enumeration that:

> ... includes all of the approaches, flights of fancy and variations through which the mind, seeking to take possession of reality, accepts it as it is and denies it; measures and dreams it; surveys and parodies it; counts and recreates it within an image of reality; it is a representation of the world.[1]

The story unfolds as a Grail quest in reverse.[2] The enigmatic title suggests images of adventurers and pirates but never brings them into clear focus. The narrator's mysterious expedition leads nowhere. Unlike Percival, he is not even afforded the slightest glimpse of the Grail he is seeking. His erratic voyage staggers along like a nightmare and has nothing of the purposeful sweep of the adventurers of knight errantry.

Pinget lets his narrator-protagonist lean on every linear prop that the genre of travel journal offers, only to pull them out from under him. He parodies the digressions that punctuate most such works by including Fieldingesque spoofs of long-winded biographical chapters. The digressions in *Graal Flibuste* serve no emblematic or symbolic purpose. Instead of advancing the unfolding of the story they obstruct it. Pinget stretches his rubbery extrapolations so far as to make the narrator seem to be spinning off-the-cuff improvisations as he goes. Authors of fanciful travel stories such as Henri Michaux' *Elsewhere (Ailleurs)* often blur normal boundaries between the real and the imaginary, the animal and the human. In this vein, the narrator notes that hybrid creatures combining alien and familiar forms make up the fauna of the kingdom that he is exploring. Pinget carries this tendency to a point so extreme that he can include as plant and animal names subconscious associations of images and puns, many of them highly suggestive. The *"flora"* including *"les verges-douces,"* ("soft rods"), *"les oublieuses-d'amertume"* ("forget-me-ills"), and *"les joies-du-matin"* ("morning joys"), are rarely what they seem. Even the domestication and feeding of pets often provides surprises:

> You feed squirrel-candles nuts and white blackbirds. They are kept not far from the square where holidays are celebrated in a small hotel whose English garden provides them with greenery and coolness on weekends, as well as the space necessary for their gambols.[3]

There are no self-contained categories in *Graal Flibuste*. In this story of an imaginary voyage to an imaginary land populated by imaginary creatures everything flows together.

The novel opens with an enigmatic introductory chapter—enigmatic because it records the observations of a drunkard whose field of vision swims before the reader's eyes, introductory because the blurry description foreshadows the jumbled journey to follow. Pinget muddles the focus further by switching the point of view of the scene frequently and without warning from the man to his cat. The reader, already confused, finds it difficult to determine whether the center of consciousness is man or beast:

> A drunkard is sitting at a table with a bottle of wine in front of him. He has a red nose, a hat on his head, and a look lost in the

contemplation of things. He wonders why he is there, he shrugs his shoulders and makes a vague movement with his forearm from time to time.

The cat thinks that his master is stupid not to have drowned him yet. He is hideous, he smells and his large head bothers him in all of his movements. We make a good pair, he thinks, I am a ridiculous monster and he's a failure, which is the same thing.

The drunkard pours himself a glass and drinks. He looks up and sees the cat perched on the shelf. Why that shelf, thinks the drunk, the cat is all I have to put on it. He squeezes breadcrumbs into a pellet and throws it at the animal who gobbles it. The drunkard thinks he hasn't thrown the pellet and makes another which he throws again. The cat gobbles it again and moves, he sits on the stove, which is always cold. At least, the cat thinks, he won't reach me here, he can't turn around.

The drunkard pours himself another glass and drinks. He doesn't see the cat on the shelf any more and wonders what has become of him. He starts thinking that perhaps he swallowed him with his wine. That's drunken ratiocination. So I swallowed that cat, he says to himself, here I am, all alone. Upon considering his solitude, the drunkard starts to cry.

The cat thinks that the stove is uncomfortable after all and goes back onto the shelf.

The drunkard pours himself another glass and drinks.

The cat washes for lack of anything else to do, his head bends, bends, he no longer has the strength to hold it up and he falls down. The drunkard hears him fall. He thinks that the cat wants to kill him. The cat misunderstands a sudden movement of the drunkard, he thinks that he wants to kill him too. He jumps on the stove.

The drunkard vomits. Here comes the end, thinks the cat, he will give me my soup pretty soon if all goes well. But there are some evenings when nothing works right, when thoughts and movements end in a blind alley. I think that those kinds of evenings multiply the older you get and, one fine day, like an unwound clock, you mark the terminal hour of the preceding evening; you are dead in your bed. (pp.7–8)

Pinget adds to the ambiguity of the chapter by describing an obsessive scene that appeared in the earlier narratives and will recur in the later novels: for years, it seems, the drunkard has been writing a letter that he is unable to finish. Like Juan Simon in *Mahu or the Material* he refuses to entrust the letter to the mails. This brief allusion to the earlier work and to the world of Fantoine and Agapa gives rise to several questions. What is the relationship between the kingdom of Graal Flibuste and the inventory of Pinget's fictional province? Does the account that follows the preface constitute the drunkard's mysterious letter to the world, or is the first chapter related to the rest of the text only by their common quality of obscurity? By leaving these questions unanswered, Pinget heightens the novel's ambiguity, challenging the reader—as best he can—to relate *Graal Flibuste* to his previous excursions through Fantoine and Agapa:

> The ceiling starts to come down. A battle, thinks the drunkard, they're on the whites' side, I'm red, I'm beaten before I start. Back! The cannons are on the other side, the sea will extinguish the cat, the enemy, what's he got in his mouth, my letter, he's going to destroy it, he's going to swallow it, the only, come here so I can strangle you, the letter I was waiting for, the whites don't believe in it any more. So many years, so many years with this bottle for a letter which hasn't come. . . . Sailor, tell me if that letter got through, it's damp, wet-through in the bottom of your pocket, nothing else except the cat tracking me has more importance, than that letter on the edge of the water.
>
> The drunkard goes to sleep on the table and the wine carries him off to the country of the dead bodies of letters. Many letters don't reach the person they're sent to, they wait in the post offices, then the angel of letters assassinates them. It's the angel enemy of love, the dry angel with paper wings.[4]

The journal begins as the traveller describes the architecture of a temple dedicated to "Graal Flibuste." From the start, the description's humorous improbabilities mock the matter-of-fact naturalism of traditional travel literature. They also produce a vaguely sinister effect reminiscent of Kafka's *The Castle*. Pinget provides enough physical details to call the landscape and the building to the mind's eye. The temple is there, in the valley. But the shifting images describing it and the unusual combination of whimsy and gallows humor make the effort to discover its function or meaning seem perilous and threatening.

After evoking the familiar spirit of this strange domain, the explorer hires a coachman, Brindon, and his horse, Clotho, so as to be able to move about more rapidly and comfortably. Brindon (*"brin d'homme,"* "Everyman"?) is a swashbuckling, picaresque jack-of-all-trades. Like Yorick's servant, La Fleur, and Don Quixote's Sancho Panza, he plays a dual role in that he helps the narrator through difficulties, as a good servant should, but he also understands the folly of their common enterprise more clearly than his self-deluded master does. The name of Brindon's horse also hints at the novel's rambling, mocking nature. The original Clotho, of Greek legend, spun the threads of fate, meticulously entwining men and events in the rich cloth of destiny. But the meanderings of Brindon's nag are more random than predestined. By filling the narrative with flashbacks and foreshadowings Pinget ridicules the traditional chronological approach and its illusion of cause and effect. The story of the voyage progresses in as hit-or-miss a fashion as Clotho's gait. The narrator tells the reader only those episodes that strike his fancy and he jumbles them arbitrarily, but his joke boomerangs and his playful tone takes on a hysterical edge as his adventures accumulate pell-mell without advancing him toward the end of his tale.

The pastiche of traditional travel-narration connections between episodes tangle into a hopelessly snarled cat's cradle. Coherence and verbal clarity rally momentarily during a description of a model dairy symbolizing order, as do the Norman farms in Gide's *The Immoralist*.[5] But in the ensuing account of a visit to a ceramics factory the narrator's concentration lapses and the scene flickers from his mind. As he sets out to "do" another point of interest, to fix another milemarker in his jumbled journey, the narrator explains that:

> The [ceramic] workshops were about a kilometer away and we went on foot. Brindon explained to me that we were going there to please me because it didn't interest him. . . . My interest awakened therefore the closer we got to the artist's lair . . .
>
> Here we are. A simple shed of corrugated iron. We go in. "Can I help you?" says the janitor. And that's all. There was nothing, nothing, nothing.[6]

Pinget turns ever-more-sweeping handsprings on the base that the conventions of the travel story furnish, replacing sharply focused images with blurred outlines and clearly delineated episodes with shapeless digressions. From one chapter to the next, puzzling non sequiturs take the place of the conventional linear progression, challenging the reader's habit of seeing experience in terms of cause and effect. In Pinget's text, non sequiturs are not ends in themselves; they help to evoke a fictional *world* that is hostile to habit and convention and where combinations of impressions remain ever fresh and ever changing. Even the name "Graal Flibuste," the verbal keystone of the text's structure, has only loose and relative "meanings." It signifies something that "exists" and has "meaning" only within the novel's framework, like the name of Melville's ghostly whale. The narrator's fumbling attempt to examine his title's etymology leads to a mental circular voyage of nondiscovery into the past and into primeval myth.

When the narrator launches into a long digression centered around Graal Flibuste's family tree, the constantly shifting spectrum of the genealogy (in which bits of myth, folklore, and wordplay collide), generates a freewheeling, Rabelaisian prose. The genealogy traces the god's ancestors back to a long-forgotten physical union in which man and beast, gods and monsters, and animate and inanimate creatures all mingled freely. Miraculous births do not explain all the twisted branches in Graal Flibuste's gnarled family tree. Nevertheless, the author executes a variety of verbal contortions in attempting to unravel its intertwinings down to the smallest twig. All the creatures he mentions must be related, in one way or another, because they derive from a common source in the primal coupling that generated all life; the trick is to run down the missing links. So the narrator gropes about, seeking to uncover linkages beneath the tangle, just as the reader of *Graal Flibuste* seeks to relate its chapters and episodes to some linear progression or other. But both narrator and reader reach an impasse when the deity's ancestors proliferate as swiftly as the narrator's adventures and Pinget's biblical parody explodes into verbal pyrotechnics with a list of gods from some obscure, long forgotten tongue:

>Affaful begat Boute-Boute.
>Boute-Boute begat Lapa.

> Lapa begat Miamsk.
> Miamsk begat Loin.
> Loin begat Peute.
> Peute begat Peute-Peute.
> Peute-Peute begat Cornette.
> Cornette begat Vallée-Sanzi.
> Vallée-Sanzi begat Tourte.
> Tourte begat Tarte.
> Tarte begat Bonne-Confiture.[7]

Pinget carries the parallel between the traveller's genealogical investigation and the destruction of the travel journal's convention of linear progression a step further. In both cases, consulting outside experts is futile. The answer to the riddle of the sense and purpose of *Graal Flibuste* lies within its pages, not in a separately published gloss. Nor will scholars or genealogical tables be of any use to the narrator seeking to find his way. Pinget portrays erudition as the dizzy handmaiden of confusion *(Scholaria begat Discordia)* by punning on the names of the authors of learned treatises.[8] Their macaroni logic differs not in the least from the narrator's painful non sequiturs. He must rely upon his own inadequate resources to define or achieve his goal. But in the local folklore of Le Chanchèze confusion is a sign of vitality. According to legend:

> Silence begat the Idea, the Idea begat the Word, the Word begat Discord. This mythology is the only one in the world that made discord a benevolent deity. Discord in old Chanziotte is a symbol of freedom regained.[9]

Pinget's pastiche in this passage and elsewhere is amusing; it entertains, startles, and occasionally annoys. Yet its very facility makes one wonder why he found it worthwhile to toy with the conventions of a type of narrative so long fallen out of fashion. Certainly travel literature no longer occupies the lofty position in the hierarchy of literary genres that it held in the eighteenth (or even the nineteenth) century. Reporters write accounts of their excursions for newspapers and magazines. Passengers may read travel stories on train or plane when, as travellers themselves, they are too tired or distracted to face anything more challenging or disturbing. The telling of an epic journey satisfies man's desire to grow, to make discoveries, and to feel that what he has learned is of fixed and permanent value. Its movement to a conclusion conveys the reassuring impression of a familiar recurring pattern: exposition, conflict, and resolution reflected in the syntactic pattern of subject, verb, and object. Perhaps the stirring epic is now sold in shabbier, more mundane guises in train stations and bus terminals, because the harassed twentieth-century voyager is only too content to sink back into his seat and seek refuge temporarily in a genre that shields him from the uncertainties of a relativistic world.

The voyage in *Graal Flibuste* offers, however, not the comfort of habitual ways of seeing things but, rather, the stimulus of "rediscovered freedom." Its episodes slip and slide by without ever leading to a climactic event. Instead, as Marthe Robert wrote of *Don Quixote*, Pinget's favorite novel,

> . . . the ups and downs of the plot . . . do not link together, they repeat themselves and add to each other helter-skelter in such a way that they are interchangeable, and far from converging toward an ending, they seem to be designed to put it off. . . . There is no gradual passage from one development in the plot to another, only a repetition of identical changes of fortune which literally condemn the hero to go around in circles.[10]

Refusing to confine the quicksilver of reality within a fixed form, Pinget deliberately frustrates the reader's expectations of what a story should be. Thus his narrative will not reassure us through its concision, nor will the chapters of *Graal Flibuste* move toward a satisfyingly complete conclusion so as to give us the impression that we actually experience life in this way. The assumptions that hold the text together disintegrate gradually until all of them are undermined by association. The target of the parody widens, giving the impression that reader and protagonist alike are straight men in a gigantic farce. Little by little, as Olivier de Magny observed in *Esprit* (August, 1958),

> The expedition of *Graal Flibuste* asserts itself as a voyage parody, and the impossible kingdom, whose flora and fauna are studied "scientifically" in such a way that they create a verisimilitude that is poetically laughable, makes the "real" kingdoms of this world with their plants and animals . . . topple over into absurdity, as well.

Pinget's sense of parody also leads him to explore the relationship between life and literature. In *Graal Flibuste*, he does not probe the protagonist's world so much as he does the protagonist's attempts to find a way to describe it. The sclerosis of his model offers a distinct advantage. Authors of travel journals frequently rely on the tricks of traditional narration so heavily that the bare bones of structure show through. Pinget, the experimental novelist, pushes the travel narrative up to and beyond its limits in order to show the drawbacks of that kind of fiction and to suggest an alternative. Like Gide's *The Counterfeiters*, *Graal Flibuste* is therefore a novel about the novel. Brindon's master actually turns "good form" inside out, as Gide's novelist character claims he will in the book that never gets written. Both works describe a narrator-protagonist's search for a completely satisfactory narrative form. Travelling and telling express the same insatiable desire, since one can never tell all, and death or silence wait at the end of the journey. The narrator's quest dramatizes the artist's attempt to impose an order on the world (recalling the early experimental novels of André Malraux), and the voyage provides a metaphor for the artist's attempt to fit material into an established form, or to create a new one.[11]

Pinget's traveller chooses to tell about the wanderings of his imagination through the journal of a voyage described from day to day. He seeks support in the forms of the literature of the past, but that potential guardrail collapses under him. For support, he turns to the rules and patterns of conventional fiction—only to be mocked and frustrated by the gulf between the coherence of the world of books and the chaotic impact of experience. But, even though fiction from the past has proved an unsatisfactory guide, he does not give up his obsessive, Mallarmé-like quest for order. He sets out to find his way by trial and error, so that the reader who is trying to string the episodes of *Graal Flibuste* together experiences at second hand, despite an initial frustration, the excitement and disappointments of a stylistic experiment in three parts.

Pinget relates pastiche to the theme of a novel about a novel by making the three stages of his narrator's experiment correspond only roughly to the departure on the epic voyage, adventures experienced during it, and the voyager's return. An overly precise parallel would have undermined Pinget's challenge to the traditional novel's linear development. Such is not the case in *Graal Flibuste*. The protagonist's feelings about his narrative method and his hopes for its success ebb and flow in an irregular fashion, but the process breaks down into three distinct, if overlapping, phases. At first, the narrator makes fun of the conventions he has rejected and is delighted to have broken out of the linear, logical structure of "well-made" fiction. He piles non sequitur upon non sequitur and accepts his coachman's critical remarks with good humor, as he frolics along the high road of life like Tom Jones on his way to London. Doubts beset him, however, when the outlines of the book he is planning vanish capriciously. He alerts the reader to the possibility that the search for words with which to define his constantly changing environment may collapse:

> I have progressed backwards so to speak [he says,] and I find myself with less at my disposal than a newly born baby. Since I have decided to write, I certainly mean to delay the death sentence that I will be obliged to pronounce against myself, but I insist upon warning the reader that this book, after the fashion of the man who composed it and contrary to custom, is diminishing in importance as it grows.[12]

The narrator's confidence in his effectiveness as a storyteller returns to sustain him, however, and it carries over into the second, or adventure, stage of the quest. Instead of simply flouting existing conventions, he begins to use the rigidity of linear narration as a springboard, searching for a structure flexible enough to contain his material without distorting it. The tone of his description of Clotho's metamorphosis in a scene of constant change is almost euphoric:

> Here he is starting to grow, and grow. First gray, then yellow, then snow white, then to diamondlike transparencies. His head touches the ceiling, it bursts through it like paper, then the roof is no more than a little collar on the gigantic neck, the body a cathedral, the feet pillars. A sumptuous tail unrolls and sweeps the air. "Clotho! I stammered, stay with me!" I saw his feet ready to leave the ground, they stamped, but Clotho did not fly away. Then there was no more stable, no more village, no more friends, nothing but that horse burst-

ing triumphantly into the dark and, I, watching him like a weakling. The entire circulatory system was visible behind the crystal, I saw the heart beating and the arteries palpitating, the blood flowing into the veins. He turned from red to gold, he touched the points of the compass. It was no longer Clotho's life but the life of the firmament, the movement of a world with a thousand million stars, the movement of universal gravity. Then I heard the voice of heaven thunder, but how can I transcribe a celestial Word?[13]

The traveller adopts Clotho as his Pegasus, or the incarnation of his Muse. Instead of trying to reduce his journal's confusion, he decides to increase it. He exults in the flexibility of open narrative structure, which previously had worried him. Clotho's gyrations encourage him to continue to advance by indirection. Chaos spills over from the genealogy chapters into the narrative as a whole, with the sign of the horse in the ascendant. The traveller accentuates the disjointed, random quality of his tale in the second part of *Graal Flibuste*, as if he hopes to stumble upon some sort of organic unity. His increasingly fanciful and haphazard adventures meander like the genealogy that never reaches its goal—the birth of Graal Flibuste.

The third stage of the narrator's quest for form, the part that, in the epic, would describe a successful return home, ends in apparent disaster. The narrator's burst of confidence subsides. Doubt returns, redoubled. The countryside frightens him, as the line of demarcation between dreams and nondreams bends and stretches:

> One summer evening when I was daydreaming, I went all the way up to the cemetery. A large cherry tree was planted in the middle of it, covered with cherries.
> The moon bathed the landscape, the air was warmish, I heard the fast-running stream jumping and the nightingale singing. At the time I was in love with a girl who lived in a village not far from here; I thought about my girl. The splendid cherry tree held out its fruit to me which I ate by the hundreds in one of those voracious fits to which those of my age were subject. I fell asleep under the tree and awoke at the crack of dawn. Only then did I see that the cherries were the eyes of the dead. Their eyes bleeding at the end of their stalks.[14]

He begins to understand that he cannot bring any of his adventures to a conclusion, despite the advantages of his method. Where anything is possible, nothing is sure.

Frustrated by his failure to construct a coherent episode, the narrator returns to Graal Flibuste's lineage. The fresh list of characters and deities becomes even more breathless, and the fear grows that even the limited objective of the digression may become lost in the material's complexity. Even so, the genealogy stutters to a halt. As the narrator's mind wanders, encounters and anecdotes form the nucleus of a coherent series of chapters, but the narrative constantly trips over its own convolutions. As allusions to previous chapters, or to Pinget's earlier books, lodge in the mind like the jumbled fragments of a remembered dream, shadows from the past flicker and fade. *Graal Flibuste* may be the text of the drunkard's unfinished letter mentioned in the introduction, or a draft of the message that Mahu refused to mail, or part of the letter that M. Levert will struggle to write in *Le Fiston*.

The book's enigmatic fragments, because of their tantalizing incompleteness, stimulate the mind, but they will lead nowhere. The reaction of a liberated prisoner illustrates the narrative's self-destructive tendencies when the shocking gift of freedom almost drives the formerly condemned man to suicide. The customs and interests of "Le Pays du Vent," the next territory visited, provide Pinget's protagonist with yet another set of analogues to his story's disintegration. The natives' fascination with puns, inverse progressions, and nonsense riddles intrigues him. Their rambling tales remind him of his journal's directionless exposition. Telling such stories can be exhilarating. It can also develop into a deadly disease, into a "verbal madness," whose victims mutter rambling monologues until they starve. The narrator considers this disease (to which Pinget will allude later in *Around Mortin* and *The Hypothesis*) as a very real threat—and for good reason. Its symptoms are a logical extension of the growing frenzy of the narrative and the stylistic hysteria of his own journal.

The traveller eventually remarks, in a bitter parody of pseudo-mystical prose, that his diary, so fluid and promising at the beginning, opens onto a labyrinth from which he cannot even begin to imagine an exit:

> I, who thought to settle in the Country of the Wind, charmed as I had been by my first contact with it, all of a sudden decided to leave it post haste. There was nothing true, nothing to attach you if you felt like leaving, either in the landscapes or the people; you didn't know in the morning if you were still asleep or not. The unusual situations there were perhaps only imaginary. You were tricked by yourself more than by others. You couldn't count on anything for sure and I rapidly got disgusted with these fantasies. . . . Our nature certainly is disconcerting. It yearns for freedom and once you offer freedom, it feels caught in a vice. . . .
>
> To let myself go on the wind, that master of error and disillusion. I did all I could to achieve the [weightless] state of a straw that the slightest breath carries here and there, for fear of staying where I was without folly or horizon. But what I took for possibles were only impossibles, and the state of a straw ["*fĕtu*" in the French text] that of a foetus, save the comfort of the pun. Where has Beautiful Chance taken me, and what storm has been given me to confront? No storm and no place, except in more and more closed circuits, labyrinths which I took at first for noble blind alleys, but which were only dead ends.[15]

He no longer describes change in terms of growth and metamorphosis, but in terms of physical decay. The early prophecy that the text may fall apart starts to fulfill itself in the experiment's third stage. But the narrator has pursued his quest too far to turn back: panic quickens the traveller's pace, and the whimsical romp takes on more and more of the terrifying breathlessness of a forced death-march. The boundless kingdom of make-believe, for which the narrator has sought so eagerly, closes in on him, and he can no longer brush aside Brindon's criticism of his narrative.

When the traveller sets out toward the sea, however, there is a suggestion, albeit a slight one, that *Graal Flibuste* may possibly build to a conclusion—that the voyage may end with the author's successful discovery of a satisfactory narrative form. Given Pinget's conception of the novel as "quest," that suggestion can only be a tantalizing illusion. Probing for an ending, Brindon's master describes the maritime landscape with unusual wistfulness as he follows a road leading toward the sea. The ocean stretches as far as the eye can see, kissing the sky in the distance and closing the horizon. Water and sky form a line beyond which all else is invisible. The scene suggests in visual terms the repose that one feels at a journey's end. But, paradoxically, as the narrator approaches his goal, his desire to end his travels or his diary wavers. As the fear of being unable to bring his journal to a close mounts, the desire to settle on the ocean as a terminus falters. According to Brindon, the narrator fears reaching the ocean because he is unable to describe it. Stated in more abstract terms, the traveller cannot close his account on a note of finality without rejecting the free-flowing form of expression and the conception of experience that are the narrative's very essence.

Just as the narrator seems about to flinch from the consequences of his quest, just as the pressure to betray the aleatory aesthetic by taking on a coherent conclusion seems irrepressible, the scene changes. The hint of a climactic ending and the reflection of the sun on the waves vanish like a mirage. On the horizon, a large triumphal portal replaces the sea, and the weary travellers make their way to it, choosing it not as a destination but as an arch leading to unknown adventures and meanderings:

> We advanced about a league amidst fields of wheat and oats. The door towered over us like a Himalaya. It was built in the middle of a space that had been stripped bare of plant life and we saw that it marked the entrance of a city whose suburbs, which were Lilliputian at that distance, came right up to its pilasters ... Wheat and grains were everywhere beneath a clear sky which was nothing like the seaside horizon; even the salt which the wind stuck to our lips had disappeared. This door with its provoking dimensions certainly guarded more than the entrance to a city. We kept on advancing. As if through the effect of an hallucination the colossal architecture seemed to come up to strike our eyelids; the detail of its frescos and enamels, of its bas reliefs and its figures modelled in the round appeared to us to be the fruit of a totally unknown art. Three cornices, more brilliant than gold crowned the masterpiece.
>
> We had eyes only for these wonders during the two hours we put in to approach it.[16]

The arch, with open space before and behind it, frames Pinget's conception of the novelist's task in general, and of his own work in particular. Pinget leaves his traveller unfulfilled. The quest for a form continues. The end of the journey is not in sight, since the act of enumerating reality will never be equal to its task. The narrator continues his endless catalog with a description of the arch.[17]

The wonders of the antivoyage arouse curiosity, and the traveller continues calmly to paint in words a picture never to be completed. Pinget varies the inventory of his fictional world by presenting the recurring elements in the folkloric framework of the imaginary voyage. He develops the theme of the author's impotence by expanding experiments with language. The spontaneity and suggestiveness of the spoken and the written word, so essential to Pinget's continuing catalog, reach a sort of paroxysm in the giddy enumerations and recapitulations of *Graal Flibuste*. The narrator's attempt to paint a clearly delineated word picture of the alien kingdom through which he passes breaks down. The reader is permitted to get only a hazy impression of the land the journal describes.

Pinget deliberately emphasizes the ambiguity of the traveller's extravagant word associations and images in order to bring into play the ambivalence of language, just as Lewis Carroll and Edward Lear did in their nonsense rhymes.[18] A language's available sounds and signs can neither penetrate to the heart of things nor relate them to each other. They can only point out objects or assign rather arbitrary labels to them. The novelist's search for a way to understand and control leads him to make list after list. Normally, naming, classifying, and cataloging are acts of a would-be possessor. The one-to-one relationship between word and object in the Book of Genesis, for example, is reassuringly simple and conclusive. Adam rules God's creation first by giving its members names that carry both moral and linguistic authority; Adam does not deal in poetic approximations or improvisations. Pinget's traveller's verbal constructions, on the contrary, do not master what they describe. As in allegory, the prose is hazy and polyvalent. Two of the characters, for example, are named "M. Songe" ("Mr. Dream") and "M. Ducreux" ("Mr. Hollow"). The similar sound and reversed vowels of the words "*céramiste*" and "*camériste*" provide the one tenuous link between two chapters. At another point, Pinget puns on the slang expression for girl friend, "*Nana*," by playing with the sounds "*Maman*," "*Anna*," and "*Ex-Nana.*"[19] Words meant to define trail off into fuzzy imprecision. The narrator's loss of linear control acts itself out periodically in his prose. In the chapter "Dame Nature," for instance, he uses "nature" in so many contexts that the word ceases to be an intelligible verbal sign and disintegrates into an arbitrary arrangement of sounds. Once again, the very existence of "natural" relationships teeters in the balance. As is the case with his experiments with narration, Pinget's verbal fantasizing opens a linguistic Pandora's Box. Freedom from logic and convention produces exhilaration expressed through free-flowing wordplay and engaging whimsy. But exultation soon gives way to anguish, and humor yields to irony, as the framework of habitual, narrative, and linguistic structures collapses.

There is a clear analogy between the elliptical structure of Pinget's fictional world and the circuitous progression of *Graal Flibuste*, for Pinget constantly redescribes and reclassifies the inhabitants of his imaginary province. He varies the topography of this strange land, from one novel to the next, like the unsatisfied musician, described in the chapter entitled "The Organist," who

> . . . played for God alone the phrase seven thousand times seven times repeated, hammered out, cut short, dissected, fused, taken up again as if, once it had foolhardily left his brain it must, by the torture he inflicted on himself by repeating it, return to the original nothingness for having remained inaudible, and carry him away too, him, the musician, in the hiccup of its ultimate variation.[20]

Like the organist's piece, and like Gide's *Urien's Voyage* [*Le Voyage d' urien*], *Graal Flibuste* disintegrates completely with the last page and begins to return to the void from which the narrator's imagination has drawn it. So the third stage of the traveller's stylistic experiment calls into question, all too successfully, man's ability to formulate, and to express in coherent terms, "reality" as he perceives it. But even as he makes sport of linear narration, Pinget mocks his own fumbling, maddeningly circuitous movement. Like Montaigne's ideal skeptic, he doubts his own doubting and questions his own questioning. Each successive novel forces the reader to change his interpretation of what he has already read. He must be as wary of trusting fixed compass points in Fantoine and Agapa as Brindon's master is in the realm of *Graal Flibuste*. The Pingetian narrator will continue to be bewildered. He will lose himself in the maze of variations that a scene calls to his mind. The seemingly puckish voyage journal marks a turning point in Pinget's efforts to renew the novel. The ongoing inventory of his imaginary world will turn more and more inward, like a text of Brindon's master, which repeats and contradicts itself almost to the point of denying its validity. Yet the whole somehow gains vitality and momentum from the integrity of the chaotic process. Having pushed his quest to the gates of ivory in a pseudo-adventure story, Pinget proceeds to explore the gates of horn through a pseudo-autobiography in his next work. As we have observed, *Graal Flibuste* faces in two directions at once, like Doctor Dolittle's Pushmi-Pullyu. The voyage to the outer limits leads to a vantage point from which the outlines of novels to come loom in the distance and the events and characters of earlier works swarm on the shadowy plane behind. Old and new acquaintances mingle. Just when shards from a shattered world seem about to come together, the ending shows that the author has no intention of letting that happen. He cannot, or will not, describe a comprehensible community, as Balzac or Faulkner would have done. His voyage becomes more and more self-consciously introspective and, after *Graal Flibuste* has shown that space cannot impose limits on the imagination, *Baga* forms a counterbalance to the centrifugal journey to the outer limits of Pinget's province, with the scudding sea and the mysterious arch on the horizon. In *Baga*, Pinget explores the confinement of mind in a carcass of meat. The endings of both novels open out onto horizon upon horizon of fantasy and conjecture, and their composition marks the end of the author's first and most clearly surrealistic phase.

BAGA

As in *Graal Flibuste*, Pinget entitles his next work, *Baga* (1958), after its most shadowy and mysterious character, and once again the work centers around a voyage of self-discovery in which the narrator makes repeated and inconclusive efforts to write his memoirs. The central character wants primarily to present to posterity a truthful, if slightly flattering, image of himself. But the composition of his self-portrait opens onto a continually expanding inquiry. As he tries to discover his identity and to explain his past by projecting a series of autiobiographical daydreams, *Baga* follows the unfinished memoirs of a man questioning his own dignity in the flickering light of his life's major events:

> I am a King. Yes, a King. I am King of me. Of my crap. I and my crap, we have a King. I mean the crap of my mind. For I have a mind. A mind which craps itself up. I've given up having it scraped out. You get so you don't want to move. After a certain age, you don't want to move any more. I still mean the mind, but it's the same thing. You get used to it. You find corners. You curl up. You caress your knees.[21]

Seeking to find out who he is, not where he is, the narrator sets out on an exploratory voyage through memory and imagination. Pinget replaces the vague outlines of the *Graal Flibuste*'s countryside with eleven mythomaniacal daydreams, each of which reflects a stage in the narrator's voyage of self-discovery. He projects himself into a succession of fanciful avatars and slips into varying roles to see what suits him best. Obsessive reinterpretations of the same act or event replace the disjointed travel episodes, and achronological exposition and arbitrary shifts in tense and person create the kind of ambiguity that Pinget achieved in the travel journal by dislocating linear progression.

The memoirs develop coherently—up to a certain point. Then, as the protagonist tries to explain his friend Baga's possible treachery, the narrative branches off into a labyrinth of self-contradictory hypotheses. Whether they take the form of centrifugal enumeration or that of centripetal investigation, Pinget's novels develop through the opposition of disintegration and proliferation, and the expression of that process through words is both a creative and a destructive act. If *Graal Flibuste* marks the end of the Book of Genesis of the world of Fantoine and Agapa, *Baga* suggests analogies linking the reader to Pinget and his characters as they try to discover landmarks in that unfolding fictional province.

As the story begins, King Architruc is describing his daily routine. His monarchy quickly takes on a down-at-the-heel character reminiscent of the slightly scabrous atmosphere of eighteenth-century erotic literature. (Architruc would feel quite at home at Mangogul's court in Diderot's *Indiscreet Jewels* [*Les Bijoux Indiscrets*]). After breakfast, Architruc lolligags in bed until noon. Following a lackadaisical toilette, he straggles through an uninspiring court routine and then sits down at a table to gulp down a roast of beef. Here the perspective changes unexpectedly to the point of view of a courtier, who ridicules the king's entourage (including the Duchesse de Bois-Suspect and the Princesse de Hem, both of whom were mentioned in *Graal Flibuste*) and mocks Architruc's boorish manners. Since the initial "h" is often silent in French speech, the first two letters of the princess' name presumably would not be pronounced. She becomes therefore "La Princesse de M[erde]" ("The Princess of Shit"), in keeping with the ironic juxtapositions of royal and bodily functions.

Almost from the outset, then, the narrator takes on the dual roles of actor and critic, two contrasting points of view that create an undercurrent of burlesque or satire that undermines the narrator's self-confidence. If Architruc is a king at all, he is one in name only, like Ionesco's Béranger the First. Behind man's carefully grounded assumptions of regal identity, a clown lurks and leers at the artifice, and a death head's beetling brows protrude beneath the layers of Harlequin's grease paint. Architruc nervously turns the subject away from self criticism, as if frightened by the exposure of his lack of dignity and the questions it raises: he describes an incident that seems to have occurred shortly after the luncheon scene in the second part of the memoirs. A delegation bearing an ultimatum has arrived from Novocardie, a neighboring state, and the king fears war. In a rambling, would-be-Churchillian speech, the king exhorts his people to remain confident, but he is cut short abruptly by his prime minister; hurt by the memory of being interrupted, Architruc breaks off telling about the war and withdraws into the past. He finds solace in reliving his coronation, and it is at this point that he gives the first of several contradictory explanations of why he named Baga to high office in the first place. By this account, Baga apparently had cured the nervous prince's upset stomach just before a crucial moment in the ceremony. Gratitude coupled with a fear of subsequent bouts of indigestion prompted Architruc to name him prime minister despite the Queen Mother's unexplained objections.

The king's thoughts then shift back to the impending meeting with the Novocardians. Baga has warned him of their bellicose intentions, and the ambassadors do, in fact, deliver an ultimatum, threatening to annex La Vallee du Chanchèze, the site of the temple to Graal Flibuste described in the previous book. They justify their action by claiming that Architruc has ignored their government's repeated requests to exterminate the rat population that is ravaging their side of the border on the other side of the valley. In the manner of the Rabelaisian warrior kings—and our even more sophistic modern "wagers of peace"—Architruc denies ever having received their petitions, declares a national alert, and proclaims that the war to follow is a strictly defensive one. The dreamlike account of the ensuing battle recalls the satiric buffoonery of King Ubu's epic sorties and alarums.[22] For comic effect, Pinget juxtaposes the hyperbole of the commander-in-chief's exhortations and the insignificant forces and objectives involved in the one-battle campaign. Architruc sets out for the front in a sputtering, commandeered taxi laden with picnic provisions, rallying his subjects to join the army as he nears the disputed valley. Baga remarks, in a caustic aside to the king's patriotic cant, that the government has been making big profits from the rats of Le Chanchèze without his sovereign's knowledge or approval. In fact, the prime minister has allocated a large portion of these secret funds to the purchase of armaments, a clear case of the cause of war providing prewar economic spoils.

Baga's remark strikes a discordant note and sets his sovereign to thinking. The king wonders whether the claims of the ambassadors may have been valid after all, and whether Baga had kept their protests from reaching him. The outcome of the battle, in which the king wins a stunning victory by driving hordes of ravening rats into the enemy's ranks, momentarily quiets his doubts, but they eventually cause the narrator to mistrust the accuracy of his initial version of the war's outbreak. Architruc's suspicion turns the memoirs inward upon themselves, to questioning their own veracity, upsetting the work's chronological exposition, and causing a double crisis of confidence for the narrator. In time, the king comes to suspect Baga of treason and tries to mull over events to find another possible explanation of his prime minister's conduct. Yet the following scenes, which fill out the book, never treat the period in question. The feeling grows that Architruc dreads having his suspicions confirmed, though he returns to writing his memoirs with the firm intention of trying to get at a truth that seems to fall apart even as he grasps it:

> It's painful, I wanted to go as far as possible. To play the game, as they say. You certainly could see that I didn't believe in it, couldn't you? What is there to believe? From what moment is everything false? The Ambassadors? No, I remember having spoken to them. Our departure at night? My taking command? I don't know any more, I don't know anymore. This sleepiness which is coming over me.[23]

The narrator's drowsiness is symptomatic of his desire to withdraw into a state of unconsciousness, and Architruc proceeds to spin ever-wilder fantasies in a game of hide-and-seek with himself. Later in Pinget's cycle, he will reappear as a crazy old eccentric, confirming the impression that mythomania throws his "kingdom" in and out of perspective. Be that as it may, the king of night- and daydreams has a place of honor in Fantoine and Agapa, for imaginative falsehoods can cause one to stumble upon an unexpected truth (as the haphazard traveller discovered in the cuckooland of Graal Flibuste). Pinget dwells on Architruc's stubborn attempt to draw from his imagination a role, a kingdom, or a past in which he can feel complete. Yet the narrator cannot satisfy himself with the world he has created, any more than Pinget's giddy province can totally please its inventor as a complete, all-encompassing unit. After the girdle of words built to lace himself in has burst at the seams, Architruc starts again, postulating yet another identity with each unit of his memoirs. The world of Fantoine and Agapa grows in a similar manner, with each novel correcting, rejecting, or modifying its predecessor's material. Dissatisfaction with the incongruity between truth and appearance sets Architruc's imagination churning. The first reaction is negative. Architruc prefaces his first reconstruction of the world with the self-critical description of his body (cited in the introduction), lingering on details that the normal (cursory) morning glance in the mirror skips over with a shudder. His penetrating stare lays bare the pathetic clown shivering in the robes of complacency and habit worn by many of all stations.

The second reaction is more positive. When disgust for his body leads the narrator to write memoirs of the dream life that he would have liked to have lived, his text bursts out of the restrictions of chronological structure and follows a freewheeling pattern. Architruc stresses the change of outline before presenting his first avatar.

> After the war, for the war did take place but not as I said, another one, slow, lasting years and years, a war like leprosy, you couldn't do anything, you decomposed, I slept all the time, you didn't have newspapers anymore, rats came as far as the city, the enemy finally left us alone and barely fifteen hundred people remained in the Kingdom; after this sickness Baga woke me and I had gotten so thin. I would have had to. . . . I would have had to. . . . I don't know. I left. I have been in the forest. There, I am in the forest. I am writing that. No, I have written. Or I was writing.[24]

Soon Architruc gives himself another fresh start. Now he is living alone in a hermit's cabin in the woods—a recluse writing anxious letters to the world he has fled. The desire to come to grips with the past, not the desire to communicate with others, causes him to write; indeed the correspondence will never reach its destination because he has no correspondent! The memoirs take on the form of a diary. Bored, he sets out to find the court musicians and spends, or imagines that he spends, a year with them. The unexplained mystery of Baga's conduct eventually draws him back to a description of life at court, and the next unit covers a dialogue between the king and the prime minister that fails to clear up the role of each in the declaration of war. It only confuses the issue further by hinting at more sordid and complex interpretations. Architruc states his affection for Baga in a way that suggests that their friendship may be homosexual, and Baga's bland assurances of innocence ring so false as to incriminate him still further. (The name "Baga" sounds a bit like the English word "bugger," but that translingual connection is very dubious at best.) Pinget also suggests that Architruc may have been aware of his friend's intrigue and had only feigned ignorance so as to be able to pretend innocence later, if necessary, after a military defeat.

OUTER LIMITS—INNER LIMITS

The sixth unit opens with an allusion to a previous work by Pinget and a flashback in the novel's chronology. A King Gnar, a minor character in *Graal Flibuste*, and his adviser, a snake (both literally and figuratively), read and comment upon the letters that Architruc wrote in the forest. The section closes with two passages in which the narrator tries to define the purpose of his text. He seeks to keep intact his sense of who he is by telling a story, much as the traveller in *Graal Flibuste* did:

> Dear Malaise. Excuse me for calling you that but that's more or less what I feel. Perhaps you did not exist outside [me]. I watch over you at the bottom of myself like an old kidney bean. I become lucid again now and then, I must have written nonsense to you. A bean which might have sprouted but the sprout rotted. It was marvellous that plant hope. We would have made soup together. How young we were! But I prefer growing old after all. I keep you, at least. All that is inexplicable. You know I sleep a lot. . . . I'm taking up this letter again after sleeping. Fortunately I fixed my thoughts on paper. Yes, I let you in beyond the seas of my sleep. Beautiful image. If I abandon you I would have the impression. . . . God it's hard to talk in metaphors. You forget what you meant. I write to you through a love of phrases. You are a phrase at the bottom of myself which I look for the way a blind man looks for the edge of the sidewalk. Let's develop [that]. The edge of the sidewalk so as not to fall flat on his face. But in my case I invent the sidewalk, I need that little danger. . . . I am in the process—shall I tell you? of looking for something new to say. I am like a bird dropping which might think the world smells bad. Good night.[25]

The narrator returns once more to the subject of the Novocardian war, but he is still unable to reconstruct exactly what took place. He adopts an orphan, Rara, contradicts the announced purpose of his memoirs and disinherits the nephews for whom he had originally intended to write. Parenthood, even by adoption, fits into Architruc's search for himself, for he wants to project yet another image of himself through Rara. The narrator then describes a Kafkalike dramatization of repressed guilt where he imagines that he is in jail. In the drab prison, days and nights overlap increasingly until every entry in the prisoner's diary bears the same date. When he learns that Rara works in the prison kitchen, Architruc manages to visit him there, but he can no longer remember whether he is Rara's foster mother or father. Joy turns to sorrow as he realizes that his plan to project himself onto an heir, like his attempt to write coherent memoirs, has ended in failure.

The eighth unit introduces yet another version of the events forming the novel's core. Architruc appears before an examining magistrate investigating his past. He introduces fresh material to incriminate Baga and to defend himself in the matter of the Novocardian war. But the content of his testimony is less important than his painful attempt to make sense and not change the subject.

> [You say] come to the point, your Honor, come to the point. . . . I'll find it, but give me time. To tell all like that isn't easy. They ask me to justify myself. . . . Do they ask me to justify myself?[26]

A third and even more unsavoury version of the prime minister's role slowly emerges from the hearing. Architruc claims that Baga was once his (Architruc's) mother's lover and suggests that he (Baga) had the king murdered in order to rule through his widow. Then Architruc alleges that he fell in love with Baga and made him prime minister in order to entice him away from the queen. The judge, finding it impossible to give the interrogation any direction, has the prisoner led away under guard. A relatively realistic account of a picnic reception for the visiting Queen Conegrund checks the memoir's lapse into incoherence momentarily, but the dichotomy between appearance and reality returns when the deference that Architruc shows toward the queen only serves to throw into bolder relief the coarse side of this gluttonous old nymphomaniac, which is suggested by her name.[27]

The king's self-denigration and his desire to find a way by which to express the purity of his nature eventually reach a climax. Architruc sets out with his prime minister to build a castle in the country. For no apparent reason, the king suddenly feels released from his body. He follows the scent of flowers and floats on the air toward the retreat of Sister Louise, into which he is accepted. At this point the book's style changes. The sentences become shorter and describe more colors and sense impressions. The slightest detail serves as a pretext for a moralizing homily or a simplistic religious symbol. The change in style follows an unexpected metamorphosis in Architruc's nature. He simpers more, and shaves less, until he awakens one morning to discover that he (or should one say "she"?) has changed sex!

The goose-girl piety of Architruc's latest avatar enables Pinget to probe yet another zone, one in which language gives off a penumbra of double meanings and repressed desires. The religion preached by Architruc's mother superior stresses a lesbianized Christianity. The groans of her mystical prayers frequently have a physical as well as a metaphysical timbre. In Sister Louise's community, woman, not man, was created in God's image, and the postulant sisters are more attracted to each other's bodies than they are to the mystical body of Christ. The women mend, pray, and read the sermons of "R.P." (Reverend Père? Robert Pinget?). The zealots save Marie, a local girl, from the clinches of her fiancé in order to clutch at her themselves, and the narrator closes the episode ironically praising the physical and spiritual union of two women. "Blessed be the pure in heart . . ."

When Architruc's male hormones return from their leave of absence, quite as mysteriously as they had departed, he is no longer welcome at Chez Soeur Louise, and so he decides to go home and continue his memoirs there. He finds Baga anxious to show him a castle that was built during the king's absence, but he is too tired to record the details of his inspection. The monotonous court routine continues to grind along; nothing has changed. The pathetic mummer's quest for identity, the scrofulous sovereign's search for dignity, the dazzling succession of avatars—it all ends with a retreat into the mediocre, numbing refuge of routine.

For all his feverish mythomania, the narrator of *Baga* never finds answers to the questions "Who am I?" and "What happened?" Yet the process that the narrator's mind follows overshadows the paucity of his quest's results. In *Baga*, Pinget does to time and identity what he has done to place and space in *Graal Flibuste*. He distorts chronology and perspective, much as Max Jacob did in *Le Roi de la Boétie*. From one day to the next, Architrue keeps changing his configuration of the world, scrapping old illusions and advancing new hypotheses, as if trying to furnish a room whose dimensions keep shrinking and expanding by turns.

> Certainly you laugh, you are amused, even very amused [in *Baga*], although sometimes the author's verve gets tired and runs thin. But in the final analysis the elaborate tricks of Robert Pinget expose trickiness. . . . It is a novel which raises doubts about the possibility of writing novels.[28]

The composition of the memoirs opens a Pandora's Box of possibilities that, instead of concluding with a portrait worthy of hanging in Sartre's Bouville town hall, recall the open gates at the end of *Graal Flibuste*. Even the narrator's name remains amusingly and annoyingly vague, "Architruc" being the French equivalent of "Mr. Super-thingamajig." At one point, Pinget suggests that "Architruc" may be the approximation of an approximation— a mispronunciation of "Archiduc," perhaps.

Named or nameless, the protagonist doggedly continues his inquiry, even though his self-consciousness undermines each successive role. He does so not out of a sense of heroism but because he has no alternative. He attempts to reduce the apparent chaos of experience to some kind of sense, as any human being, freighted with an active but insufficiently clairvoyant intelligence, might do. His memoirs record the collapse of the solutions he proposes, solutions teetering between stupidity and vulgarity, fantasy and poetry. *Baga* serves a similar function in Pinget's fiction, scaling down the dimensions of the kingdom of Graal Flibuste to the confines of a rat-infested valley. The dissatisfaction causing Architruc to project and discard one avatar after another parallels whatever it is that inspires Pinget to expand and contract the contours of his fiction with each successive novel. Having traced, in his first books, the outlines of a fictional province that is growing and changing, Pinget now begins to turn his quest inward, and the second phase of Pinget's experiment is about to begin. In *Baga*, he begins to transform his exploration into a limitless inquiry, stressing the analogies between the attempt to create a world, the protagonists' struggles to write their texts, and the reader's attempt to link the whole. Americans have a saying, "If you can't find something nice to say, don't say anything at all"; in France, on the contrary, one of the worst faults to be found in an otherwise active intelligence is the lack of *"le sens critique,"* the sense of disproportion, the sense of the ridiculous. Pinget's first books focus a witty and deep "critical sense" on the conventional novel, denigrating and spoofing its weaknesses. Yet already in *Graal Flibuste* and *Baga* one feels a powerful current of affirmation of both the healing power of writing and the adventure of innovation. That current will grow stronger as Pinget, having razed the house of fiction to its foundations, turns from wrecking to building.

part two

Twisting Mystery's Tale

374

rewrie photograp la gauche

Fenpied moins ratili;   600 ; 30
                        000   20

fenêtre ouverte,

~~soir~~ ~~possible~~, ciel rose   du soir
~~nous~~ toit ~~pierre~~, ~~on~~ héron=
de lies qui tournoient d'en face
                        très haut, c'était le
bau fixe, mes ~~journées~~ arrosées de pernod, nous
remettions au lendemain le bricolage à la recente,
l'histoire du capitaine bonhomait de
                       dans nos derniers son image transformée
~~pratique au jour~~ nous le retrouvions à l'écran
~~tant~~ tant simple, ~~c~~
                 ses vrais yeux, son vrai
s'ouvrire, comme ~~les jours où~~ aime revus
                 longtemps
après ~~autrepa~~), ~~B~~ nul pulsé ici
                           & n'ai qui nous

3 From Quest to Inquest

Monsieur Levert (Le Fiston)
Clope to the Dossier (Clope au dossier)

Françoise, who in the world are the funeral bells tolling for? Oh, my goodness, it must be for Mme. Rousseau.—Proust, *Combray*

... I always had an extreme desire to learn to distinguish the true from the false, to understand my actions clearly and to proceed with assurance in this life.—Descartes, *Discourse on Method*

So Watt did not know what had happened. He did not care, to do him justice, what had happened. But he felt the need to think that such and such a thing had happened then, the need to be able to say, when the scene began to unroll its sequences, yes, I remember, that is what happened then.—Samuel Beckett, *Watt*

It had happened several times, indeed quite often but never in such a clear, characteristic way. You work in a given direction, all the more stubbornly in that you are less sure of yourself and have less data in hand.

You tell yourself that you remain free, when the time comes, to turn round and search in another direction.

You send inspectors right and left. You think you are getting somewhere and then you discover a new clue and you start moving cautiously forward.

And all of a sudden, just when you least expect it, the case slips out of your grasp. You cease to be in control of it. It is events which are in command and which force you to take measures which you had not foreseen, and for which you were not prepared.

> In these cases there are a few uncomfortable hours to get through. You rack your brains. You ask yourself whether you didn't set off in the wrong direction from the start, and whether you aren't going to find yourself faced with a blank wall, or, worse still, with a reality different from what you had imagined.—Simenon, *Maigret Gets Angry*

In his first, his surrealistic, manner, Pinget uses parody to probe and dissect the cadaver of the "well-made" novel. As we have seen, however, the aim of his spoofs, however outrageous they may be, is to revive, not to destroy. In both *The Fox and The Compass* and in *Graal Flibuste* he burlesques the notion of the novel as a successfully completed quest by mocking the epic-voyage genre. In Architruc's antimemoirs he turns the narrative tradition of autobiography inside out. In his next four novels the more patently whimsical elements disappear, but Pinget continues to rely on humor as he veers between destructive and constructive poles in his approach to fiction. In the second stage of his quest Pinget twists and distorts the familiar linear plot into unexpected shapes, developing a variation of the mystery story in which form and content come into a more satisfactory and less precarious balance. Pinget first brings his talents as a parodist to bear on the detective story in *Monsieur Levert* (*Le Fiston*, 1959), followed by *Clope to the Dossier* (*Clope au dossier*, 1961). Both works are related to Fantoine and Agapa's unfolding chronicle, developing as investigations of a past event, as did Architruc's scrutiny of Baga's motives. *Monsieur Levert* (or *No Answer*, as it is titled in the Calder & Boyars translation distributed in the British Isles) resembles *Baga* to a greater degree, whereas *Clope to the Dossier* anticipates *The Inquisitory* (*L'Inquisitoire*). Taken together, the two works change the outlines of Fantoine and Agapa as the reader has known them. Changing the configuration given to his work as it unfolds, Pinget makes the chronicle swallow its own tail by altering the mystery-story format, for in these investigations the narrator questions the validity of his own basic premise. Having written first under the guise of a voyage to nowhere, then under that of a mythomaniac's fruitless search for identity, Pinget now turns to the detective story and treats it as a played-out butt of ridicule. His ambivalent treatment of the mystery-story model strengthens the link between author, narrator, and reader stressed earlier. Pinget's protagonists—and his readers, following the protagonists from novel to novel—lose their way in the clouds of contradictions that roll over Pinget's province. They keep trying to make precise meteorological observations, but the weather changes too fast to be mapped. Even so, the desire to take one's bearings in a tantalizing, ambiguous world persists. As the disoriented traveller discovered in *Graal Flibuste*, inhabiting a partially comprehensible environment without trying to understand it is intellectual suicide, and Pinget's seekers strenuously reject that passive alternative. Instead, the voices speaking in *Monsieur Levert* and *Clope to the Dossier* press ahead with their investigations and are undeterred by the inconclusiveness of their findings. "Outside of what is written is Death," M. Levert exclaims succinctly, returning to the endless inquiry and the directionless letter that he knows he will never finish.

Levert's remark points up a fundamental parallel between exploration of the stammering, inconclusive nature of the verbal process and investigation of the fugitive, the unknown. Pinget's Keystone Cops, instead of running down the "truth," play hide-and-seek behind hypotheses. Because of Pinget's well-coordinated stylistic devices, the locus of mystery lies more in the characters' word associations than in events tracked down and remembered. An early printing of *Le Fiston* had no page numbers, depriving readers of conventional reference points and possible resting-places along the way. Extremely long paragraphs rework the initial "given." Each could stand alone, yet each is linked to the whole (however tenuously) and mirrors the relationship of all of Pinget's books to the ongoing chronicle. In retrospect, the paragraphing gives the impression of a landscape strewn with fragments of some collapsed or unfinished structure. The increasingly disjointed paragraph linkage in *Clope to the Dossier* elicits a constant and strenuous mental effort to relate parts of the material or just to "keep the place," and Pinget confuses matters further by weaving fact and supposition together through frequent shifts from the present tense to the conditional. The passages linking episodes through cross-references, repetitions, puns, and parallel scenes soon become muddled, producing an increasingly disturbing sensation of déjà vu.

Eventually, suppositions overlap and fuse like the contours of Fantoine and Agapa themselves. The narrative scrambles itself to such a point that it no longer matters whether the action under investigation actually took place or not. Perhaps the protagonist is piecing it together out of the whole cloth, like a novelist dreaming up a story. The inventive, inductive thought process takes over as subject and object as Pinget depicts man as a compulsive, comic-strip storyteller striving mightily to fill verbal balloons only to have them burst under the pressure of his hot air. In short, the inquiry of Pinget's investigator lies somewhere between the capers of Groucho Marx as Captain Spaulding in *Animal Crackers* and a modern Oedipus shouting the answers to riddles into the wind. Or to use another figure, his protagonists walk a tightrope of words over the depths of silence and chaos and dare the reader to follow.

Le Fiston, Pinget's first mystery-story spoof, begins with a basic affirmation, a geometrical premise as suggestive as the opening statement of a fugue: "The shoemaker's daughter has died." The entire novel will grow from the articulation of the tone of voice speaking this sentence and the elucidation of an ill-defined crisis that is evoked by it. The intonation of the opening statement drops at the end. The nameless narrator gives a curt, sparse account of the funeral of Marie Chinze, the dead girl in question. Crisp factual details replace the surrealistic curlicues of *Graal Flibuste* and *Baga*.

After expeditiously presenting the characters attending Marie's funeral (much as an Agatha Christie would list the murder suspects), the narrator recounts the movements of various groups after the service. Marie's older brother, Roger, his pregnant wife, and another couple return home by car. Roger's wife is carsick en route. Next we meet Mme. Pacot, her husband, and their daughter Alice, another branch of the Chinze family. By chance, Alice meets George, her lover. George's obvious vulgarity displeases Mme. Pacot, and when the family gets home, a quarrel breaks out over Alice's choice of friends. The girl takes advantage of the brouhaha to slip out to see George.

The narrator next reports on the activities of the priest who said the funeral Mass. The rectory's disagreeable retainer, Odette, prepared lunch for the curate. After the meal, he took the bus to

Sirancy to make some sick calls. The scene switches to a café where the Moule brothers, Victor and Pierre, banter with a waiter about sex. Pierre Moule is engaged to Simone Brize. The brothers then return to the farm where they live with their mother.

There follows a fussy, cluttered word-picture of a villa owned by a certain M. Levert. Who is this man? What connects him with Marie Chinze? The answers, if any, lurk in shadows as yet unexplored. Phrases from the description of the garden will recur later in slightly different form. Their sharply etched outlines give the scene the eerie intensity of a painting of a nightmare landscape:

> The garden lies in front of the house, a neat formal garden. First comes a gravel terrace surrounding the house. On the street side it is fenced in with a low wall with a railing on top that forms a little courtyard. On the other side there are different-shaped beds surrounded by boxwood hedges and planted with flowers or grass. The little paths dividing these beds are gravelled too. Some are shaded by rare trees once planted at regular intervals in the beds but several of them have since died. Those that are left spoil the garden's symmetry. After the flower beds comes a wide meadow full of daisies in summer. Then there is the Furet woods that run down to the river. The oaks are a hundred years old.[1]

Eventually the narrator links Levert vaguely to the act or movement around which he has been building the story. At about ten o'clock on the morning of the funeral, Levert met an old woman gathering wood on his grounds. She told him that the church bells were tolling for the shoemaker's daughter. After leaving her, Levert sat down on a bench in the grape arbor of the garden, took out a notebook, and began to write. As he wrote, a bird sang overhead—a detail that the narrator will repeat later, again and again, without distinguishing past and present. Levert goes inside to continue his writing, and the text includes a meticulous inventory of the house's layout and furnishings. At four o'clock, the old man's sister and her daughter Francine pay a call. Once again the uncle asks who has died, even though the woodcutter and his maid have already answered the same question.

Levert, it turns out, is writing a long letter that he can neither finish, send, nor abandon (much like Porridge in *The Fox and The Compass*, Sinture in *Mahu or the Material*, the drunkard in *Graal Flibuste*, and Architruc in his hermit avatar in *Baga*):

> He writes every day to his son who went away almost ten years ago. First he makes a draft, then he writes the letter. When the letter is finished, Monsieur Levert files it away, for he does not trust the mails. Then too a letter might be inconvenient for its addressee, so inconvenient.[2]

As the narrative continues to focus on Levert, scrutinizing his movements and actions in ever greater detail, Pinget suddenly turns the inquiry inside out by revealing that Levert is himself the heretofore anonymous narrator. Up to this point, the narrator has been speaking of himself in the third person. Actually, it now seems, the letter he is composing is the novel itself, and the reader, without knowing it, has been perusing a draft of the work:

> After the visit Monsieur Levert went on with his letter. He was tired and thought for a long time. He must not have heard the hall clock strike because he jumped when his housekeeper announced dinner at seven-fifteen. Already, he said, I'm not through, I'll have to work tonight. After the meal he did go back to his desk. He seemed even more exhausted than before. He wrote slowly, checking against his notebook, consulting the dictionary. At eight-thirty the telephone rang and he answered it. Then he went on with his letter. The living room was dark, quiet, the housekeeper had gone upstairs to her room. On the mantlepiece Europa, abducted and motionless, hurled defiance at the dreams of escape.

> Dear son. I'm starting over. Face drawn, shoelace untied, coat unbuttoned, hair ragged, eyes red, head empty. This prison where I am. It's starting over. The hand writing you. Off the track. The track of the track of the. Head. Heading. Dash against the wall, crash spots on the wall, holes. Holes from nails. Wall pegged with holes. Moving away, coming back. My head pegged, these holes in my head, the wall. I didn't want I did want. Writing you. As if the night in its mercy had managed to manage to collect under this same roof in its infinite mercy. Managed to collect under the same roof Pain. This letter will never be mailed.[3]

FROM QUEST TO INQUEST

Following the revelation of the narrator's identity, certain questions arise about Levert's story. The text may indeed be a letter written to persuade a runaway son to come home. But if so, the reader wonders, why did the lad leave town ten years ago in the first place? Why does Levert speak of Marie Chinze's funeral at such length in a letter supposedly dealing with "family news"? Perhaps Levert's son is imaginary—a desperate attempt to furnish an empty life with purpose. Anguish and loneliness break through the speaker's voice, but their cause remains obscure. Levert sees himself as a father seeking justification through his son. "I was looking for my son," he writes. "I am orphaned." Fitfully, he runs down the reactions to Marie Chinze's death, hoping to stumble upon answers to these questions.

Minet Chinze, Marie's brother, plays a central role in the following scene, in which he mourns his sister while looking out a café window at the train station, peeling potatoes, and reliving in memory the arrival of Leon, a friend who spent a summer with the family ten years before. In memory, he meets Leon's train and shows him his room on the second floor. Impressed by the "tall athletic blond fellow with a Northern accent," Marie sets the table as if for a party. During the summer, Leon and Marie fall in love but, somehow, the match never quite comes off. Minet, after recalling that Marie had refused another suitor after Leon's departure, turns his attention back to the potatoes he has been peeling.

As in *Baga*, the narrator's suppositions now begin to double back on themselves, muddling the chronology. The next scene returns to the woodgatherer's movements after she spoke to Levert on the morning of the burial. She stops to chat with Sophie Narre, the town gossip, as the mourners are filing out of the church. Pinget has mentioned Sophie, the village magpie who professes to have knowledge about everybody in the earlier books, and who will pop up regularly in later ones. ("Narre" calls to mind *"narrateur,"* as Bernard Pingaud pointed out, and through that name Pinget refers back to the busybody, conventional novelists caricatured previously.) Winks, lowered voices, and suggestive silences spice the gossip's chit-chat. Sophie Narre hints that Levert may have once been Mme. Chinze's lover and Marie their illegitimate daughter. Like the names of so many of Pinget's characters, "Levert" suggests multiple associations: *"le vert galant,"* rougish flirtatiousness, *"le verre,"* the glass ever-present in his hand, *"le vert,"* the green of youth, growth, and rebirth. Sophie Narre's insinuation would seem to be in character, and it is passed along without comment. But Levert changes the subject abruptly (nervously or guiltily, perhaps?) to a description of another piece of property that he owns. This time, overly precise detail gives the impression that Levert is trying either to reject the previous episode's innuendo or to regain his composure by mindlessly rattling off facts.

In describing this second piece of property, which is at Sirancy, Levert follows the same order used in writing about "Les Roches." There is an old, sulfate-blue coachhouse at the southeast corner of the grounds. A broken-down watering trough lies in a heap in front of the door. The shed has been converted into a combination laundry and haybarn. It is only after giving a long rundown of objects in the rooms of the villa that Levert starts to reminisce about his life there with his wife and son. Mme. Levert (if indeed there ever was one) seems to have been a temperamental heiress who withdrew more and more from her husband after the birth of their son, Gilbert. The father apparently overcompensated for her rejection by lavishing all his affection on the boy, and he admits that he spoiled his son, particularly after the mother's death. He even went so far as to accompany the boy on drinking bouts. Then, one day, Gilbert ran away without warning, leaving behind only a short note telling his father not to try to trace him.

This bland description of Gilbert's departure is quite unconvincing. Many spoiled children enjoy threatening to run away—a time-tested trump card in the game of "Blackmail Parents"—but they seldom leave home for good. Furthermore, the reader is forced to wonder whether, and if so how, Marie's funeral and Gilbert's flight, the narrative's two pivots, are related. As Levert gropes for a possible link, he begins his letter anew. He starts on solid ground by describing his house. (Does he need the illusion of a firm factual foundation for his reconstruction of the past?)

> I'm starting over, son. First comes the bookstore on the right, then a door. Across on the left, a garden, then a lamppost and a second

door with that German concierge. What I might have been if I hadn't been your father. If I had been no one's father. Reconstructing my memory by spelling out this love for no one every day, once you had left my paternal roof there remains this love of this letter of this hand writing, I'm starting over but will I have the strength. The shoemaker's daughter is dead.[4]

The step-by-step investigation soon loses itself in a mental fog, however, just as Levert loses his balance and bumps into lampposts after drinking heavily. Descriptions of the two properties overlap and eventually become indistinguishable. Levert repeatedly obscures the linear perspectives of time and place, imagining that he is writing in the grape arbor, or mulling over his sister's worries about his sanity. Through it all, the accumulating sense of guilt gives the letter a sense of progression:

> ... what they want is for me to confess, not one spring, they bothered me with questions about that girl, that girl, the shoemaker's daughter is dead, the funeral, you used to know her didn't you, no letter that I know of.[5]

The "maybes" and "perhapses" begin to take more definite form as the old man quaveringly formulates the hypothesis implied by Sophie Narre's allegation. Perhaps Marie Chinze was indeed Levert's daughter. Perhaps Levert's guilt over the affair drove Levert to transpose his son and Marie's romance into the imaginary affair with Leon. Perhaps the discovery of a close brush with incest chased Gilbert away, killing a grief-stricken Marie. Describing a nightmare in which Mme. Chinze confronts him with his guilt, Levert stammers:

> Aunt Pacot and Alice are sitting on the sofa, old Chinze and Minet are sitting in the two other armchairs. Out of the bag she is clinging to like floating wreckage. Madame Chinze takes a bottle of pills which she sets down on the table next to the little lamp. She says: They say your son knew her or me, it's almost ten years since you last saw me, now I can tell you. Marie was sitting beside him and that's the way it started, that swimming race with Yvonne and Henriette. He put his arms around her. I knew what they were saying, I'm telling you. Your pills. Next to the little lamp. I've never been jealous, I liked her. I say you were there. At that funeral. Monsieur Levert. I say. And Sophie Narre. Sophie Narre. So-phi-narre. So-phi-naaaaaaaare. So-phiiiiiiii.[6]

The antecedent of the pronoun "she" becomes polyvalent here. "She" is alternately or simultaneously, Mme. Chinze, Mme. Levert, and Marie Chinze. The "druggist's tube" refers to allegations that Mme. Levert, not Mme. Chinze, took drugs. Marie's partner after the swimming contest could have been Leon, George, or Gilbert. In sum, Levert's bumbling inquiry has unearthed a scandal as melodramatic as Faulkner's violent chronicle in *Absalom, Absalom*, and for a moment it seems that he has only to offer final supporting proof to conclude *Monsieur Levert* with a neat and cathartic mystery-story "finish." But then the verbs slip into the conditional, affirmation skids into conjecture—and Levert flees his desk. At this point, Pinget throws the progression of the crime novel into reverse gear. Levert steals away to the cemetery intending to put his inquiry into its final form, leaving behind his desk and his hopelessly scrambled notes.

> Afterward Monsieur Levert must have been thinking about all these things. Together. You suppose what he was thinking, knowing on one hand the story of the funeral and on the other that of the lost son, knowing in snatches what Sophie Narre said about the son's relations with Marie or with the mother, nothing definite, the story is scattered here and there in different hearts.[7]

The cemetery scene does not however, wrap up the book or the investigation. Levert does not unburden himself of guilt on Marie's fresh grave. The troubled graveyard monologue reveals the novel's real subjects, namely, the functioning of the story-telling consciousness and the use of words to conjure away death. It serves to shift the novel's emphasis away from the discovery of *why* Levert is writing and *to whom*, for the old man realizes more clearly than any of Pinget's earlier protagonists, that it is writing alone that can keep him relatively safe. The previous books have served as exercises leading up to *Monsieur Levert*, and the book's very first sentence posits the material from which the author will develop variations in years to come. As Levert remarks, while trudging down the road in the moonlight:

> Even reduced to imagining what you might have seen. To being what you have not been. Sometimes the one sometimes the other,

> approximately, obsessed by your own dead, ten years and out of this so-called lottery the story will come out mixed with what you might have been if you hadn't been. His father. His son. His daughter. His neighbors.[8]

And he observes a few pages later, after a new series of suppositions.

> He throws away a cigarette. Phrases about other people. Unbecoming. Monsieur Levert would disappear between the lines, his sister the clan, this jumble no one believes except the hand writing,[9]

The old man pauses before Marie's grave, his wife's tomb, and continues to recall the past, trying to sort out the jumble of parents and children, husbands and wives, maiden names and married names that each stone represents. The passing of time has obscured people's identities. Families have forgotten the dead. The letters on the markers have become illegible. Levert rambles on, adding inconclusive suppositions about the past—anything—so as not to have to end it.

He works on his next version in a bar, hoping that alcohol may help clear the cobwebs from his memory. As in the introductory chapter of *Graal Flibuste*, the effects of advancing drunkenness reflect and intensify a sense of disorientation. The tipsy narrator's words glide furrily into unintended puns and give voice to admissions that he is trying to repress. The narrator's initial statements seemed straightforward.

> La fille du cordonnier est morte. L'enterrement a eu lieu jeudi dernier. Il y avait la famille et quelques personnes. Madame Chinze, la mère, était recouverte d'un crêpe noir, on ne voyait rien d'elle et c'était tant mieux. Le père avait un châpeau melon à la main. (page 7)

> The shoemaker's daughter is dead. The funeral was last Thursday. The family was there, and a few other people. Madame Chinze, the mother, was so wrapped up in black crepe you couldn't

see her at all, which was just as well. Old Chinze had on his black suit and carried a derby.[10]

Now, eighty-one pages later, he cites the paragraph almost verbatim. At this point in the text, however, a slipping tongue and a drifting mind have made words bleat curious sounds.

> . . . ou disons morte la fille du nier du la fille à nier. Aveugle. A nier. La nier du mordofille est corte. L'enterdi eu a jeu linier derment. La Chinzille et pelquame ersonnes. Famère étout recremoire un pauverte von nelloyait mientant nieuxvelle cherpinze lostait coirume oireau echon memain lonla fetit plusemme.[11]

> . . . where so-called funereal where so-called funeral the shoemaker's daughter the maker's. Blind. The maker's. The doeshaughter's baker is mead. The thurlyal few stal worsly. The chanzily wether and a fur pafel. Chadam inze smother wasso repticlap bake beavertall. Westicell. Cold chazzon. Sack boot darryda barry. Seesawter wins thef. Fald ithikye.[12]

The resulting gibberish sends English readers of French sputtering to the dictionary repeatedly until they realize that Pinget is holding language up to a distorting mirror. The linking words or indicators of declension are systematically slurred over or eliminated.

> Cherpinze lostait coirume oireau echon memain lonla. [Le] père Chinze [av]ait [son] costume noir [á la] main [et un] chapeau melon. fetit plusemme. [il est] plus petit [que sa] femme.[13]

Not only do the "tool words" disappear, but entire prepositions as well. The dislocation of the last syllable of *"cordonnier"* ("cobbler") springs free the verb *"nier"* (to deny), a Freudian slip that brings Levert's repressed paternity to the surface. The fatherhood he struggles to deny finds its way, willy-nilly, into words. In fact, Jean Roudaut is correct in affirming that:

> This short passage constitutes a sort of reduced image of the organization of the book. One therefore can find in it images of cutting back [that are] particularly clear if we compare the "scrambled" text and the original page.[14]

The use of words in the passage approaches the extremely open-ended hebephemic verbalizations of schizoids, in which words stretch their shapes to the point of becoming structureless. Turns of speech repeated earlier in the text have foreshadowed Levert's idiosyncratic usage. For example, he repeats over and over, "the music was wiping the glasses," a phrase that makes sense only in the light of a confused transposition: the passive *result* of the humming sound made when rubbing the rim of a goblet is transformed into the active agent of the hand drying the glass. Samuel Beckett's Lucky, a fellow sufferer of Levert's affliction, collapses after saying his piece. A full rest stop, in the form of a blank page, halts *Monsieur Levert* after the narrator's combined breakdown/breakthrough. The indefatigable Levert cranks up his reconstruction again from the beginning, claiming that he must correct certain inaccuracies so that Gilbert does not come home under false pretenses. The possibility still exists that he may yet fit the pieces of his puzzle into a coherent whole, but the probability of his doing so diminishes rapidly as he goes back over the short vignettes that open the story and adds a variation to each one. Now he claims that Roger and his wife did *not* go home immediately after the funeral, and that it was another lady, not Roger's wife, who was carsick. According to this version of events, Alice Pacot could not have seen George because he was visiting his mother. The priest's retainer's name is now given as Martha, not as Odette. The curate did not eat at the refectory at all, nor did he take the bus to make sick calls; he went off on his bicycle to visit a friend. Levert also retracts what he said about Paul and Victor Moule: a woman waited on them in the café, not a man; they do not live alone with their mother, but share the farmhouse with a third brother and his wife.

Up to this point, Levert follows a familiar pattern, that of first stating facts (however contradictory), and then making suppositions. So precisely does he follow the earlier draft's sequence that, despite the clash of new details and old, his assertion that this text is simply a setting straight of the previous account seems valid at first. The precision of the corrections leads to the hope that Levert will reveal the element, or scene, that is blocking a solution. But when he returns to the Minet Chinze episode he starts to interpolate new material, imperceptibly abandoning systematic corrections and elaborating on the original. He cuts the long flashback to Leon's summer visit. A second Odette appears, one who is to be confused all too easily with the curate's retainer. This second Odette is the wife of Louis, the bartender. Levert wavers between staying within the earlier outline and taking a completely new tack in the passage corresponding with the first version's talk with the woodgatherer. Phrases and fragments used previously appear in a jumbled mosaic, side-by-side with fresh exposition. The chronology becomes hazy, just as did the distinctions between one hypothesis and the next at the end of the first draft.

As repetition accumulates, the elusive material slips between Levert's fingers once again. His eggbeaterlike memory blends into one the two separate visits from his niece. In one of the text's more flagrant contradictions, the niece now claims never to have seen the house at Les Roches, whereas she was said earlier to have paid a call there ten years before. Even Marie's burial and Gilbert's flight lose their clarity of outline. Levert confuses his maid's, his sister's, and Marie's funerals, and he writes to his son as if he, the son, were only a composite, a dream figure—part George, part Minet, part Leon:

> It was you, you had come back. Or your cousin George or Minet the Chinze boy, you were leaving. You asked for your gun hidden in the shed. Someone came back. Your mother was leaning over the balcony in a bathrobe, her hair down, she saw him coming, she screamed. That was a mistake. The war was over.[15]

The more Levert tries to get his bearings, the more confused he becomes. His inquiry trails off into illogical verbal associations spinning from *"tomber"* ("to fall"), and verbs with the root *"–poser"* ("to pose" or "place"):

> That's not all Levert said, I still have to tell it to my son. He picked up his notebook but he was laughing so hard he dropped his pen. The notebook too and the table too and the scraps of the dinner and the floor too. The whole house was shaken, the walls fell, the maid fell, the evening fell. So many fallen even so. All these graves. Very well kept up. With one's own strength. One

> has strength Levert said, with a twist of the wrist you make everything fall and the rest. The maid was waiting for the fit to end. With a suppository she supposed. You're going to take your suppository she said and you'll fall asleep. I suppose, Levert said. I suppose. I suppose.[16]

The old man repeats himself so frequently that it becomes almost impossible to tell where one draft of the letter ends and the other begins. At first, short phrases crop up, such as: "two, three high-class whores, a harem, why not" and "that disease is typical of our time." Then longer fragments, and even entire episodes, creep in. Levert describes a visit that Rodolphe Potter paid George, Alice Pacot's lover, ignoring or forgetting that he has told the same story about Minet and Leon. Now it is Potter who is the "tall, blond athletic fellow." George introduces him to his sister who sets the table for a party. Potter and the sister fall in love. And so it goes.

A cracked mind's hall of mirrors refracts the words of Levert's letter from various angles and in unexpected combinations. The tactile reality of the long lists of furniture is no longer reassuring. The substantiality of the objects mentioned is no longer convincing. No doubt Levert is imagining them as he stares at the blank wall in front of his desk. If he can furnish the forgotten rooms of the villa, perhaps he can fill his life with memories of the son he perhaps never had:

> These houses are all alike henceforth, rolled up folded back, their rooms painted, their stones polished, their gravel. The vinegar in my mouth. The father's house, old mother, or sister, old brother, on the chest a little lady in an evening gown. There's no longer any reason. To define or localize the object the character which has never stopped. To go away, to be in order to go away, to be gone. This sun will kill me. Monsieur Levert at his work table, Monsieur the wall counting its holes. Mademoiselle Ariane her letter wandering down the hallway, the labyrinth the imbroglio. Will be moving until death follows nothing else to see warming up except the hand writing.[17]

The narrative was designed to catch the past and the self, to hold them so they cannot escape. But as Levert states:

Will disappear the we also also, I all alone henceforth Hypothesis. Not to move any more to go back into the wall. To feed on plaster. In the field of vision of the marble hand no longer writing. No one to say it. Each room, each staircase turning where it stands, immutable order. In the same way each one at home or on the road Sophie Narre at her window, Toinette Lebru serving drinks. They would not move again. They would not die again. No one to know. Eternal life to furnish with accidents. No more vinegar in my mouth. It would be over in an instant. One has no more curiosity. One suffers without a second thought. One is here. Still more reminiscenses. Worthless hypothesis.[18]

He composes a telegram to Gilbert, floundering in the mass of information:

> at various dates which I do not give in order, the unexpected arrival of my niece, meeting woman in the woods, the news of the funeral, the tedious pursuit of unknown persons of both sexes, the memory of the houses my wife and I lived in, the visit to a cemetery, the confusion at different dates and for different reasons of characters relating facts and gestures of other characters at such and such a date, the substitution of names, the writing of a letter, and the urgent duty of creating for myself other habits.[19]

Scuttling out from behind the pretense that he writes in order to call someone *else* into being, Levert continues. As the corpses of Marie, his wife, his sister, and the maid pile up around him, Levert struggles to justify his life. First he imagines his son as a "success," as a prosperous, self-made man with a comely wife and presentable children. Then Levert projects his own death as seen through his son's eyes. At this point, Levert has grabbed at a fistful of endings and there should be no room left in the story for Levert himself—and yet his heart keeps beating. The fiction, a fragment of Pinget's consciousness expressed in words, provides solace, not salvation.[20] Outside words lies nonbeing. Levert keeps on writing, powerless to write himself out of the book.

> Death is never assimilated; silence is never possible, the accord is always retarded. The son never comes back to fill up this distress. ("I have not digested my death; *Monsieur Levert*, p. 130). And if he did

come back, would it not be to condemn? Would it not be to digest death to give in to it, to commingle oneself with it in suicide?[21]

Speaking of the criss-crossing *"allées"* in front of the post office that his letter will never reach, the narrator describes a pattern suggestive of *Monsieur Levert*'s variations. The inside of the post office provides another visual analogue, as Levert ticks off a list of specific functions served by each of the numerous service windows—a veritable Cartesian dream of order, with a place for everything and everything in its place. Every contingency is provided for. Unfortunately (as in most French post offices), many of the windows are closed, temporarily or permanently, and the customer must fall back on his ingenuity to thread his way through the bureaucratic maze.

The novel ends with images of intersecting lines extending to infinity. Echoes and repetitions shape the ebb and flow of Levert's quest. They spin a circular riddle without a definitive answer, like the flowerbeds, which give the impression of being a "periphery of infinite solutions." Did Levert have a son, or not? Was Marie Chinze the shoemaker's daughter or Levert's? With unspoken questions, Pinget saps the credibility of his title and the validity of his first sentence. Like Architruc and his mythomania, Levert admits that delving in the past provides a momentary "stay against confusion" and in the book's closing words he concludes:

> Farther away the road or the roads and the mountains where you can get lost, where you get lost, where you are lost. All that remains, a landscape, all that remains is lost. Should I go on, son, should I start over what's the use. He'll come back you know, he takes after you, this letter that I would have posted tonight. It remains like what no longer exists. Except for what is written there is death.[22]

Thus the novel ends on a paradoxical note, affirming the "written," despite its manifold insufficiencies.

CLOPE TO THE DOSSIER (CLOPE AU DOSSIER)

None of Pinget's works exasperates the reader intent upon "making sense" of a text more than does his next narrative, in which he extends two devices used in *Monsieur Levert* to undermine the making-sense approach with veritable elephant traps. Switching frequently between tenses and points of view, experimenting with jumbled chronology, loose paragraph construction, and repeated phrases, Pinget makes his second antidetective story even more ambiguous than the first. In the end, he not only leaves in doubt the *"action"* that the protagonist is trying to piece together; he makes it almost impossible to make *any* definite statement about the plot. *Clope to the Dossier (Clope au dossier)* paints an anguishing picture of the strained relations between writer and community. The reclusive artist and the gregarious common man eye each other suspiciously. The writer drives pen across paper from behind ramparts of solitude, wondering how to justify his isolation to those around him. Doubts and guilt chain him to the desk. Is the chronicler merely the shabby scrivener of everyday Fantoine, or is he the seer of a magic land of Agapa (*"agape,"* or unselfish love)? Waves of tenderness and hatred surge through the text, holding the reader's attention through sheer intensity of feeling. Once again, uncertainties shroud the book's relationship to earlier narratives, to the nature of the event discussed, and to the narrator's identity.

The parallel between the anguished-writer characters and Pinget himself stands out more and more sharply. As the text's intricacies erase the story line, Pinget focuses more directly on the verbal process and brings to the foreground the interplay of sounds, images, and puns. *"Clope"* (meaning "cigarette butt," in French slang) picks up an image that Levert used in describing his "letter":

> He throws away his cigarette. Phrases about other people. Unbecoming.[23]

Clope to the Dossier dramatizes a failed experiment, a novel that doesn't get written. In it, Pinget treats the theme more abstractly than in *Mahu or the Material*, *The Fox and the Compass*, and even in *Monsieur Levert*, and a "Proceed with Caution" warning must be posted before the abridged summary to follow, for the investigation-decoy of *Clope to the Dossier* leads to an even more snarled briar patch and to a far stickier Tar Baby.

Ostensibly, the narrator of *Clope to the Dossier* sets out to reconstruct a single act: he concentrates on the firing of a shot, rather than on the interlocking reactions to the death of Marie Chinze. The novel's episodes unfold in a spiral, snail-shell pattern that pivots around the axis of that precise moment. A four-cycle series of scenes corresponds to M. Levert's "drafts." The first begins just before the report reverberates. As the novel begins, three men—Mortin, Phillipard, and Verveine—are sitting in a café gossiping about Clope. Their conversation indicates that he is a bachelor of undetermined age who lives by himself. As the three agree that "living alone's no life," and as they wonder aloud whether the recluse isn't a little crazy, a flock of wild geese flies over the building. The center of attention then shifts to Clope as he guns down one of the passing birds. Two slightly different versions describe the events immediately following the shot. It is impossible to know which version is accurate, since they differ in only a single detail of timing. In the first, Clope's dog, Kiki, finishes eating his share of the kill while his master is storing the rest in the cold cellar. In the second, the dog has not quite finished when Clope returns. The café patrons assume that Clope is the one who has fired the shot and predict he will get into trouble for poaching.

The narrator takes care to make clear the specific word, gesture, or image linking the events presently described to the first cycle. The account proceeds coherently, with occasional digressions embroidered around a particular character. After the café episode, Simone Brize (Pierre Moule's fiancée in *Monsieur Levert*) is introduced. The couple is now married, but Pierre is almost always away, working as a cook on a merchant ship, and Simone keeps herself busy looking after the apartment and their son, Guillaume. She did not hear the shot (Clope's?) because, just as it was fired, she dropped a large frying pan. The narrative follows the direction of Simone's glance out the window at Judge Pommard's house. The judge did not hear the report either (his wife was moving furniture), and he goes back to reading a legal brief and sipping beer, after calming the fears of the cleaning woman, who says that she heard a shot as she was entering the house. The overlapping scene that comes next resembles the alternative versions of the behavior of dog and master after the disemboweling of the goose.

First the narrator mentions a M. Bille, who is reading a legal document while sipping coffee; he hears a loud bang over the noise his wife makes as she goes about her housework. The scene momentarily shifts back to Judge Pommard, reading quietly, and then to Simone Brize working in her kitchen. The fact that a tacit transition is made from one scene to another through a shared action or movement, or through an association of words, makes it clear that the jumbled text follows some sort of order and is not a haphazard account.

The intrusion of the apparently irrelevant phrase "eardrum damaged" interrupts the story's flow. Pinget will use this recurring phrase later to suggest the narrator's proximity to the point from where the shot was fired, for if the protagonist's ears are still ringing, he must have been close indeed. The repetition of the phrase will betray one of Clope's frequent prevarications when the narrator resumes his exposition.

At the center of the next scene, M. Toupin, an old, half-blind beggar, is standing halfway across a bridge, wearily turning the handle of his hand organ, while two brothers-in-law walk by. There is a flashback to Simone Brize in her kitchen, and then, as the conversation of the passersby fades, Toupin hears the shot. In the rapid changes of scene in the next pages Pinget's jerky, restless, highly cinematic technique is strongly felt: cut to Clope fretting about being punished, cut to the Pommard house, cut back to the café as a carpenter replies "Yes, Sir" to the judge at the very instant that Verveine is saying those same words to a customer. The narrator interrupts to complain how very difficult it is to reconstruct accurately the actions before and after the shot, but his "clarification" only serves to trouble the twelve vignettes that bracket it. It is so full of puns and double meanings as to be virtually untranslatable:[24]

> Eh oui le temps vilain temps vilain temps vilain temps de mon temps voyez-vous, eh bien oui quoi le temps passe il y a beau temps je dis bien tout ce temps tout ce temps passe et quel passé ah là là un temps pour tout un temps un sale temps ne trouvez-vous pas le temps d'aimer et le temps de mourir alors qu'est-ce que vous croyez bien pire bien pire on a le temps de croyez-moi mourir mais pas d'aimer il

est bien temps grand temps vous m'entendez et tenez tout ce temps qu'on perd à vouloir en gagner mais oui à tant le temps qu'on a mis à ne pas le perdre vous m'entendez mais allez leur faire entendre allez donc leur faire entendre allez donc.[25]

Ah yes the time/weather nasty time/weather nasty weather nasty weather of my time do you see, well yes what the hell time passes it's been a long time I mean to say all this time all this time past and what a past my oh my a time for everything a time miserable time/weather don't you think the time to love and the time to die so then what do you think much worse much worse you have the time to believe me to die but not to love it's time high time/fine weather you hear and what about all the time we waste trying to save time why yes figuring at so much the time we spent not wasting it you hear but just try and make them see just try and make them see damn it.

After this outburst, the narrator launches into a second cycle of scenes. In theory, they all take place prior to those just presented; in fact, the gaps between the end of an episode in the second cycle and its beginning in the first cause considerable confusion. He begins: "Before the geese flew by, what was she doing. Simone Brize. Her marketing." After following Simone from store to store, he retraces the movements of Mortin, Phillipard, and Verveine. Then, after a short sequence in which the judge jumbles a neighbor's name, the narrator turns to Pierre Moule, who is making coffee in a ship's galley, and to Clope, who is sharing breakfast with Kiki. The novel goes further back into Simone's morning, covering her thoughts and actions from six-fifteen to the moment she left the house.

Pinget's vision transforms Simone's daily movements into a clumsy, endlessly repeated ballet as she straightens up, cooks, and puts things away. The monotonous rhythm of her chores reflects the ebb and flow of the novelist's struggle to find order in chaos. The common purpose uniting writer, character, and reader makes itself felt most fully here. The individual "frames" of the slow-motion film showing Simone's attempt to keep herself and her child clean blend into each other, much as Pinget's books do. No sooner has the mother taken care of her needs, than the child has soiled himself again. The cycle of routine accelerates. Caring for an infant, Simone cannot skip a step and the precise description of her actions heightens her unspoken despair. The narrator shifts to the conditional tense as he describes her goings and comings in the apartment before leaving to buy "eggs, carrots, oranges, milk, salt."

The novel follows yet another attempt to order experience as the narrator reproduces a long conversation between Judge Pommard's father and M. Toupin, two elderly gaffers trading stories about the old days. Pommard and Toupin try feebly to brush away the cobwebs from the past, much as Levert did in *Monsieur Levert*. The tone is gently humorous. Levert's death is announced in the course of the garbled exchange, in which the speakers agree on practically nothing else; they do not agree, for example, on the make of the first car in town, the date of a local election, or even where they were stationed during the war.[26]

> Ah Germaine Pisson, said Pommard, she married well, Levert, do you remember the pasta people. I thought *she* was the one who had the money said Toupin aren't you getting mixed up with the father. The father are you crazy I knew him like the palm of my hand the father, sowed his wild oats, the Legion and the rest. So then Levert's son said Toupin. If I told you said Pommard if I told you that he died like a dog last year they found him in a ditch think of it in a ditch Spiffy Jim Levert.[27]

A revolving door of questions blocks access to the halls of memory, and the interlocutors stumble and dust themselves off again and again over the curb of the same queries. Old age and slipping dentures slur their syntax while whistles, grunts, and shortness of breath cut short their quavering elegies.

In the next scene, the narrator turns to another artist-character's search for form. This time, he moves back in time from the gunshot, and then reverses direction and builds toward it. He describes Maurice, a young artist painting the bridge where M. Toupin panhandles. Women on their way home from the market stop and say hello, and the narrator lists them from the most recent to the earliest arrivals, shifting from the present tense to the conditional as he gets further away in time from the shot (and thus reversing the procedure of the preceding scene). Simone Brize is the last to cross the bridge. An unspoken revulsion of unending routine unites the mother repeating the same actions day after day and the artist sketching the same scene at all hours. Their only communication is an understanding glance:

> Toupin said to Simone "ah the poor boy take a good look hard worker poor fellow just think he starts all over every day do you understand that." Starts what all over said Simone. Starts everything see every day a new canvas or is it a sketch you'll see go look, go on look you'll see, do you understand that. But Simone did not look surprised . . . something like a way of understanding each other existed between her and the painter, he in his daubing her wiping her baby's bottom doing her cleaning and waiting for Pete every day like something that starts up again . . .[28]

The phrase closing the first cycle tops off the second series of nine scenes.

> Eardrum damaged. I'm listening. A sort of a sort of. No nothing.

The feverish narrator now throws himself into a third parallel line of investigation, one that ranges still further into the past and future framing the shot. Maurice serves as a point of departure. Trying to imagine the artist's thoughts, the narrator writes,

> . . . he wouldn't be able to keep from thinking that he'd be famous some day precisely because of these endless new starts which only seem to wind up in dead ends. Then he would go on toward the bridge which he would finally get to unless we must have him meet someone else. He would say hello to Toupin and begin his canvas. And in his inner eye Toupin would see file by, a single suggestion at first, the last of the people he may have seen go past erased by the next to last then by the previous one and by the others and he would follow them by turning his crank backwards simple distraction . . . one would wonder simple hypothesis if Maurice and Toupin wouldn't do the canvas together, a backward canvas on the top painted with these women passing by and their little routine and another painting of this misery under the shade trees of which this one, last born of the morning's coffee and the night and of a sick feeling would be only a poor copy . . .[29]

The rich but apparently meaningless jumble of sounds of the hurdy-gurdy being played backward highlights the disintegration of linear coherence. None of these hypotheses lead to conclusions. Instead, scenes overlap and flow together, just as in M. Levert's drafts. Fragments from the Simone Brize episode recur in the description of Mme. Mortin's morning routine some three years later. The heightening, repressed sexuality of the earlier scene finally comes into sharper focus:

> Elle aurait mis le lait sur le feu le jour commencerait à poindre, elle serait restée assise ou debout le temps qu'il fallait qu'il aurait fallu au lait de bouillir ou serait allée au jardin où elle se serait attardée avec l'impression soudain que le lait aurait profité de sa liberté pour déborder le polisson de la casserole rentrée donc et voyant qu'effectivement dirait oh oh et se precipiterait sur la casserole cependant que lui ne se ferait pas faute de s'imminscer dans toutes les fentes de la cuisinière arrivant jusqu'au trognon . . .[30]

> She would have put the milk on the burner, day would start to break, she would have remained seated or standing the time needed the time that would have been needed for the milk to boil or would have gone to the garden where she would have lingered a while with the feeling suddenly that the milk had taken advantage of its freedom to spill over the scamp from the pan having gone back inside then and seeing that in fact would say oh oh and would rush over to the pan meanwhile he/the milk wouldn't dream of missing the chance to mix into all the cracks in the stove/cook getting right through to the core . . .

The two characters overlap even more when Mme. Mortin jots down, on her shopping list, the familiar items, "eggs, carrots, oranges, milk, salt."

The text slips still further from "fact" to supposition as the narrator muses: "Simone when she goes to bed what does she think about." Naturally enough, she thinks of her husband, conjuring up sensual fantasies alone in the dark. She worries that Pierre may have taken this job because she could not satisfy him in bed (as already insinuated in *Le Fiston*) and worries about the possibility of his having mistresses. Simone jerks awake after dreaming about divorce, suicide, and death. As the third cycle, comprising three scenes, closes, the penumbra of ambiguity concerning the gunshot has grown ever more mysterious and threatening.

Pinget utterly confounds the unwary reader who dares to hope that the conclusion of *Clope to the Dossier* will clarify the investigation. The narrator asks far more questions than he answers, momentarily putting aside the syntactical mask of the conditional tense and speaking, at last, directly. In this vein the text concerns itself with a brief gathered to defend Clope from a crime or crimes unknown.

> Eardrum damaged. Calm down. Most of it is done. They can accumulate their proofs. Dossier locked closet. Clope's innocence. Counterproofs. Calm down. Let's finish it off.[31]

The narrator tries to nail down his case by checking Clope's movements on the night of the shot. But he cannot establish the precise location of any of the characters at the critical moment.

> Elles aurait dit qu'il serait sorti mettons vers onze heures moins le quart et serait allé se promener du côté du chantier. Quand il a relevé la tête, il a vu les oies et tiré. Elles auraient dit que Simone Brize aurait bien entendu le coup de feu en train de boum crrrrrr Guillaume crrrrr Guillaume crrrrr Brize aurait bien entendu le coup de casserole qui serait tombée juste à ce moment préparant son repas et celui du petit regardant vers la mer molle morte par ce coup venait de se flanquer une balle. Du nerf. Toupin tournait sa manivelle il aurait entendu il dirait qu'il aurait entendu Jacques Cheviot et son beau-frère dire qu'ils pourraient retourner en arrière voir si le coup de feu ils l'auraient entendu s'ils étaient passés en même temps que l'étudiante sous le deuxième plantane s'ils retouraient donc en arrière l'étudiante ne serait encore qu'à disons cinquante mètres et Toupin aurait pensé si Jacques et son beau-frère reculent d'un mètre de plus ça y est crrrrrrrrrr. Du nerf.[32]

> They're supposed to have said that [Clope?] went out let's say about quarter of eleven and took a walk by the work site. When he raised his head, he saw the geese and shot. They are supposed to have said that Simone Brize heard the shot perfectly well while she boom crrrrr Gruillaume crrrrr Guillaume crrrrr Brize is supposed to have

heard perfectly well/of course the business/noise of the pot which is supposed to have fallen just at that moment preparing her meal and the little fellow's looking toward the sea/she dead calm by that business/noise she just shot herself. Toupin was turning his crank he's supposed to have heard he would say he heard Jacques Cheviot and his brother-in-law say they could go back and see if the shot if they had heard it if they had paused at the same time as the girl student under the second shade tree if they returned then backwards the student would still be only say fifty meters away and Toupin would have thought if Jacques and his brother-in-law go back one meter more there we go crrrrrrrrrrr. Calm down.

Reexamination unearths another shard from shattered remains of linear logic in the novel's concluding, fragmented pages. While going over his investigation for the last time, the narrator alludes frequently to Clope's mother. Clope, apparently, associates her with the gunshot. He also seems to connect her and the old coach house described minutely in *Monsieur Levert*. The lawyer for the defense, the curious voyeur, the writer, or whoever is in fact pursuing the inquiry, describes the search for an object, possibly a gun, linking the shot, the mother, the son, and the made-over laundry, all incriminating Clope—perhaps:

The coach house. First this wash-house painted door jammed by the gravel got to push, the humid smell on the sloping earth this fall-like steam this taste of getting in out of the cold, the wash to boil in the washing machine, a woman in wooden shoes leaning over the basin. The smell of wood to go down at night she will not have finished before she never had finished before, to carry the gasoline lamp. And out of this steam suddenly to come out the woman saying I do not wash any more I am dead don't you see that I am dead and to go lie down on the sand who slowly sinks in closing again over her slowly. They would be here letting herself be absorbed by the sand a coal in her mouth and the eyes put out by the firebrand. Look in the rotted closet newspapers gray with the damp and the equipment of the still in pieces the beautiful copper dull beneath the grime and under the table stuck to the basin between the foot and the drain pipe the hand grope around through the soft muck. Through the bars the same light to have set down everything come back with her and say it's not worth the trouble any more what he was doing there they would finally lead him away take back as counterproof that useless morning fish the glasses frame out of my pocket and my mother to take them back come to sit down and to put them on and to tell me let's go back over it together, open the dossier there, they won't find anything against you. Suddenly she got up saying don't you see that I am dead, she was going to lie down on the sand which slowly I had no more strength when everything would be accomplished.[33]

This association of events is panned through a third time, suggesting strongly that the key to the explanation of the mysterious gunshot lies within it:

Shot. Kiki bring back the dead bird. Getting up suddenly I'm dead don't you see I'm dead.

The tangled skein of hypotheses will not be untangled; the writer spends his last gasp in a desperate, circular attempt to unsnarl it, but the hoped-for *quod erat demonstrandum*, or "this case is closed," never comes.[34] On the contrary, Pinget weaves the threads of the inquiry together even more completely by means of multiple antecedents, disconnected tenses, contradictory affirmatives and denials, and lack of punctuation.

La verité quand elle sera sèche cette nuit-là était-ce avant était-ce avant sans pouvoir sur ce qui a été dit sans pouvoir ce n'est plus elle avant cette main je la couperai elle m'aurait dit lisant tu vois là avant c'est toi sans pouvoir elle m'aurait dit lisant c'est toi ce dossier il faut ce dossier plus le temps non plus le temps plus le temps plus le temps plus le temps.[35]

The truth when it/she will be dry that night was it before was it before powerless over what has been said powerless it is no longer the truth/she before this hand I'll cut it off she would have told me reading you see there that's you powerless she would have said to me reading it's you this dossier you need this dossier plus time not the time any more plus time plus time plus time.

The foregoing review of the material that Pinget scatters through *Clope to the Dossier* has necessarily been merely a cursory summary of the content, rather than a full review. In its complexity, *Clope to the Dossier* foreshadows a technique concentrated in *Fable*, where, as Jean Roudaut observed:

> The book combines, in all possible ways, a series of elements given initially in order to circumvent the reductive action of time. He rhymes together, not words, but situations.[36]

Pinget widens the focus here by sustaining conflicting versions of the gunshot and the narrative ostensibly intended to explain it, to the point that the reader is left uncertain about the novel's basic outlines. The link between *Clope to the Dossier* and *Monsieur Levert* remains tenuous but enticing. Pommard and Toupin refer to Levert's death, and the dossier contains piles of his letters. The exact circumstances in which the gunshot occurred, the identity of the speaker or speakers, and the dossier's purpose pose equally puzzling enigmas. The shot's victim was a goose—perhaps. Or it may have been Simone Brize, or possibly it was Clope's mother. The narrator may be Clope, a lawyer responsible for Clope's defense on charges of poaching or murder, or a novelist roughing out the draft of a book. *"Dossier"* can also mean "the back of a chair," so the title may refer to Clope's sitting as he writes, or to Clope's being "on the spot." The title leaves all these possibilities open. It alludes directly to a legal brief. *"Clope"* may refer to the narrator's name, or it may refer to the sound that is made when a discouraged writer drops a manuscript into a well, as if he were flipping away a cigarette butt. (Pinget will subsequently develop this latter alternative in his play *The Hypothesis*.)

Whereas the repetition of shopping-list items and such phrases as "living alone's no life," "they will take him away eventually," and "eardrum damaged" erodes the demarcation between the narrative's cycles, the barriers to human understanding seem insurmountable. Characters shout at each other over the walls of their prisonlike lives. Words twisted in transmission from English to French give Simone Brize's expressions a zany, hit-or-miss quality. She speaks, for instance, of *"ouisqui,"* *"ouell boy,"* and a *"djip."* The narrator achieves a similar effect by giving different names to the same character. In one scene he calls Mme. Mortin's maid Claire, and then Annette, and he refers to Judge Pommard's neighbor as

Bonnet-Bonvin, Bouvard-Bompain, Bompard-Bovin, Bonnard, Blancpain, and Bonvard.

This dilation of language depicts dialogue as the projection of sound rather than as communication. The chaotic exchange between Toupin and Pommard that is set in motion by a misunderstanding of the expression *"pension alimentaire"* ("food pension") is characteristic:

> Did she get a food pension asked Pommard. What said Toupin. A food pension did she get a pension with the divorce. My word I know they put her in a "pension" and that she was poorly fed there said Toupin just think a little girl two years old if it isn't a shame. I don't mean the girl said Pommard I mean the mother. She remarried said Toupin but the little girl stayed in the food "pension" for a long time how time flies . . .[37]

Pinget often runs episodes together by beginning a scene with a pun on one of the words immediately preceding. Thus he toys with two of the meanings of *"tirer"* ("to pull" and "to shoot") when describing Mme. Pommard and her maid as they make a bed.

> Elle voulait dire qu'Anne Dothoit avait tiré sur son mari. Tirez moins fort dit-elle vous me tuez. Elles tiraient toutes les deux sur les draps . . .[38]

> She meant that Anne Dothoit had shot at her husband. Don't pull so hard she says you're killing me. They both tugged at the sheets . . .

Puns also appear in parallel scenes describing the same action performed by different characters. When giving an account of the housecleaning in the Bille family, Pinget writes:

> Mrs. Marble was looking for a pendant under the piano. She said that pendant couldn't just have flown away. You lose everything said Marble.

The parallel episode that follows begins:

> Pending that time when Julie Loser folding the next to the last sheet or was it the last.

> Mme Bille cherchait un pendant d'oreille sous le piano, elle disait ce pendant n'a pourtant pas pu s'envoler, tu perds tout dit Bille.
>
> Ce-pendant que Julie Pommard pliant l'avant dernier drap ou était-ce le dernier . . .[39]

Though it is possible that the hyphenization of *"cependant"* ("pending that" or "while") was dictated solely by the hazards of page layout, and that the author was not punning *"perdre"* ("to lose") and *"paumer"* (the slang expression for "to lose"), Pinget's proclivity for verbal acrobatics makes accidental echo improbable.

By the end of the book the narrator's identity has become immaterial, and so have the nature of the crime and exposure of the "criminal." Pinget makes *Monsieur Levert* and *Clope to the Dossier* into an extended *"procès verbal"* in a double sense, moving toward a plotless narrative by parodying the detective story. On the one hand, he transcribes the protagonist's attempt to build a shield between himself and Death,

> . . . as you would do with furniture in front of a door which is going to be forced a huge number of memories as a defense against the intruder.[40]

Overlapping scenes invite the reader to intervene actively. He can sift through the words and rearrange the garbled syntax as he pleases. The punctuation of the text and the division of blocks of experience and of run-on sentences are left open for him to explore. He is also free to experiment with the cadences that determine the timbre of the speaker's voice, be he lawyer, father, novelist, poacher, or all of them simultaneously. On the other hand, Pinget exposes verbalization as an approximative exercise, and he makes felt the menace of absurdity and silence beneath it. While celebrating the free-form possibilities of language, *Monsieur Levert* and *Clope to the Dossier* produce an effect similar to that of Beckett's *Molloy*, of which Bernard Pingaud wrote:

> . . . we tell ourselves to ourselves every day. But we do not think every day (in fact we almost never think) about what is hidden behind these stories, about what they presuppose. Namely, for exam-

ple, that *there are* events, adventures, characters . . . and that you can tell all, that you can tell the truth, that the world is, in fact, the way it appears in books. Now the world isn't that way. Or more exactly there isn't *one* world which the *récit* is supposed to imitate. The world is already language.[41]

Pinget has moved from the light-hearted fantasies of the early books to experiments with narrative technique. Under the cover of parodying the detective story, he comes closer to exploring the joys and anguish of language itself. Later, he will move into a zone in which prose and poetry intertwine.

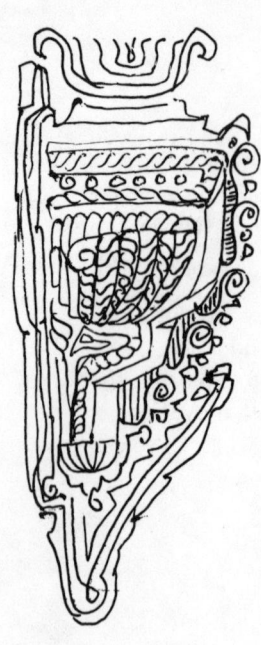

4 The Lumber Room of Memory

The Inquisitory (L'Inquisitoire),
Someone (Quelqu'un)

... I converse with myself about politics, love, taste or philosophy. I let my mind go to its most libertine extravagances. I let it follow the first idea, mad or prudent, that comes along ... like young bucks dogging it after a courtisan, step by step. ... My thoughts are my mistresses.—Diderot, *Rameau's Nephew*

The raison d'être of the *récit*, of every *récit*, is not what is true, but what seems to be true. The trouble is that this close to the bone "all propositions are reasonable." Each variant becomes reality in turn. More precisely, there is no more conflict between *récit* and reality. The *récit* is the only reality. It's no use going back and comparing the differing versions. ... Each hypothesis cuts down the preceding one before being abolished in its turn by the next one. The key to this fabulous universe is formulated in this implicit definition: "what is said is never really said because it can be said again differently." The *récit* shows itself for what it is, a pure invention, a verbal universe.—Claude Lieber, "Lecture de *Quelqu'un*" (*Littérature*, no. 10)

After *Clope to the Dossier* Pinget seemed on the verge of discovering a structure complimentary to his style, a structure that would make his treatment of language more dramatic and provide a more effective framework for his recurring themes. That is not to say that the works of his first period necessarily suffer by comparison with the later books. Like any experimental writer in revolt against past narrative conventions, Pinget's relationship to his literary heritage is stormy and complex. As Germaine Brée has pointed out, the early books work out the issue of outmoded forms through parody, providing a bridge between the rejected old and the innovative new.¹ But the appearance of *The Inquisitory* in 1962, when Pinget was forty three, showed that he had found his own voice and that innovation would thenceforth take precedence over parody—though Pinget's humor is (blessedly) never absent. *The Inquisitory* piqued the reviewers' curiosity and won notoriety and critical acclaim for its author. It was in the running for almost every major French literary prize and fell just short of first place in one vote after another. Grumblings that critics were too retrograde to understand the "new novel" leaked from behind the closed doors of prize-committee deliberation chambers. The resulting hint of a quarrel between the *"anciens"* and the *"modernes"* widened Pinget's public.² The book's mastery of technique justified the hopes of those who believed in Pinget's promise. Jérôme Lindon described *The Inquisitory* as:

> A sort of summa in which the different aspects of Pinget, apparently disconnected up to now, come together.

The format of the detective novel is changed in one important detail. Pinget presents the text as a stenographic record of a preliminary hearing into the direction, or directions, that a subsequent criminal investigation will take. Through the interview's random development, Pinget restates the themes of the inconclusive effort to give significance to the past and to the affirmation of being through speech. The dialogue has the character of a combined "interrogation" and "repertory," suggested by the neologism of the title. And since *The Inquisitory* is set in an anterior, more fluid stage of the deductive process, the questioner struggles to:

> force, run to earth, unmask, a complex and opaque reality through the process of an episodic Socratic dialectic method whose 'detective' theme functions only to permit a perpetual beginning. [A method] . . . which alleges drawing a new piece of information from each subsequent piece of information, a new detail from each detail in an inquiry whose proportions eventually escape all limits.³

A "summa" grows out of the questions and answers, which constitute a sweeping, mock sketch of people and places cramming Fantoine and Agapa. As the book's jacket blurb put it:

> A throng of faces, events, and passions, the picturesque chronology of a universe in full provincial activity, emerges little by little under the uninterrupted fire of an implacable questionnaire. But the voice that is speaking reveals less perhaps by what it says than by what it leaves unsaid, and you soon guess that its truth has a false bottom.

Olivier de Magny's imagistic description of *Graal Flibuste* is particularly apropos of this novel, for *The Inquisitory* accretes layers like a palimpsest and, as the author superimposes a reappraisal of his earlier works on the basic interrogation, the narrative's layers grow along with the novel's groping prose.[4]

"Yes or no answer." So the book begins, as an interrogating voice asks the first of more than two thousand questions, badgering the answering voice of an almost deaf old man. The first sentence's imperative suggests that the subject must not only reply but must weigh his answers carefully. A preliminary series of exchanges shows the investigator seeking information about the missing secretary of the owners of the Château de Broy. He has chosen to question the reluctant informant for several reasons. For one thing, the old man worked under the secretary at the castle for many years. For another, he used to peek through keyholes to fill the loneliness caused by old age and poor hearing. The servant's deafness permits Pinget to make certain verbal associations and puns. As the critic Albert-Marie Schmidt observed, "this infirmity transforms him into an incomparable maker of puppets." Pinget pits the curiosity and wiliness of both voices against each other from the outset. The questioner tries to ferret out what the old man has discovered, repeating questions and doubling back over answers. Shifts in lines of questioning divide the material into blocks comparable to M. Levert's drafts and the cycles of scenes in *Clope to the Dossier*.

The first questions pick at the daily routine at the château, the location of rooms and staircases, and the general tone of the parties held there. The interrogator gradually zeroes in on members of the staff, the relationships among them, and their acquaintances in town. He seems particularly interested in the secretary. The old man responds openly to questions that show the secretary in a bad light, implying that he was involved in a ring dealing in stolen or forged paintings. Although the old man seems cooperative, the interrogator's technique of skipping from one subject to another gives the impression that his confidence in his informant is less than complete.

Soon, however, he turns his inquiry toward the two bachelor-playboy owners of the château, dropping the house and servants temporarily. The subject admits reluctantly that his former masters consorted with younger men of less than distinguished backgrounds, citing a certain Chantre in particular, and also an unsavory hotel-keeper who came calling with a motley assortment of sleazy theatrical people. He recalls with obvious disapproval that once, while unloading the car, he stumbled onto a collection of pornographic pictures. For the moment, the questioner lets that libidinous sleeping dog lie (as well as insinuations that the owners were homosexuals), and asks about the more respectable guests. Why, for example, were the dinners at the château all stag affairs? The servant balks at giving direct answers when the questioner's insinuations tend to threaten the reputations of his former masters.

When the old servant mentions the town's inhabitants, many of Pingent's now-familiar cast of characters come briefly to the fore. The Princess of S ("La Princesse de Hem"), the Duchess of Doubtwood ("La Duchesse de Bois-Suspect"), Miette, an antique dealer, Miaille (all names that will recurr in *Fable*), and the local doctors—all rubbed elbows with his masters. Medicine leads the conversation back to Chantre, who is currently finishing his internship. Did a quarrel with the château's owners cause the young man to intern at Douves rather than at nearby Agapa? When pressed, the answering voice spins evasive arpeggios, and the questioning almost substantiates the supposition that the château harbored an illicit ring of some sort—almost, but not quite. The shadowboxing continues when his antagonist lets the old man retreat from another verbal corner. Still, the interrogator keeps sparring relentlessly, looking for an opening.

He finds it when a well-placed digression relaxes the old man and he lets his guard down slightly, whereupon the questioner dredges up the subject of medical care. Why didn't the playboys see the local doctor? What kinds of injections did they take? Were there any syringes lying around the house? A series of similarly leading questions about the behavior of foreign guests hints that the château may have sheltered a narcotics operation. A return to the list of doors and passageways reveals that the servant has failed to mention the secretary's office. Was the missing man involved with the homosexual Minette in illicit operations with antiques, or with the realtor, Ballaison, in land speculation? More slick (and sick) sleuthing to no avail:

> . . . in an interminable remembrance in depth, a Mr. X (identified summarily as a retired-deaf-valet) traces . . . the thorough inventory of what he has done, an inventory that passes through exasperating descriptions of the Château de Broy, where he worked, and its furnishings; the whole is broken up with shadowy references to the place's masters, about whom the interrogated-interrogator remains almost completely silent, while, page after page, this pregnant silence imposes on the reader, through gossip's deductions, a shabby, unverifiable anecdote about two old millionaire queers who like wild parties. And so, this Château de Broy, with such a two-bit mystery, is like an empty box. And little does it matter that the discourse be a memory, a conjurer's trick or a continuing process of creation giving itself the lie. In *The Inquisitory*, one discovers his life made of full nothingness and empty being, in a vast metaphor of stripping away. A meaning present sheerly for the beauty of the image given rise to.[5]

The simplicity of the interrogator's questions eventually makes one wonder if he is asking them in good faith. He doubles back, apparently hoping to catch the old man in a lie, an evasion, or a contradiction, and the interrogation turns inward, as the secretary's disappearance fades into the background. The questions probe and jab at exposed rag-tag leavings from the old man's past. The inquisitor takes on the task of forcing him to reintegrate his identity. The blankness of retirement and death terrifies the old man. So he ducks behind the shadows of memory, hoping that muttered litanies of bric-a-brac will ward off the realization of his insignificance and the approach of death.

The servant appears in a different light when he reveals, under pressure, that he was once married and has been a widower for ten years. The master and mistress in the house where he and his wife began service communicated with the Great Beyond. The lady of the house volunteered her services as a medium after the death of her servant's eight-year-old son. The boy's father, convinced that the source of the séances was diabolical, opposed them in vain, and he accused his master and mistress of casting spells that later killed his wife. Persistent prodding forces the old man to admit that he drinks heavily and then pushes him to irrationality: he has an hallucination that the devil has come to carry him away, and the conversation almost dissolves into terrified whimpering.

The next questions quiet him down, but only after his unstable, potentially dangerous side has been disclosed. The interrogator now begins to discuss a series of murders involving necrophilia. Is the questioner seeking to back his adversary into a confession? Was the old man involved in these crimes? The investigator manages to link him to one of the convicted murderers, but only tenuously: they had once worked in the same household. The subject's fatigue and incoherence, real or feigned, obscure the truth. He complains that:

> ... all the time you're asking me questions it seems to me I'm back in the café on my chair as if I was talking about something else something else somewhere else I'm not here any more we could invent other people no matter who yes make them say anything we liked it would be just like what happened between the real ones all of them in our heads they're dead, your questions give me the impression we're forcing them to speak but mistakes are not important they'd talk just the same whether it's true or false and we'll still be in the same boat when other people ask questions about us, someone will answer them this or that it won't make any difference our life will have been our own and no-one can do anything about it other people I mean, and whether you ask them yes or no the result will be the same they'll mix you up with me I'll be the one who asks the questions and you'll do the answering true or false what does it matter ... the truth has been left a long way behind it was just where we didn't expect it, perhaps because it was too simple and we've been racking our brains to say something different because of our efforts and we get left with a fine mess that

has nothing to do with the truth and perhaps that's what our life
is, like a sort of boxroom we lumber up with things we don't want
any more we say they're our memories it's helped me to get where
I am and twenty years later we turn them out again and we've no
longer any idea what they mean, papers photos notes notes all these
notes.[6]

The mongoose tries to bore in and catch his victim in a lie. The cobra seeks to tire or hypnotize his attacker. The old man answers defensively and at cross-purposes. He shies away from describing a wing of the castle that he previously had said was uninhabited, and he almost refuses to go on at all:

> Another twenty rooms and then there'll be still more and you'll tell
> me to describe them, and more and more kitchen servants tell-tale
> tittle-tattle secrets of the bedchamber families mile upon mile of
> streets and stairs and lumber-rooms and junk-shops of antique
> dealers grocers butchers of skimping and scraping everywhere in
> our heads how dreary it all is always starting all over again why,
> all these dead people around us all these dead people we third
> degree to make them talk when will you have finished I haven't
> asked anything, am I always going to have to start again the eve-
> nings in the bistro in the street what how why[7]

Finally, the questioning voice drags an admission out of the old man: a certain M. Pierre lives in one of the castle's towers, takes his meals alone, receives few visitors, and observes the stars. A saintly hermit, like Father Blanès in *The Charterhouse of Parma*, M. Pierre prefers celestial contemplation to the human hurly-burly. When forced to speak of M. Pierre, the old man refuses to jump from subject to subject, undercutting his earlier answers:

> . . . you see someone do something straight-away you jump to con-
> clusions we must be mad there are no conclusions except those we
> imagine at the moment or that we're determined to call conclusions,
> the true ones are nothing like them they get mixed up with every-
> thing else and that's life but it's a slow process and listen though
> I'm on my guard your questions still make me slip up, I still fall
> into the trap it does happen and give my opinion and draw con-
> clusions in spite of knowing it's all tommyrot . . .[8]

THE LUMBER ROOM OF MEMORY

The questioning voice tries to tie the loose threads of the investigation together by getting the old man to describe his employers' annual lawn party. In so doing, he rattles all the castle's skeletons, reviewing hints of scandal that momentarily gave the *"procès verbal"* a sense of progression: the owners' alleged homosexuality, the secretary's use of the house as a center for a drug ring, the possible complicity of a member of the household in murders. The recapitulation fails, however, to prove or disprove *any* hypothesis about what really was going on—if anything. Yet the investigator continues undaunted, trying to whipsaw the elusive piece of information out of his victim alternately reassuring and threatening, commiserating and cajoling, him. All to no avail. The adversaries struggle on in a verbal skirmish that seems to be getting nowhere and apparently could go on indefinitely. The novel ends, appropriately enough, on a note of fatigue:

> Answer, have you envisaged some way of seeing Monsieur Pierre again
> Never I wouldn't dare disturb him unless
> Unless
> As I dreamt one day one morning I was walking along my little lanes
> Go on
> I took one I didn't know before and there's Marie in a garden with our child and she says to me come in and I go into the kitchen where I find Monsieur Pierre
> Go on
> He asked us to dinner we had all night long to talk about the stars and another night and then another and
> And
> We were going to talk for a long time
> Go on
> I could hear everything I could hear everything I was telling him all the names Cyrille came to shake me
> You were dreaming in the café
> I don't remember
> You'd fallen asleep in the café
> I don't remember
> Has it ever happened that you fall asleep in the café

> Answer, had you fallen asleep that day in the café
> I don't remember
> Answer
>
> Yes or no answer
> I'm tired[9]

This résumé of the novel, it must be emphasized, reduces it to its least rewarding level of meaning, that is, to speculation about what did or did not "happen." The reader's sense of motion as the questions swirl and double back on themselves and lurch forward has barely been suggested and must be experienced through the text to be appreciated.

Up to now, our discussion has only skimmed the surface, accepting the identities of the interlocutors at face value. At the outset, there are no "characters" as such but only, as Léon Roudiez pointed out, a speaking voice and an answering voice.[10] The "character" of the old man is in constant evolution, creating itself as it breaks and retreats into silence. In his next book, *Someone (Quelqu'un)*, Pinget will caution against taking the detective/suspect relationship between the voices too literally:

> Let no one come tell me that I'm answering questions. Because they said it. They had it said. About my other lives when I was trying to get rid of them. He's answering questions, see. It must be the police. There's a detective tone, he's obliged to answer, they're forcing him, they're hounding him. Stupid stuff like that. Must have got messed up in my editing. To be that wrong, to give an idea that false. It's damned annoying.[11]

Pinget's spoof of reviews taking the cops-and-robbers aspect of *The Inquisitory* at face value reinforces what should be obvious from close reading: that the interrogation's importance lies elsewhere. The thrust and parry of question and answer does more than simply stir the addled memories of a confused servant. It challenges the validity of Pinget's entire chronicle by reexamining the world of Fantoine and Agapa, and it comments implicitly on man's use of words to exorcise his fear of emptiness and death.

The dialogue only *seems* to take place between a police functionary and a suspect. It is the interplay between a novelist and his material that causes its fundamental tensions. *The Inquisitory* is 489 pages long, a length that reversed a trend of increasing brevity in Pinget's production. None of his previous books exceeded 250 pages, and those following *The Fox and the Compass* got shorter and shorter. Pinget stressed this aspect of the work in an interview with Denise Bourdet, pointing out that *The Inquisitory* transcribes the constant questioning of the world he is drawing from the void:

> That threatening little phrase, "yes or no answer," I was addressing it to *myself* to force myself to get on with my book.[12]

The Inquisitory confronts the reader with a review of life in the familiar setting of Douves, Crachon, and Sirancy. The old man's gossipy tongue trips over the names of Mahu, Mlle. Lorpailleur, Latirail, Sophie Narre, Brindon, Clotho, Architruc, Toupin, Pierre Moule, M. Levert and his son, M. Chinze, Clope, Cruze, Verveine, Mortin, and Phillipard. It might appear that the reader would need some sort of biographical glossary to sort out the characters, and such a guide actually exists: *Nomenclature of Persons from Sirancy-la-Louve, Agapa and Their Environs Mentioned In the Transcript (Nomenclature des personnes de Sirancy-la-Louve, d'Agapa et des environs mentionnés dans le procès' verbal).* In a satirical response to critics' misreadings of Pinget as a twentieth-century Balzac (and an inept one at that), the Editions de Minuit put out this genealogical index in 1962 as a spoof of the Castex Repertory of the populace in Balzac's *Comédie Humaine*. But Pinget's "summa" was never intended to clarify. Instead of straightening out Fantoine's labyrinthine environs and its unpredictable citizenry the text adds new and tantalizing vistas and dead ends. The old man refers to events central to *Monseiur Levert* and *Clope to the Dossier*, but rumor and hearsay cloud his observations. Contradictions obscure the rare bits of factual information, and incoherence, mendacity, and ignorance distort what "facts" there are:

> Whereabouts is Fantoine
> About six miles from Sirancy in the direction of
> Veriville there's still a Mahu there who must be
> the crackpot's nephew he married the Clope girl

> they run the café, it's the brother-in-law Chinze
> who put up the money they hadn't a bean neither of them
> my gentlemen always used to say that Fantoine
> was the home of all the local good-for-nothings,
> I must say the population in my day was a pretty
> job lot, on account of it was so isolated I suppose
> in the old days people usen't to move around so
> much it's a poor bit of country this side the
> land's no good there must have been a lot of
> inter-marriage
>
> And this Chinze
> A cousin of the cobbler's the father of Marie
> Chinze no-one knows what she died of everyone
> wondered at the time, Levert was more or less
> mixed up in it or his son we never knew Levert's
> wife took drugs he finished up in a ditch, Marie's
> brother that's Minet
>
> And the Clope girl
> The daughter of a boozer who used to doss down
> in the station he had to be chucked out.[13]

The culling of material moves simultaneously in several directions. It explains and confuses, blocks one line of development only to begin another. For every moot point clarified, the dialogue casts doubt upon a previously acceptable hypothesis. At first, *The Inquisitory* sweeps along with the momentum of the final volume of a series: the early meandering ties together loose ends, and a resonant finale seems to be in the offing. Later, however, discords and contradictions develop, and the dialogue eventually recalls old Topsey's hurdy-gurdy played backwards in *Clope to the Dossier* or the ducklike squeaks of a rewinding tape recording. Carl Bjurström stressed the harmony of *The Inquisitory*'s prose and structure in *Critique:*

> It's a language which flows along without discontinuity, with constantly renewed invention. A prose which surges forward at the very moment it is coming apart, giving birth to slips of the tongue and bloopers which are often irresistibly droll. This constant contrast be-

tween lassitude and vitality, wear and tear and invention, stupidity and perspicacity, banality and extravagance, vulgarity and mystery is a powerful driving force of humor and anguish.[14]

Pinget's prose achieves the halting quality of *Monsieur Levert* and *Clope to the Dossier*'s language by playing up speech distortions caused by deafness. The old man garbles clichés because he has never heard them properly, and his spoonerisms give the clichés new life. He swaps *"cuisine"* for *"cuisse"* in a common expression:

> Quand on ne sort pas de la cuisine de Jupiter il faut tâcher d'y rentrer
>
> If you spring full-blown from Jupiter's head [= "john"] you don't have to clean it out.

Syllable slippage confuses *"clergeyman"* and *"kleptomane"* [*"clergyman"* and *"kleptomaniac"*]; *"nymphomane"* and *"nymphatique"* [*"nymphomaniac"* and *"nymphean"*]; *"misanthrope"* and *"misancroque"* [*"misanthrope"* and *"misancroak"*]; *"strip-tease"* and *"tripe-tease"* [*"Striptease"* and *"tripe-tease"*]; *"Ross Royce"* and *"Rolls Royce"*; *"somnifères"* and *"somnifèvres"* [*"sleeping pills"* and *"sleeping bills"*]; *"Venus Aphrodite"* and *"Venus Amphibite"* [*"Venus Aphrodite"* and *"Venus Amphibious"*]; *"études de seminaires"* and *"études d'inseminaires"* [*"seminary studies"* and *"insemmination studies"*]; *"clavesin"* and *"claquesin"* [*"clavechord"* and *"clackachord"*]; *"cottes de maille"* and *"crottes de maille"* [*"sheath of armor"* and *"shits of armor"*]. By simply displacing an accent *"Menerve"* [*"Minerva"*], the goddess of wisdom and the arts, becomes *"Ménerve," "m'énerve"* [*"Irks me"*].

In short, the preliminary hearing leads nowhere. The interrogation never comes up with the key question. The grand synthesis obscures everything. Individual words release Roman-candle showers of meanings, and the scrambling of titles of famous works of art suggests that the sacrosanct humanistic tradition itself is vulnerable to chaos, and confusion, and derision. The stable, predictable orbits of the constellations observed by M. Pierre are a universe away. *The Inquisitory*'s circular dialogue and its volatile prose posit a world denying and contradicting itself.

As the investigation unfolds, Pinget distorts the mystery-story format by inundating the reader with material, thus calling into question both the novel and the cycle of which it is a part.[15] The interrogation develops through a pattern of repetition that is capable of indefinite expansion, like the organist's phrase in *Graal Flibuste*. Jérôme Lindon's prediction that the novel would mark a high point in Pinget's development proved to be accurate. *The Inquisitory* underscores the novelist's paradoxical quest. Speaking architecturally, *The Inquisitory* supports the weight of the arch from *Between Fantoine and Agapa* to *Clope to the Dossier* and lays the foundation for austere buttresses of the sparer arcs to come, and as Olivier de Magny asked in his postface to *Graal Flibuste:*

> And so does this swarm of anecdotes, all these manias, these palavers, these interests and these calculations, these ups and downs, these deviant appetites, these shady dealings, these gay parties and these foul crimes (which you never finally can count and whose exact motives you can never discern), do they all conceal with their illusory diversity a deeper, enigmatic, anguishing similarity, a sealed anonymity which no question and no answer can reduce? The old servant has spoken, and in the the same motion wiped out what he has said, denying the possibility of the novel which the inquisitors are eagerly forcing him to write, but which he buries under the ash of answers whose meanings he challenges or no longer understands.[16]

SOMEONE (QUELQU'UN)

Pinget's next novel begins with a more concrete kind of rummaging. If a man reaches into his coat pocket for his keys and finds that they are no longer in their accustomed place, his immediate reaction is one of surprise and dismay. Frustration can soon turn to panic if memory fails to explain their disappearance. *Someone* (1965) begins when the narrator realizes that some notes that he needs are missing from his desk and consists largely of his muttered remarks as he searches in vain for the missing piece of paper. The tone of the convoluted ruminations becomes more querulous as the protagonist reconstructs his movements and his troubled voice slowly brings Pinget's province back to life.

> You check three times if a door or a window is shut or if the gas or electricity is turned off, you know very well that it's off and you

> start over three times, even more, telling yourself that perhaps you didn't look carefully the last time or you were thinking about something else.[17]

The quest begins in the immediate past, then ranges further afield. Lost scraps of information leave chinks in the rejected treatise (a *"mémoire"* in French), an obviously ironic illusion to the seeker's sievelike rememberer. The search for these notes sets off an inventory that grows like Topsy:

> If I say that perhaps it's not that paper that I'm looking for but another one it is for the following reason. I just tried to re-edit my botanical paragraph and I succeeded very well. I had all the information I needed. I'll go on tomorrow. First I'll finish this exposé, saying that paper but it's surely another one, just as indispensable in any case, don't worry, just as indispensable.[18]

The narrator lets his thoughts ramble, hoping to trick his memory into releasing the paper's location by pretending not to concentrate on it. As observations accumulate helter-skelter, the monologue opens onto a far broader, parallel inquiry. The speaker engages in a dialogue between echoes of his memory and the tired pounding of his heart. He strives to pack the trunk of remembered experiences for the imminent voyage of death. The narrator's name, "Mortin," coupling as it does the root *"mort"* ("death") with the reassuring diminutive *"tin,"* reflects a desire to make the prospect of death bearable, or at least familiar. The narrator complains that it is:

> As if your existence always had to form a compact little parcel which you could grab in a hurry and take along everywhere. And that's not even an image, I shouldn't say as if, that's the way it is. That's the way it happens. Your existence in a suitcase, neatly packed, well catalogued so that you have what you need just in case. So you pack your bag endlessly, you're always in the process of making something into a parcel.[19]

As he stumbles around looking for his notes, the narrator describes the broken-down suburban boardinghouse in which he lives and of which he is a part owner. Pinget paints the *"Pension"* as a way station between past and future. Its inhabitants, a listless collection of retired failures, wait for death, more or less consciously. Humor keeps the portrayal of their foibles from running either to excessive cruelty or to pathos. They knit, they sort bills, they hoard toilet paper—anything to pass time and to ignore its flight. The protagonist keeps himself busy writing and mulling over his past. His garrulous *"exposé"* could end only in its author's death, a death similar to the last stages of "verbal folly" described in *Graal Flibuste*.[20] Methodical precision and the searches it sets in motion help him to deal with insecurity. As he ticks off for the fifth time the activities of the day on which the notes disappeared, he writes:

> It is therefore almost certain that I did not go to the kitchen. Or go back to the refectory. Why would I have gone back there? Did Mme. Reber want to tell me something? No. She goes down to the garden around ten these days, she doesn't go back to the refectory. Well that's it. She was going down to the garden and she asked for her chair . . . And when she was settled in it I asked her if she hadn't seen my paper. I specified stack of paper . . . So she not treat me always as an inferior I added that stack of paper was of considerable importance, an entire paragraph of my *"mémoire"* depended on it.[21]

The other residents of the house share the narrator's fascination with the past, but their attitude toward it differs significantly. The protagonist uses the search for the piece of paper as a pretext to permit his memories to pass in review; he hopes to make a dramatic discovery through the mnemonic device of the *"exposé."* His companions try to hide from reality in a carefully composed world of idealized recollections. Stale anecdotes about an idyllic youth in Alsace or a honeymoon in Italy ward off the menace of passing time. They exchange words. The reflex of sociability is moribund, not dead. But they are as withdrawn as the senile grandmother, who is described with characteristically astringent irony:

> The daughter-in-law said to the grandmother to get her out of the way while she did the housework, go watch television. But the grandmother was senile and the daughter-in-law put her in front of the set without turning it on. It didn't make any difference. And toward the end when she was even worse she put her in another corner, not in the living room, turned toward a blank wall and she

told her look at the television and the grandmother looked and she left her alone.[22]

The narrator's obsession with writing gives rise to eccentric habits. His snooping and muttering exclude him from the boarder's circle, and they obviously doubt his mental stability. His only companion is a retarded child, Fonfon, another unfortunate who is cut off from the fellowship of others. The text strays into imaginary conversations as the narrator dreams of telling his life story to a neighbor. If only he had *someone* to talk to! He describes the trivial routine of the *"Pension"* with the detachment of a spectator—the comings and goings of the cook in the hallway, the jockeying for position when setting out a lawn chair, the crash of a potted plant being dropped, or the grotesque preoccupation with fashion on the part of women who will probably not live out the year. The narrative follows the voice's querulous questioning through all this trivia. The broken-down boardinghouse does not stand in contrast with the bareness of the protagonist's life, as did the castle's richly furnished decor in *The Inquisitory*. Nor do the speaker's questions put him onto the trail of lurid scandals.

Yet the narrator's droning, dogged voice does more than hold the reader's attention; it wins his respect. *Someone* could not possibly venture further from the conception of "Literature" with a capital "L," or sting more sharply the notion of the novel as "pretty writing." The speaker's exploration of his world's limits has a compelling integrity, sordid though the account may be.

> Putting things into focus, that's what I like best. . . . Precision, what a wonder! But people don't understand. They think it's beauty or sumptuousness or love or God knows what. It's precision. Finding *"le mot juste,"* finding exactly the right word, why it's divine! I should say in passing that "caca" ["poop"] is often the most precise word.[23]

The observer records his companions' empty lives with mordant humor, but also as a fellow sufferer. He does not sit in judgment. Disillusionment has caused his misanthropy, not cynicism:

> Before, when I wasn't working on my little writing I was like everybody. I talked, I experimented I lived as they say. I bored

> myself shitless. That's the right word. Or rather not entirely. I bored myself shitless, but I kept saying to myself that I was going about it wrong, that I didn't have an open mind, that I wasn't seeing things as they are, that I could get a lot more out of them and that I would change. Things and people I mean. Especially people. So I made the pleasure last if you can say such a thing. I floundered around in other people's "poop" telling myself that I wasn't seeing clearly, that I had to be more attentive, kinder too, forget myself a little, love them a little, help them a little, so that they open up a little. Hell. The more they opened up the more of it there was. At one point I couldn't take it any more, I was suffocating. And I withdrew into my own.[24]

Writing later, he reaffirms his membership in the excremental confraternity of humanity:

> I'll stay on like a child on his potty, he keeps waiting to get up, the mother looks to see if he's done his duty, he still hasn't done anything, she sits him down again until he delivers his poopy. I want to be the child, the mother and the potty at the same time.[25]

The recurring dung-heap imagery underscores the themes of passing time, compulsive talk, and shifting contours:

> Incessant outflow, discharge; scatological images whose significance is evident recur regularly in this book. The long soliloquy of Someone is nothing but . . . a true diarrhea of existence. In his somewhat coarse language Someone says "The future is like the runs, it empties you, it kills you."[26]

The blend of frankness and reticence, of integrity and irony, enables Pinget to carry out:

> a fictive operation that makes sordidness tip over into courage, meanness into lucidity, and rottenness into love, without apparent transition.[27]

The authentic concern of the protagonist's voice compels interest in what he says, and, as the text winds itself into convolutions and arabesques, hope that the appeal to the subconscious may cause a relevant fact to bob to the surface generates a certain suspense. The nameless narrator might just remember, for example, where he put the notes, write his memoirs, and thus become "Someone" at last. The double quest represented by a scene in which the narrator rakes through a manure pile might just possibly wind its way to either one or the other of two possible resolutions. The speaker might eventually find a sympathetic, understanding listener in answer to his recurring wistful lament. He writes of this possibility:

> "Just let them understand me, let them put themselves in my place. I wonder if someone would want to. . . . If only I had someone! Someone to read over my shoulder, but that would be too good to be true."[28]

Or he might possibly discover that he has been *"Someone"* all along. The narrator withdraws further into recollections as the first alternative fades out.

> It's getting more and more insipid. But I've got to go on anyway. It's when you lose hope that the miracle occurs. I may very well find something which has nothing to do with my paper, even less with my life, and which puts me onto a trail. . . . Something unexpected, flashing. And even if that doesn't make me find this paper, too bad, I'm not giving up on it, no, but I'll get interested in this flashing thing as well. Could it cure me of my everlasting heartsickness perhaps? Change me? Transform me? A new me which would come out of this trifling, a being all pure, all grace, all smile. It sometimes seems to me that I've just missed it, that if I hadn't been obliged to let myself get all tangled up in our existence I would have become this being and that it's still sleeping somewhere, in limbo, perhaps in my body but above all don't look for it, don't lean over my spleen, keep talking, dissecting ineptitudes, force myself, and something that I will have forced myself even more to say, without any connection with the being, that's what it would cause it to come out, to surge up like a rocket.[29]

But the extended mnemonic device of the monologue never sets off the hoped-for association of ideas. The review of the past does not uncover secrets that redeem the present. The yellowed snapshots of posed figures, forgotten arrivals, and joyless outings do not unlock the door to a Proustian treasure-trove. Although the narrator struggles (without success) to place the isolated moment of each picture into a coherent continuum, the perusal of an old album is terrifying rather than reassuring. It parallels the speaker's fruitless foraging in the garbage pail, where he picks over rotten tid-bits in search of the missing piece of paper.

> All these zucchini and eggplant skins, the rotten parts of tomatoes, the spit out nerves of beef steak, the disgusting leftovers of casseroles, the lettuce cores . . . the ravelled remnants of the rag bag mixed in with fat balls of dust already greasy with the juice from plates . . . I looked at everything. Reber yelled at me put on gloves to do that job. Gloves, gloves, I had to have gloves, . . . Am I the type to handle life with kid gloves?[30]

"Mettre des gants" ("to put on gloves," or as we say colloquially, "to handle with kid gloves") means, figuratively, to act with restraint, decorum, or good taste. In making this aside, Pinget is probably justifying the crudeness of his language and the sordidness on his material at this point.

The narrator looks his empty routine in the face without flinching. Whether poking through the debris of the past or scavenging through the refuse pile of his present uselessness, he remains barehanded. He permits himself only one distraction, a rented television to amuse Fonfon. Everyday, the bug-eyed neophyte viewers identify themselves with Captain Corcoran, the hero of a television serial, and they become "somebody" for the fleeting duration of each program:

> I thanked God for having given me this idea. Perhaps I was going to save Fonfon like that, with the television. But I was saving myself too, I might have been able to save myself perhaps . . . Corcoran saved the princess, she was in love with him, he burned cities, he galloped along in the wild countryside, he took command of armies, and there was this pet tiger, everything, everything, we held our breath, we were the friends of the captain, we dressed his wounds, we advised him to return to the palace where his fiancée was waiting for him, and he went back, he married, he went away again to defend the poor. He conquered all the empires. And for a month it was like that. We *were* the television, we saw palm trees

wherever we walked, sunsets on the minarets, perfumed nights, ships strewn with cushions and we set out for the tropics. Fonfon remembered from one time to the next, not I, he was the one who ended up telling me the story. We were coming back to life.[31]

But the speaker cannot afford to rent the set indefinitely, and so the escape from tedium comes to an abrupt end. He keeps on talking, however, though he knows by now that the notes are lost forever. He has no alternative, and he groans pacing the floor reviewing the events of the day:

> I want to conclude straight away with a view of the whole a sort of "tour d'horizon" which closes off all exits, that's normal, that's the horizon's job. But it's false.

He can no more bring his text to a close than could the deaf servant lost in the dim hallways of the past.

> Nothing is ever concluded in this life, not even in one like ours. It's not because you think that the horizon is within reach that it exists. It's a vision of the mind or of fatigue, it's all the same. There is no horizon anywhere.[32]

As Adolphe Grégoire observed, in *La Revue Nouvelle:*

> If one could give the work, in the beginning, the configuration of a spiral descent to the depths, as soon as the essential quest is revealed to us and all hope of seeing it reach its goal seems illusory, the structure bursts, ravels out, fragments itself for lack of breath and fatigue, up to the point of erasing itself without any reason and opens onto a gaping void.[33]

The dogged monologue assimilates itself with the earlier novels through a series of cross references.

> In one of my other lives, careful, I've only had one, I mean one of my *"exposés,"* I said I was the king of my crap. That meant the same thing, reading between the lines. In short, I note that I'm not coming out of it.[34]

The quotation comes directly from *Baga*, as does the attitude of self-derision. The speaker also searches the grounds of the boarding house only to admit, like the narrator of *Clope to the Dossier*, that "all hypotheses resemble each other but they don't all lead to the same place."

Once more the quest leads inward—to nowhere.[35] The speaker joins the growing brotherhood of Mahu, Porridge, and M. Levert. The words of his predecessors blend, as Pinget's characters seem more and more like different intonations of the same voice. Other parallels can be drawn to what has come before. Once again, the title indicates what the book is *not*.[36] Porridge finds no compass to guide him. *Baga* deals with Architruc, not Baga. Clope opens possibilities instead of circumscribing them. Levert loses his son (if he ever had one). The narrator of *Someone* fears that without someone to listen, he's nobody. Yet the novel gives these recurring themes a fresh and effective expression. The narrator avoids the free-flowing fantasies that characterize *Mahu or the Material* and the mythological twists of *Graal Flibuste*.

Yet here, as so frequently in Pinget's novels, the subconscious plays an active role. The speaker used stream of consciousness to trick the memory into releasing its secrets. Instead of stringing together surrealistic images, Pinget suggests the powerful presence of the unconscious by focusing on the protagonist's observations. He eliminates inventories and descriptions almost completely, depicting the boardinghouse as a bare shell.

> There to be honest I really should mention everything that is in the shed and that I inspected and walked around. But I don't want to give myself over to inventories any more. I did it before with my conscience, what patience it took! In my other *exposés*, to help me to concentrate, hoping that it would strip bare my subconscious, that it would open paths toward the essential for me. Lots of luck! Completely useless. Objects are good for nothing if you're after the soul. You might think right off that they help us to get our bearings, to concentrate, I repeat, God-damned foolishness. You get caught in your own game, you fiddle-faddle around with the description, you lick your chops but in the end you're Simple Simon like before.[37]

The novel creates and sustains the illusion of a living voice exploring, through words, the physical and metaphysical limits of its environment. Pinget brings to life a voice searching for a language with which to express itself. As Ludovic Janvier wrote of Beckett:

> To make him take the road toward the self, the writer made a traveller of his character, and he made him even the writer of his voyage. . . . Once the voyage is abandoned, the character finds himself immobile and, in his silence, all he has is to live the extreme experiment of the writer in front of his blank page: to add to himself word-by-word in hopes of being born.[38]

part three

Approaching Silence

THIBS

Des gros propriétaires ils ont des terrains tout autour de Straung ~~toys~~ les grand parents étaient encore paysans ils avaient la ~~pièce~~ ferme des côté de la route de Camp entre la grand route et le chemin Philibert. Le père c'est le père d'Augustin qui a acheté la maison de la place. ~~Trevor~~ La pure ~~modeman~~ un fermier dans la ferme Augustin continue à gérer ses biens avec son beau-frère Fouron le cousin de Marseille ils sont tout le temps en train de discuter pendant des heures un terrain ou une maison et acheter ou ~~vendre~~ c'est des gros clients de Balcain.

Et Gaston Letourneur et ~~le~~ ce t'épenir Sonfiar?

Gaston c'est un autre coureur cycliste Il a ouvert son magasin Il y a dix ans Il ne pouvait plus faire de sport à cause du cœur il a avec lui un de ses copains Pierrocks dit le frère au blanchisseur qui était aussi coureur cycliste ~~...~~ Il fait les réparations quand Il n'est pas au cygne c'est un vieux garçon ~~................~~ comme on dit dans les quarante-cinq toujours en train de rigoler et d'entuber bizarre son voisin Sonfiar qui n'rait toujours au bistrot sa femme elle lui fait la vie une fois c'meul s'il veulent faire entrer la coopérative. ~~..........................~~ à ce propos, un lemaq de Lisque significative des petits qui vont ~~..........~~ peut-on pleur ça pas maintenant ça il bufft prendre un peu le bon temps avec Pierre

5 Words on Stage. Pinget's Theater

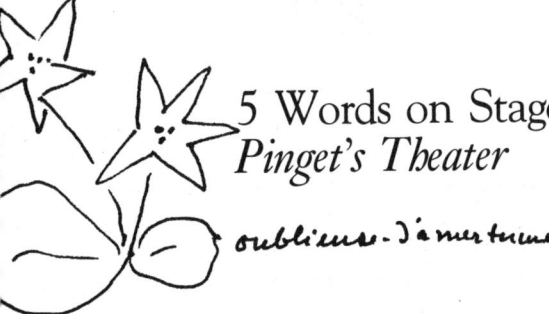

THE TEACHER:	Sounds, Miss, must be seized in mid flight by the wings so they do not fall into the ears of the deaf. And therefore when you decide to articulate, it is most highly recommended to raise the neck and chin very high, stretch up on tip-toes, here, like this, do you see?
THE STUDENT:	Yes, Teacher.
THE TEACHER:	Be still. Remain seated. Do not interrupt. And it is also recommended to emit sounds very loudly, with all the strength of your lungs associated with the strength of your vocal chords. Like this; watch: "Butterfly," "Eureka," "Trafalgar," "papi papa." That way the sounds filled with warm air, lighter than the surrounding air, will fly up and out with no risk of falling into the ears of the deaf which are the veritable gulfs or tombs of sonorities. If you emit several sounds at an accelerated speed, they will grab onto each other automatically, thus constituting syllables, words, even phrases, that is more or less long groups, purely irrational assemblages of sounds stripped of all meaning but for that very reason capable of maintaining themselves without danger at a high altitude in the air. The only words which fall are those loaded with significance, weighted down with their meaning which always eventually succumb and fall.
THE STUDENT:	... into the ears of the deaf.—Ionesco, *The Lesson*
BELA:	I mean words ... how can I say ... the very fabric of our ... you understand ... cart death along, transport it in a vehicle. ... or lead up to it, which all comes to the same thing.—Pinget, *Abel et Bela*

Since the late 1950s Pinget has written extensively for both radio and the stage, and his interest in these media has grown steadily. An adaptation of his 1962 radio play *Around Mortin* was performed on French National Television in 1971. *Dead Letter (Lettre Morte)* (1959) and *Architruc* (1961) have been included in the repertory of the Comédie française. The British Broadcasting Corporation and Radio Stuttgart have produced Pinget's radio plays.

He began his theatrical activities in 1959 with a French translation of Beckett's *All That Fall (Tout ceux qui tombent)*. (Beckett later returned the favor by doing the English translation of Pinget's *The Old Tune* [*La Manivelle*].) In 1970 Pinget accompanied the Tréteau de Paris company to New York, serving as a consultant in the production of *Architruc* and *Dead Letter*, and in 1972 the dramatist turned actor and appeared on stage in a Paris production of his *Abel and Bela (Abel et Bela)*. Considering Pinget's growing fascination with tones of voice and the generative, runaway quality of words, it is easy to understand his being strongly attracted to the theater and his increasing involvement in it.

Furthermore, Pinget obviously enjoys moving back and forth from one genre to the other. As a general rule, his dramatic pieces follow the novels chronologically, reworking or developing themes and materials already treated. *Monsieur Levert* and its theatrical analogue *Dead Letter* both appeared in 1959. *Architruc*, the stage version of *Baga*, appeared three years later. Since Pinget wrote the novelistic and theatrical pieces more or less simultaneously it is small wonder that the three manners of expression, or periods of development, into which the novels can be grouped apply to the plays as well. *Architruc* falls into the first, surrealist manner and is in the same spirit as *Between Fantoine and Agapa*, *Mahu or the Material*, *The Fox and the Compass*, *Graal Flibuste*, and *Baga*. *Dead Letter*, *The Hypothesis*, *Here and There*, and *Around Mortin* correspond to the novelistic variations on the mystery story, *No Answer*, *Clope to the Dossier*, *The Inquisitory*, and *Someone*. Pinget's latest plays, *Identité, (Identity) Abel et Bela, (Abel and Bela) Paralchimie (Paralchemy)* and *Nuit (Night)* are closely related to his most recent narratives, which experiment with the flow of words as self-perpetuating and self-destructive sounds. Since the theatrical works cast some revealing sidelights on the theme of the quest in the novels, many of the plays will be treated here from that point of view. The following brief glance at Pinget's plays will therefore recapitulate the development of the quest theme in texts of his first two periods and serve as an introduction to the experimentation with narrative in which he is engaging at this writing (i.e., in the latter half of the 1970s).

Pinget's theater is a theater of words. As in the French classical theater of the seventeenth century, the text is of primary importance. Gesture and action are minimal. Tone, modulation, repetition of words and phrases are at the very heart of the drama. The plays draw on the novels, in which writing, not action, is of prime importance. One may wonder why Pinget turned from prose fiction after writing *Monsieur Levert* and *Clope to the Dossier*—why he risked spreading his talent too thin by experimenting with theater at all. In 1960, Jean Thibaudeau advanced a possible explanation for the author's decision, suggesting that Pinget's dramatic pieces comment upon and prepare the direction his fiction would take (and in fact did take), particularly in *The Libera Me Domine (Le Libera,* 1968) and *Recurring Melody (Passacaille,* 1969).

> It seems that Pinget has reached a moment when, just as he was reaching the peak of his novelistic accomplishment, he was obliged to force his writing, as if to rework and test again a language-reality tension whose ambiguity and urgency the modern novel exposes more and more clearly. Pinget's work deals . . . with a contradiction between a desperate realism . . . and a baroque temptation of language, a contradiction that novelistic form alone did not suffice to hold or suspend, and that explains the recourse to the theater.[1]

Bringing the province of Fantoine and Agapa to the stage gave Pinget the opportunity to restate his themes in new terms, and to find ways to direct attention to the autocritical commentary running just beneath the surface of the novels.

DEAD LETTER (LETTRE MORTE)

Although Pinget's first dramatic pieces derive directly from previously published material, they draw freely on characters and situations presented in the narratives and use the devices made possible by the stage with increasing effectiveness. The action of Pinget's first play follows Levert's search for his son as described through the letter drafts of *Monsieur Levert*. *Dead Letter*, the theatrical parallel to this novel, makes use of several changes that smooth the transition from page to stage. For example, Pinget replaces the novel's contradictory descriptions of the funeral with repetitive dialogue. Since the audience sees an actor speaking lines, the dramatist can hardly delay the emergence of the character's voice, or hide his identity as in the novel. The first act takes place in a café where M. Levert is a frequent—and garrulous—customer; he is the kind of tippler whom bartenders dread, one with a "glittering eye" and a long tale to tell. In the novel, Levert describes going to the bar in rather vague terms; in the play, the audience actually sees him there. Scraps of conversation, the spoken equivalent of the novel's letter drafts, gradually sketch in a loosely defined subject. M. Levert has apparently been bending the long-suffering bartender's ears for years about the disappearance of the junior Levert—and he has no intention of relenting. The halting expression of his unhappiness both amuses and pains the audience. His anguish is convincing, although the specific cause of Levert's suffering is mysterious at first, and the starkness of the almost-bare set heightens, by contrast, the baroque, wandering quality of the dialogue. The characters in the play frequently try to cast what is going on around them to fit a scenario conforming to their manias. At the end of the first act, for example, when some actors enter the café, M. Levert confuses scenes from the play they are rehearsing with the story of his own prodigal son. Illusion and reality, one character and another, melt into each other, as in Corneille's *L'Illusion Comique (The Comic Illusion)*, giving the play the phantasmagorical quality of dreams and the overlapping drafts in *Monsieur Levert* and *Clope to the Dossier*.

In the second act, the play's realistic outlines give way to fantasy. The café turns into a post office, recalling the labyrinthine structure before which the novel ends, and the bartender plays the role of an employee whom old Levert pesters every day for the letter they both know will never arrive. The purveyor of illusion, be he bartender or postman, tries to convince Levert that a happier life lies somewhere just beyond the corner, just the other side of the provincial limits confining them. But the hypothesis of future happiness breaks down even as he is postulating it, and as the play ends he is repeating, mechanically: "What really counts, what really counts, what really counts."

In this first foray outside of prose narrative, Pinget succeeds admirably in bringing Levert's loneliness to life on stage. The play within a play shows the protagonist striving to relate his obsession to a broader fable, and reaching out to others with words and clichés. The play's title, *Dead Letter*, refers to Levert's unsuccessful attempts to get in touch with his son. It also implies that communication addressed to God-the-Father will lie unanswered in some dusty dead-letter office.

But the theater imposes limits even as it opens up possibilities. The physical presence of Levert on the stage and the reliance on dialogue convey Pinget's meaning with greater directness at the cost of his sacrificing many of the novel's deliberate ambiguities. When he appears on stage, M. Levert obviously has a body, a face, a way of walking (even though Pinget encourages actors to keep their "theatrics" to a minimum), and thus the disembodied voice that hypnotizes the reader of *Monsieur Levert* is trapped, on stage, in the "too, too, solid flesh." Pinget's first attempt at confronting the audience with the drama of a voice seeking a word that has become a dead letter is not as convincing as the novel. It is too easy for the intellectually lazy spectator to dismiss the play as the babblings of a demented old man, or to see it simply as an off-beat retelling of the biblical parable of the prodigal son.

THE OLD TUNE (LA MANIVELLE) and HERE AND THERE (ICI ET AILLEURS)

In the dramatic works following *Dead Letter*, Pinget manipulates theatrical conventions with growing assurance. *The Old Tune* (*La Manivelle*, 1959) transposes the cacaphony of dialogue between Topsey and Losey in *Clope to the Dossier* into a frightening, engrossing radio skit. Pinget's skill with spoken language makes his radio plays particularly effective. The almost palpable tension between speech and silence also contributes to their success. The bleak, desolate railway-station setting of a later work, *Here and There* (*Ici et Ailleurs*, 1961), expresses the emptiness of routine in visual terms. The Everyman-like central characters live as squatters in a station between undefined points on the line. A continuing departure, or a starting over again and getting nowhere, conditions the self-consciously futile desire to seek another quality of life somewhere, anywhere, "here or there." Bracketed by the past and the future, the characters' lives peter out in a twilight present, in which they pass the time shuffling through insignificant memories. The protagonists, Clope and Mme. Flan, pander to the needs of those passing through the station, all of whom share a sense of having been cheated by life. The scurrying travellers are attempting to give meaning to their passage through time, but they are, actually, simply running in place, and their efforts provide theatrical analogues to the inconclusive quests of the protagonists of Pinget's novels.

Mme. Flan could hardly care less about public affairs; her private concerns are in far too parlous a state. But she peddles newspapers from all over the world to her credulous, "concerned" customers. Her wares soothe travellers by stimulating and distracting them. Her preoccupied readers submerge awareness of impotence in their personal lives into righteous reaction to issues of the day. As a bonus, the press dispenses the comforting illusion that the well-informed members of its clientele participate actively in the rational progression of history. Clope's audience, though less numerous, also asks only to be thoroughly deceived. He pretends to reveal the occult links between the sterile lives of middle-aged ladies and the mysterious "laws" of the Tarot cards. The fortunes he tells vary as little as the stories that Pinget's narrators tell each other. But the ecstatic recipients of the mumbo jumbo are too pleased with their momentary self-importance to notice how empty it really is.

Clope and Mme. Flan remain skeptical of the panaceas that they offer, for their customers' needs are universal. Each of the two seeks consolation from dreariness in his or her own way. Mme. Flan dreams of moving to a more pleasant location. Perhaps she sneaks a glance at the enticing travel advertisements in the Sunday newspapers. The devil-may-care spontaneity in the lives of the travellers who trot back and forth in the station excites her as she equates travel with escape. Whereas Mme. Flan's projected excursions recall Emma Bovary's desperate daydreams, Clope faces the triviality of his existence with what passes for stoic realism, rejecting out of hand the notion that life is any different elsewhere. "Here or there," as M. Levert remarked in the earlier play, "these moves don't do any good." But Clope eventually lets himself be caught in the trap of domesticity. He seeks to play a formative paternal role (as do M. Levert, Architruc, and the protagonists of *Someone* and the *Recurring Melody*; if he cannot shape his own life, perhaps he can form the life of a surrogate son.

Clope's conception of language brings another theme from the novels to the stage. The sometime magic-man scoffs at the notion that a set of verbal symbols can compress experience into a coherent string of sounds. Clope quotes rules of syntax in order to obfuscate his thought, not to clarify it. The validity of grammar rests upon a shaky foundation indeed unless the connection between the phenomena that it posits can be proved to be dependable. When young Pierre, a passer-by, arrives at the beginning of the second act, the audience learns that Clope has been trying to reconstruct an event from the past by composing some kind of diary or dossier. The confidence man shares his secret with the boy after the lad has overheard one of his jumbled monologues. A father/son relationship develops, and the younger man moves into his mentor's hut. Their idyll, during which they try to find an honest man among the passing pilgrims, is cut short when Pierre suddenly departs, whereupon the old derelict abandons the skeptical aloofness advanced in the first act by setting out after his protegé, leaving Mme. Flan to fill the empty station with figures from her hopes for the future. Clope's search for his "lost son" adds another chapter to Pinget's account of the frustration of parental communication, the futility of trying to reach out to another at the most basic level. The old man's message to Pierre has no more chance of getting through than had M. Levert's plea to his boy. The first plays deal, then, with dead letters to the lost children of a world that is lost in the past.

ARCHITRUC

The play-within-a-play device is used again in *Architruc*, the theatrical development of eipsodes from *Baga*. The bitterly whimsical protagonist of *Arichitruc* gives vent to his fantasies and monomania through charades, less truculent in nature than the fantasies of Le Père Ubu, but in the same vein. The short, vaudevillelike improvisations that the Prime Minister puts on to distract his master barely succeed in holding together the play or, by extension, Architruc's life. The King of Rags and Patches and his straight man fend off death by "putting on an act," or a series of acts. Inevitably, however, the moment comes when the performance wears thin and they scramble to seek something—anything—to distract them from their all-too-apparent mortality. The major dramatic progression of the play shows Baga slowly losing his ability to impose an illusory, permanent world until, finally, death brutally bursts through the shell of the asylum of make-believe and strikes down Architruc as the "play" ends. The same controlling metaphor of the dispossessed king is used by Ionesco in *The King Is Dying (Le Roi se meurt)*. But whereas the whining of Ionesco's King Béranger becomes simply tedious, Baga's charades have a childlike wistfulness that makes the abrupt dénouement all the more effective. Moreover, Pinget's sensitive depiction of the master/servant relationship foreshadows the complex, shifting relationships of couples in subsequent plays.[2]

THE HYPOTHESIS (L'HYPOTHESE)

In this 1961 play, Pinget abandons dialogue for dramatic monologue. Or to put it more precisely, the single character, Mortin, engages in a short-circuited conversation with layers of his own consciousness and memory. At its most accessible level, *The Hypothesis* dramatizes the disintegration of a would-be writer's attempt to explain the disappearance of a manuscript. Mortin's musings point up the contrast between the chaotic mental state of the private man and the composed face he intends to wear before others, but the public mask slips as the audience watches him revise a paper he plans to deliver before a group. A filmed image of Mortin, which is projected behind him and grows in size as the play progresses, eventually bullies and dwarfs the actor, interrupting him, contradicting him, and advancing varying hypotheses until the actor, thoroughly cowed, seeks refuge in silence, muttering:

> . . . he would see march by in his head . . . all the lost chances to be silent (Pause) Too late they would appear to him as the only . . . too late as the only . . . which may have had an outside chance . . . to clear up the mystery . . . (Pause) The lost chances to be silent . . . (Pause) The lost chances . . .[3]

The earlier plays of Pinget's surrealist and mystery-story periods communicate to the theater audience the progression and doubling back that characterize the chronicle's narratives.[4] The knotted word clusters of *The Hypothesis* produce a disturbing dramatic effect that is similar to the overall impact of the novels' prose. Echoes and associations of words and ideas clog the coherence of the speaker's line of thought. For example, derivatives of the root "*poser*" ("to pose") push Mortin's monologue to the edge of a bottomless verbal quagmire, just as the conflicting hypotheses eventually do in the narratives:

> If you accept the hypothesis of the acceptance, the question could not be re-*posed* it would be all over and I would see myself if not dis*posed* of at least obliged the word indis*poses* but you must understand me to sup*pose* that which, in the mind of the author *posed* in authority, would have caused the idea of a de*position* if not to leap forward at least to firm up, that which precisely would have im*posed* the hypothesis on us . . . would have im*posed* the hypothesis on us . . .[5]

Exposing the inadequacy of rigid grids for the interpretation of behavior heightens the sense of disorientation. A spoof of the sexual, "Freudian" vision of the family gives way to an equally hilarious takeoff on the sentimental "Victorian" way of viewing the same phenomenon. Mortin's eventual mental collapse troubles and disturbs the spectator. The more the actor understates his performance, the more the audience squirms. A strong undercurrent of laughter runs through the play, but it is the nervous laughter of self-defense prevalent in an audience watching the first reel of a gruesome horror film. Mortin has contracted a severe case of the "*folie verbale*" from *Graal Flibuste*, and watching him suffer through it is as painful as sitting through the aimless, endless monologue in Beckett's *Happy Days*.

AROUND MORTIN (AUTOUR DE MORTIN)

Pinget's sense of theatrical priorities and his concern for its aural possibilities show through in his restructuring of the material of *The Hypothesis* into the radio play *Around Mortin*, which was published in 1965. Radio, of course, provides an ideal medium for theater-as-sound. The listener eavesdrops, curiously at first, and then with growing perplexity, as Pinget teases him into piecing together gossip from fragments of the conversations of unseen speakers talking behind closed doors. (It is interesting to note, incidentally, the evolution of the different ways in which Pinget treats Mortin's breakdown. He first exposes the reader to it at one step removed in *Clope to the Dossier* [1961]. He next forces the theater audience to witness it directly in *The Hypothesis*, written the same year. Finally, in *Around Mortin* [1965], using the medium of radio to offer an even more disembodied version of the same event, he confronts the listener with the choice of either participating in the scramble for a synthesis or turning off the radio and retreating to the world of personal silence or sounds that will not disturb him.)

A running account of Mortin's breakdown comes whispering over the airwaves as a private detective peeps through the keyhole and tells his confederate what he sees. Mortin's attempted suicide catches them by surprise, and their bewilderment colors the sequences that follow as the play skips ahead in time. A critic wants to write a biography of Mortin, now dead, and naturally he tries to piece the episodes of his subject's life together into a string of continuity. The nine interviews that ensue advance his research, only to send it sprawling. The "facts" garnered from the memories of those who knew Mortin soon bury the investigation in a mass of contradictions. Frequent static distorts and interrupts the voices, an aural parallel to the interference blurring Mortin's past. Pinget gives a kaleidoscopic view of truth, not a telescopic one. It is up to the listener's ear to filter out the "real" story, if it must, or else simply to delight in the interplay between the intonations of the speakers' voices and the conflict of their innuendos.

Pinget carries the pettiness and poetry of his novels' province to the stage with all the care of a man balancing eggs. That he gets home free is a tribute to his sure-handed manipulation of theatrical devices. The sets portray in visual terms the banality and the void that the protagonists strive to fill or to flee. The authors' pastimes and charades give physical expression to their relentless quest for security. The dialogue of the deaf transposes the open-ended progression of the mock-detective inquiries of Pinget's second manner. Pinget's monologues put the audience face to face with the author's continuing probe of "verbal madness." The radio play underscores Pinget's determination to carry his expedition into the caverns of verbal sound in the face of the popular success of gestural theater (did audiences ever really listen to the *words* that the half-nude or nude characters were mouthing in the exhibitionistic theater of the sixties and early seventies?), and the tradition of straight-forward, dramatic story-telling.

IDENTITY (IDENTITE) and *ABEL AND BELA (ABEL ET BELA)*

Paradoxically, although words serve as a barrier against death ("outside what is written is death"), speaking them, wasting them, propels us through time toward the ultimate silence, death. The unfolding line of a narrative is linear by conventional necessity; there is a beginning, a middle, and an end. It reminds us, therefore, of our passage from youth, through middle age, to debility and death. Cut back over the story as we may, open parentheses as we will, the end of the tale is inevitable and the same for everyone. The mouth will open—and no sounds will come. Unlike Sheherazade, we will not escape by forestalling the end with a request for "one more story." Pinget, in his third manner (that of reducing the length and the coherence of his story fragments to the barest minimum), runs his quest to earth at the level of words themselves. We no longer witness the outlines of novels fighting to eliminate each other *(Mahu or the Material)*, or differing hypotheses cancelling each other out *(Someone);* now we see words themselves stuttering in the sky and exploding like a fireworks display. The stylistic techniques used to obtain this effect are similar in the fiction and the plays: repetition, alternation, shifts in tone. But since the theater demands greater compression, we shall begin our approach to the narratives of Pinget's third manner through the plays written during the same period.

With the publication of *Identity* (1971) the identification between Mortin, the harassed, self-deprecating writer, and Pinget becomes increasingly close. The play has three main characters: Mortin, his friend the doctor, and the maid Naomi, and one minor role, Naomi's six-year-old niece. Of the play's two acts, the second takes up only a third of the text. As the title indicates, the play presents the elaborate word games through which Mortin strives to find and define his identity. As in *Architruc*, that search opens onto a series of burlesques or charades. The narrative mode is predominant. A series of stories gets told and the characters try to define their identities by the stories they tell. However, since the narrative elements have no single meaning (like the long "anecdotes" in Ionesco's *The Bald Soprano (La Cantatrice chauve)*, that particular road toward self-definition leads nowhere. What is more, different characters frequently repeat the same story verbatim. Soon, therefore, the anecdotes have meaning only as set pieces in an oratorio or as arbitrary clusters of words. Clearly they will be of no use in establishing an identity. The following operatic reprise of two anecdotes shows to what degree the narrative is deliberately blurred and scrambled. While Mortin sits mutely at his writing table, the doctor and Naomi repeat, word for word, in chorus, the scrambled text obtained by mixing two stories. They start declaiming from in front of Mortin and work their way around the table, one moving to the left, the other to the right, ending up behind him.[6]

> DOCTOR (AND NAOMI USING THE SAME TONE)
> A before leaving I fat broad beamed child went to see the widow as there are my brother I have not bad for never been able to call her his age but spoiled sister-in-law I had by the mother, the father to warn her didn't like that to be careful remembering all the time his youth . . .

> DOCTOR (Narrative tone).
> A fat broad beamed child the kind you find, not ill-behaved for his age but spoiled by the mother the father didn't like that still remembering his own youth.
>
> NAOMI (The same).
> Before leaving I went to see my brother's widow, I never could call her sister-in-law I but to let her know so she'd be on her guard, not so much for her although.

Telling shaggy-dog stories at cross-purposes does not cause the characters' identities to emerge from the mass of verbal flotsam and jetsam. But then an alternate method suggests itself. Perhaps the characters' identities can be established in terms of their roles within the play. In the theater, a character's identity—be he hero, murderer, victim, or confidant—is often defined in terms of his functional involvement in the central action. The shadowy central action of *Identity* keeps shifting, however, and the distribution of roles is constantly reshuffled. The basic situation is that someone apparently wants to leave somebody else, and a quarrel is brewing. The first version the audience sees is Mortin rehearsing his final break with the doctor despite Naomi's protests. In a subsequent scene, however, Naomi is the one who wants to get rid of the doctor. Another scene follows with the doctor breaking angrily with Mortin, and finally we see a furious Naomi threatening to walk out on them both. The other central action of the play, which provides a thread of anticipation or coherence, is the serving of a duck dinner that Naomi labors over mightily throughout the play. But this also fails to supply the characters with even the rudimentary roles of cook, host, and guest, for when the triumphant moment of bringing the bird to table arrives—Naomi serves up an empty plate!

Identity was written shortly after *Le Libera* (published in English as *Recurring Melody* in the United Kingdom and as *Le Libera Me Domine* in the United States) and is similar to it in that its movement and development depend heavily on shifting tones of voice. The characters declaim the text in tones varying from "narrative" to "emphatic," passing through "distracted," "harassed," "prophetic," "doctoral," and "downright strange." Yet in spite of the more than twenty abrupt shifts in tone called for by the stage directions, none seems to define or express Mortin's identity completely.

If stories and tones of voice fail, only words remain. The characters seem to find comfort in handling homey, vivid, idiomatic expressions with ease. They enjoy bandying such expressions and running them together.

MORTIN: Veuillez mettre la table.
NOEMIE: Veuillez pousser de côté ces paperasses et me laisser faire mon ouvrage. Monsieur est toujours dans mes jambes quand je mets la main à la pâte.

MORTIN:	Ou toujours dans vos pattes quand vous me tenez la jambe. Assez de ce galimatias.
NOEMIE:	Mon galimatias vaut le vôtre.
MORTIN:	Do please set the table.
NAOMI:	Do please set aside all those papers and let me get on with my work. You're always underfoot when I'm getting to work.
MORTIN:	Or always underworked when you're pulling my leg. Enough of this gibberish.
NAOMI:	My gibberish is as good as yours.[7]

After a while, however, the snappy dialogue leads to a number of misstatements and misunderstandings—the mistaking of *"analyse"* ("analysis") for *"Anne-Lise"* ("Anna-Louise"), for example. The stories mouthed by the actors become longer and even more disjointed in the second act, as piles of paper accumulate on Mortin's writing table and the two characters who are not speaking go through the circular motions of unwinding a skein of wool. Finally, after Naomi and the doctor have exited and screams of fright are heard off stage, Mortin runs out of verbiage, and the curtain falls as he struggles in vain literally to have the last word.

Perhaps reacting to Mortin's aphasia, the characters in Pinget's one-act piece entitled *Abel and Bela* seek to answer the question: What is drama? The audience first sees them on a practically bare stage in the process of sketching out ideas for a play. Although, as their names indicate, it is hard to know just where Abel begins and Bela leaves off, Abel is the idea man and Bela specializes in polishing the final dialogue, but they work together as a team. The plot that they hit upon, though simple, is designed to draw the public. The first scene is to show a gala gathering of the very rich somewhere in Europe, sometime between the two world wars. The exiled wife of a renowned political figure announces to everyone that they are all invited to a party at her home. The next scene shows her preparations for the party—ordering the hors d'oeuvres, setting up the bar, and so on. In act two she will begin the preparations all over again, and then the party will begin.

Abel and Bela are unable to find a satisfactory ending, however, either for the party or the play, and they are concerned that their scenario may not really be the stuff of which drama is made. In an amusing slap at the theater of gesture, then currently in vogue, the would-be playwrights toy with the idea of having the party degenerate into a naked orgy, with fornication openly displayed on all sides as the curtain falls, or perhaps by revealing that the dungeons in the hostess's castle are stuffed with dead bodies à la *The Inquisitory*. They also consider turning the play into a murder-mystery thriller.

But they eventually reject those notions, and indeed the whole scenario, as being overly "theatrical" in the bad sense of this word, and turn toward subjects that they feel to be truly dramatic in the lives of everyone, namely, lost youth, first love, and death. Each of them delivers a stammering, halting monologue on those subjects, and for the first time, the play within the play comes to life. But simply telling the truth, complete with halting silences, awkward transitions, and painful reticences, is plainly too undramatic for Abel's and Bela's purposes, and so they try to hoke things up—to "force the note," in their term. As they so do, it becomes obvious to the audience that Pinget is suggesting that the real stuff of drama is neither their scenario nor their nostalgic monologues but the flow of words, one word calling forth another, the words with which they weave the web of their friendship and their lives.

In this curiously self-conscious play, similar in many ways to Molière's *L'Impromptu de Versailles (The Impromptu of Versailles)*, Pinget states the rationale for the numerous reprises in *Identity* and the technique of repetition and alternation that he will develop to such a high degree in *Fable* and *This Voice (Cette Voix)*. Words in themselves are far more dramatic than the fabrication of an imaginary situation. The complex interrelationships of words are of far more interest and import than the situations they are used to describe. The repetition of words and phrases calls the importance of language to the attention of the audience or the reader. Abel is quite specific on this point when Bela takes him to task for repeating the same action and dialogue from the first act to the second, and he retorts, in some heat:

> ABEL: So you realize that the first act was purely gratuitous . . . and that it doesn't really begin until the

	second act. In other words, that everything is a question of words, one word can carry along another after it.
BELA:	So then it's not the second act, it's a reworking of the first.
ABEL:	It's the second act. A question of words.[8]

As the two characters continue their conversation about the theater, the very stage set of the scenario they were describing at the outset abruptly descends on flats from the ceiling, actors dressed in party clothes amble on stage and start kissing each other and undressing, and the play-within-a-play comes full circle.

PARALCHEMY (PARALCHIMIE) and *NIGHT (NUIT)*

The audience watching Pinget's performance as an actor in *Abel and Bela* was confronted with a situation as convoluted as the war of the novelists in *Mahu or the Material*. Here was the dramatist himself in the flesh, acting in a play, playing the role of a writer roughing out the play he was going to write. A similar situation takes place in the short radio play *Night* (1973). The two characters, Al and Ben, are in bed with the lights out, talking. They have lived together for many years, but their love has dimmed, not brightened, with the passage of time and the stultifying effects of routine. Al, the more sensitive and gentle of the two, is feeling uncomfortable and having trouble getting to sleep. So he has his friend read to him the very moving passage from Cervantes describing Don Quixote's death. As he listens, Al daydreams about a better life in a house in the country, and then, quite suddenly and unexpectedly, he dies. As Ben's cry of horror fades into silence, two other voices, A and B, discuss the play the audience has just heard. B seems to be the author. He explains some of the play's obscure points, and defends the work rather weakly against A's criticism, stating that everything lies in the nuances of the words. As B's voice trails off into silence, the announcer, sounding a self-conscious note that recalls the autocritical remarks that are scattered throughout Pinget's works, asks members of the listening audience to send their opinions of *Night* to Robert Pinget at his home address.

Pinget's growing preoccupation with words, also reflected in *Fable*, serves as the explicit subject of *Paralchemy (Paralchimie,* 1973). Once more, the main character is Mortin. This time he is aided and abetted by his niece, Lucile, his valet, Erard (escaped from the shabby confines of the pension in *Someone?*), and an eloquent, somewhat nutty plumber who comes to repair the flush pipe of the toilet. The title *Paralchemy,* a neologism from "para" and "alchemy," refers to Mortin's search for a superscience of words; he hopes that if he can fully comprehend words and their mysteries, he will discover a magic agent that will transmute the dross of his wasted life into gold. The introductory stage direction summarizes the subject and thrust of the play succinctly:

> The entire play, which invents itself as it goes along, is a projection of the unconsciousness of Mortin, who is a would-be playwright at the same time that he imagines he's looking for an ideal truth with the help of old-fashioned alchemy. The *"materia prima"* here would be dramatic language.
>
> The scenes follow each other very quickly, differing in tone and lighting like the accelerated process of the transformation of matter.[9]

As in all of Pinget's plays, the characters in *Paralchemy* do little else but talk. In fact, Lucile and Erard mouth the words that Mortin has chosen for them, playing the roles that he has assigned, speaking their parts conscientiously. The stated subjects of the discourse are the soul, god, art, and love, but, as Mortin states at the outset, all four are so intimately connected that they are treated alternately and sometimes simultaneously. As in *Identity,* changes in tone are frequent, and they tend to focus attention on the play's most important element—not the action, not the setting and the costumes, but the spoken text. Here, as in his recent fiction, Pinget has reduced the narrative or plot element of the play to a bare minimum. In *Paralchemy,* the goal of the quest pursued in Pinget's third period, or manner, comes into sharp dramatic focus. Mortin seeks to find words to express the disappointment, heartbreak, and stubborn hope of one who has loved language and life long and well. The anguish of a fatal quarrel, evoked in *Fable,* hovers in the background.

And as one thing led to another, the conversation having gone on very late, they were close to the hearth, their glass of wine in their hands in that house which they'd had so much trouble building, then furnishing and making liveable, both grown old between these four walls to think how long they'd been sharing the same existence with their rhumatism and their big bellies, their eyes less clear and wrinkles which make them look like the pictures of Uncle Alfred, one suddenly says to his brother looking at the ceiling, do you think, all that trouble, to have it come to this, what were we trying to prove, the other could not answer and for a long moment he will have seen a thousand shadows file by which he couldn't even have named, was it disgust, unhappiness, or resignation, bits and pieces of sentences impossible to repeat going back to different periods, accumulated in his head and without a voice to attribute them to, all forgotten, faded away like an atonal murmur, choppy, and without continuity which insists in an inopportune way on the vanity of memory and the horror of time.[10]

The roast duck, promised but never produced in *Identity*, has been reduced to a cup of gruel. As in the previous play, reprises occur frequently, with the same lines assigned to various members of the cast. The characters subject the audience to a flood of arcane allusions and an exhibition of verbal diarrhea in a garbled version of Latin, the Queen of Romance Languages. *"Primum cacare"* ("To shit being the first given") the plumber intones, in a back-handed allusion to the stool upon which he applies the tools of his trade. Martin riposts to this pseudo-geometrical premise with one of his own *"Primum Vivere"* ("To live being the first given"). *"Similia similibus similiter simulatio"* ("Similar things are more similar to similar things through simulation"), the plumber concludes, in a parody of a well-known Latin phrase used first as a Euclidian theorem and later by Thomas Aquinas in a proof of God's existence. From there the words degenerate into senseless sound as the plumber exits singing:

Anima	anima	anima
Blabla	blabla	blabla
Similia	similia	similia
Patatras	patatras	patatras

Oh my soul	oh my soul	oh my soul
Blahblahblah	blahblahblah	blahblahblah
All the same	all the same	all the same
Slam and bang	slam and bang	slam and bang[11]

Anecdotal fragments of no conceivable interest are then rattled off, discarded, and taken up again only to be junked once more. A long anecdote about a butcher and a dressmaker carries the sing-song humdrum to the edge of children's verse. Its content is so devoid of any possible interest that it hits the ear as waves of sound constituting a kind of musical tone row in prose, with repetition occurring at irregular intervals.

Of course, the research for the desired alchemy ends in defeat at the end of the first act: as the curtain falls, Mortin is asleep, having been lulled off by his own text. Clearly, he has not been able to use words to cast his experiences into either a universal fable that is understandable to all or into a legend that will pierce life's mysteries. But an inexplicable transformation effects Mortin in the second act. In the first, the audience listened to nothing but gossip, nonsense, wordplay and pseudo-science. In the second, Mortin, the doctor, and Naomi declaim an involved and mysterious parable, biblical in tone, about a shepherd. The grave, imposing vigor and enigmatic beauty of the piece recall the final descriptions in *Graal Flibuste*. The long, carefully articulated series of words produces a parable that defies précis or interpretation. It may signify something beyond the story it tells, or it may not. It may be the beginning of a fable of great moment, or a senseless, unfinished fragment, or an anguished reflection of the salvation promised in the crucifixion of the Good Shepherd. Whatever the story's meaning, however, whether or not it is "a reply to the Mandala of the Orientals, plenitude, the Universality of being, or the Prima materia," as its narrator alleges, neither Mortin, Erard, nor Lucile can elucidate it further. Like the mystical snake Ouroboros cited by Mortin, the narrative fragment about the shepherd swallows its own tail. Mortin's quest will do the same: after it has wound down to a halt, Mortin's self doubts return. He struggles to find "two or three key words, always the same ones which are starting, they also to make themselves unpronounceable." Then, in a violent *coup de théâtre*, lightning flashes, thunder rolls, and Mortin goes blind. Has he glimpsed the grail of truth that no man is permitted to see and remain untouched? Has he been the first of Pinget's characters to pursue his quest to the end? As the curtain falls, the audience knows only that Mortin has been left blind, speechless, and terrified.

The *dénouements* and stylistic techniques of Pinget's spare and unsettling dramatic pieces reflect the thrust of his later fiction. In the plays of his first two periods, or manners, Pinget relies heavily upon the audience's anticipation of being told a story. As we have seen, he does so in order to throw into question the very linguistic, artistic, and philosophical presuppositions on which the act of telling a story rests. Baga's charades and Mortin's hypotheses in *The Hypothesis* condense and dramatize the parodic elements in the fiction of the first two periods. As we have seen in *The Inquisitory* and *Someone*, Pinget's quest for a permanent truth leads him to annihilate both plot and character, as they are usually defined, and to go beyond them. Mortin and the other characters of the later dramatic works identify themselves as tones of voice. They are distinguishable entities only to the degree that they wrestle with and use words in a distinctive manner. A theater so exclusively aural as Pinget's makes very severe technical demands upon the declamatory skill of the actors. The dramatist imposes those demands because his quest has led him to strip away story and characterization in order to get down to the level of words as such. And words, and their associations (both conscious and unconscious), as well as their repetition and alteration, take center stage in Pinget's prose fiction from 1968 on.

6 Living Voices

*The Libera Me Domine (Le Libera), and
Recurring Melody (Passacaille)*

Spoken language has for the novelist all the characteristics and attractions of an infralanguage, inconsistent, mobile, above all untouched by the context of the written, the organized, accepted, law-giving form. Its vocabulary, syntax, and rhetoric are unique to itself; its essentially transductive logic provides a ground for an organization . . . that is open to incoherence and continuity.—Tony Duvert, "La Parole et la fiction."

Taking a cue from the ebb and flow of sound over the theater's footlights, the phrases of *The Libera Me Domine* (1968) and *Recurring Melody* (1969) shrink the snippets of Pinget's recognizable anecdotes almost to the zero point. Consequently, his later books take on a greater urgency and intensity, as Pinget continues to pare down the narrative pretexts triggering them. In the novels, plays, and radio pieces of his latest manner talking has replaced writing, and speaking and seeking have meshed. Some of these works give the impression of openness. Like the screen door of a country house left ajar in summer, they invite the adventurous to enter the verbalizing recesses of the author's mind; they move restlessly over familiar landscapes, and suggest further episodes. Others curl in upon themselves like snail shells, closing off further development with the finality of a storm door slammed shut against winter winds. *The Libera Me Domine* (1968), a book about summer, opens. *Recurring Melody* (*Passacaille*, 1969), a wintry novel, closes.

Nevertheless, the two have much in common as they extend Pinget's ongoing quest further toward the limits of hysteria and despair. As the title suggests, *The Libera Me Domine* unfolds as an elaborate, often poetic meditation on death, both physical death and death of the spirit. The theme is subsequently taken up again in a series of variations in *Recurring Melody*. Why cast such a philosophical, poetic subject in narrative form? Simply because only the demands for continuity and psychological analysis so essential to narrative can force the author to continue the discursive monologue that consumes and generates his work. As Pinget himself has remarked:

> In all the novels where you find "I," you have speakers whose words bring to life hit or miss both the meaning of their discourse and their presence.[1]

The compulsion to integrate the warring elements of the self through words nags at the Pingetian narrator even more persistently here than in his previous work.

In *The Libera Me Domine* three objectives set the pages turning: Mortin's frantic search for a pretext to intern the spiteful, gossiping Mlle. Lorpailleur in a lunatic asylum in order to shut her up, literally and figuratively; the recurring urge to order experience through language; and finally the attempt to bring a tone of voice to life on the printed page. Mortin ultimately fails to have old Lorpailleur put away and *Recurring Melody* ends with the writer-narrator slumped at his desk, his meandering monologue silenced by an overwhelming sense of loneliness. Yet despite their apparent failure and inconsistencies on the level of logical discourse, the two novels do succeed brilliantly in capturing a "tone"—the goal Pinget set himself in the preface to *The Libera Me Domine:*

> I say I explore the voice of the person speaking since for me the preliminary work consists of selecting from the components of my own voice the one that interests me at the moment and isolating it, then objectifying it until a character emerges from it. That character is the narrator himself with whom I identify. That's why you find "I" in my books but it is an "I" that is always different.[2]

But the depiction of the speaking "I" becomes more and more problematical, mysterious, and remote as the depth dive into the self goes deeper. The pinning down of the "I" in *Recurring Melody* is tentative and inconclusive. Pinget identifies the speaker as "someone," "a man," "he," and finally in the first person only on page eighty-seven.[3] As Pinget, himself, noted in this regard:

> ... the tone varies from one of my books to the other since the search in this domain will never be finished. To choose each time,

from an inclination for the new, one tone among the thousands that the ear has recorded, that is my lot.[4]

THE LIBERA ME DOMINE

Pinget's recurring character "Mortin" is a creature made of air. Breath rushing around his tongue and palate brings him into being. In a sense, Mortin represents the Pingetian character "par excellence" since he discovers, creates, and sustains his identity by the hows and whats of saying, not by the facts of doing or learning. As we have seen, in Pinget's world, who we are is conditioned by what we hear, and that identity is revealed in turn by how we express ourselves, whether we like it or not. Or as Mortin puts it:

> It more or less came to the same thing as saying that the whole of the psycho psychi life of our little society might well rest on one or two very vague phrases, a few remarks about anybody or anything invented by two or three people at the outside which may well unconsciously have set the general tone for years to come of the conversations or rather of the behavior of our compatriots, yes it certainly was odd, this network of gossip and absurd remarks had conditioned our existence to such an extent that no stranger coming to live in our midst could have resisted it for long and that if he had come to follow the trade of let's say baker he would inevitably have branched off into that of child-killer for instance.[5]

Pinget's peculiar manipulation of the possibilities of first-person narration achieves extreme and unexpected effects. Instead of pinning the speaker down, Pinget's use of "I" hollows out an empty core at the narrative's very center. When, in a book told in the first person, vital information placing the "I" in relation to the fictional "they" is withheld, the reader tends to seek hints to help sketch out the central figure's portrait, and a sort of archeological scrambling for clues ensues. In *The Libera Me Domine*, the informational void remains empty, leaving only the tone of voice.

> *The Libera Me Domine* demonstrates to what point the first person, if refused its former introspective and autobiographical implications, can erase, much better than the "he" (which always presupposes someone speaking it) all human referent to the fiction, any presence

preexisting the novel, any presence that might maintain itself "next to" the work to assure its unfolding, guarantee its credibility, or let itself be perceived little by little through the narration as if being reflected in a mirror gradually being uncovered. On the contrary, here the "I" becomes the person of indetermination, stubborn silence, and absence, and strangely enough, it objectifies the book by abandoning it to itself. Accumulating "voices that go nowhere," *The Libera Me Domine* is an uninhabited novel.[6]

As in his earlier work, an iron reserve stops Pinget short of thinly disguised autobiographical use of the first person. Negations cancel affirmations and reticence veils self-exposure, or quotation marks obscure the voice's identity as the narrative eventually moves to direct use of the first person. When the speaking "I" emerges at last, it is too late to give the text a well-grounded center, but just in time to focus attention on the role of language in our apprehension of the world.

What is gained by reducing the storyteller's substance to such a shadowy presence? And what keeps the story flowing if no one in particular is telling it? Paraphrase cannot furnish answers to such questions, especially since *The Libera Me Domine* has no content "a priori." Permutations of anecdotes, bursts of names, dates, and bits of village gossip bombard the reader with such frequency that talking about the book without quoting a long, representative passage would be as illuminating as striking matches in the dark. The opening pages of *The Libera Me Domine* quoted below (in Barbara Wright's fine translation) convey the headlong, discursive flavor of the book as a whole, and the superb analysis by Tony Duvert that follows shows how the accumulation of contradictory blocks of material and disconnected bits of information actually contribute to the novel's growth instead of bringing it to a halt.

> If old Lorpailleur is mad I can't help it.
> If old Lorpailleur is mad I can't help it, nobody can help it and anyone who could prove the contrary would be mighty clever.
> If old Lorpailleur is mad but is she mad, she is, claims that I was involved either closely or remotely, that I had a hand in the affair of the Ducreuxs' little boy, that I was in league with the police hence my impunity.

Had a hand in the affair of the Ducreuxs' little boy unbeknownst to anyone, my name wasn't mentioned at the inquest then here comes this madwoman years afterwards and tongues start wagging.

If old Lorpailleur is mad I said to Verveine I can't help it, nobody can help it, you must get her locked up, there must be a way, what's the use of being a chemist then, you must know how it's done, you must know someone, some authority, oh come on, you just have to pick the proper channel and then it's all plain sailing, grease the wheels, that's the expression, he answers no, hasn't the authority, anyway not the slightest idea how to, all he can think of if the worst comes to the worst is the family, he'd heard years ago that for this sort of thing, but the family's a long way away how do you expect, a sister in the Argentine, all the rest dead and buried, I said let's think let's think, it's not possible, there must be a way, am I supposed to put up with it, tongues are beginning to wag, in any case says he if they go on you'll have to go through with it, he meant the police, the law courts, so on and so forth, just because of the evil gossip of a madwoman, it's not possible, it's not possible I said.

If old Lorpailleur is mad something must be done at once.

Verveine answers well I can't do anything about it, if you can think of a way carry on, you won't find me meddling in your affairs but is she mad that's the whole point, no no don't get me wrong I'm not saying that you had any sort of hand in the Ducreux affair, all I'm saying is that someone like old Lorpailleur may well have started people talking about you for other reasons mayn't she, don't get me wrong.

Don't get what wrong I said.

Don't get what wrong I repeated, tell me what you're getting at.

That someone like old Lorpailleur at her age, fortyish, may well imagine that you given your character, given your means, I don't know, you used to work together in the old days so they told me, that was it, well then maybe at that moment she might have I don't know, she might have imagined, you see what I mean.

Someone came into the shop, I should have waited, I didn't wait, we left things at that as they say but things never stay left at that for long.

If old Lorpailleur is mad things won't be left at that, we'll find a way, there must be someone, some official channel, then it's all plain sailing, quick, the straitjacket, old Lorpailleur is in good hands.

The Ducreux affair, an old affair, a good many years ago, a good ten years ago, the Ducreuxs' little boy, four years old, was found strangled in Ferret's wood under a pile of leaves, he was wearing his little sailor suit, he'd gone out one Sunday with his parents, they were making their way over towards Sirancy, the parents were having a nap after their picnic.

He was wearing his little blue dungarees that his mother had made out of an old pair of trousers of his father's and a little red woolly and shoes of the sandals type, sandals and little socks that his mother . . .

A dear little blond boy with brown eyes strangled on the spot near Chatruse, he was found three days later, his parents' grief was terrible, the whole village was talking about it, we hadn't seen a tragedy of the sort since eighteen seventy-three.

We'd never seen anything like it.

Immediately the gendarmerie, immediately the inquest, the witnesses, the neighbours, they'd seen the little boy going out of the yard at about ten in the morning, Mademoiselle Cruze was cleaning her windows, she had a step-ladder on the pavement.

It was in July, a bad month in our parts, every sort of calamity happens to us in July, fires, car accidents, hail-storms, drownings but we hadn't had a murder since eighteen seventy-three, it's still there in the records and newspapers of the time, a fellow called Serinet shot dead by his brother-in-law.

We'd never seen anything like it.

The father was a baker, the mother too, they still are, they're still there, in the rue des Casse-Tonnelles, but the little boy isn't there any more, he'd have been fourteen, such a pretty little boy, they still talk about him even though they've had three children since, little Laure, little Frédéric and little Alfred, all very sweet children.

It's all very well to say they've had three children since, little Laure, little Frédéric and little Alfred, the tragedy they lived through you don't forget just like that, these things mark you for life said Verveine, she was a good excuse for him that customer who came in, he didn't have to answer me, I should have waited, I didn't wait, it's not possible that he doesn't know what to do, madwomen get locked up, wasn't he saying that she wasn't mad, wasn't he implying that I was telling him a lot of nonsense, what a nerve the old bugger has, you won't find me meddling in your affairs, isn't it everybody's affair, a madwoman in our midst.

It's all very well to say they've had three children since, the poor Ducreuxs, it still preys on their minds especially as the killer was never caught, he's still at large.

In spite of the gendarmerie being called out, the inquiries, the official reports, the special tribunals, so on and so forth, it's a very strange thing in this day and age, the killer is still at large, no reason why it shouldn't be little Laure's turn next, for instance, or little Frédéric's, just the very thought gives you cold shivers up and down your spine, it shouldn't be possible, a permanent menace, a poor baker's family, they're still there, living in what might well be called daily panic, no it shouldn't be possible and when the day comes that old Lorpailleur insinuates that Verveine had something to do with it I won't be the one who proves the opposite.

If old Lorpailleur is mad it's nobody's fault and things can be left at that, she goes round talking nonsense, her black dress, her hat with the crêpe round it, her yellow teeth, she lost her mother years ago, still in mourning, a maniac, on her bike going to school at half past eight, an English-type bike with upright handle-bars, she sits up as straight as an i, when the day comes that her crêpe gets caught in a gust of wind and sticks to her face round a bend just when a lorry's coming I won't be the one who proves the opposite I mean that the lorry was to blame, old Lorpailleur killed outright, lying there in the road, but also that mourning mania don't you feel there's something disgusting about it, dragging your dead around with you at the height of July, two days before the school broke up, she passed the baker's, Mademoiselle Cruze busy cleaning her windows saw her out of the corner of her eye, she doesn't say good morning to her any more, she had her shopping basket on her carrier as she had to do her shopping after school and a few minutes later there was little Alfred coming out of the yard.

Things could have been left at that.

Old Lorpailleur came out of school and got on her bike, she sat down and just at that moment let go of the handle-bars, she falls off, she lies there screaming and kicking, the children are frightened, I can still see them standing round her in a circle at a distance with their little briefcases under their arms or their satchels on their backs, when Blimbraz arrives, and then Verveine, they go up a bit closer to her, she's foaming at the mouth, it's obvious that she was mad said Madame Monneau what did I tell you, her bereavement must have unhinged her, what an idea, entrusting children to a madwoman, blind that's what we were, my little boy did tell me she was queer, in the middle of a dictation she suddenly used to call out words that had nothing to do with it, I can still hear him.

The word cataclysm or catastrophe, it seems it preys on their minds, megalomania, calamity mania, they see traps everywhere, they turn every which way to get out of them, to free themselves, to escape, something's going to pounce on them, they feel they're tied up, that's madness for you.

Something like the lorry for instance.

She was lying in the road, the kids in a circle at a distance, the poor teacher, how come she did that, the lorry driver kept repeating, she just suddenly came straight at me, she came straight at me, he was wiping his forehead with his handkerchief, the doctor who lives at the bend in the road leaning over the dead woman feeling her pulse, listened to her heart and certified that she was dead, there are already twelve people, mothers grabbed hold of their kids, come on don't look, come on d'you hear me we're going home, the kids said then there won't be any more school, in any case you were breaking up the day after tomorrow, what about next year, another teacher, get a move on d'you hear me don't turn round, they'd taken the corpse opposite to the doctor's before the morgue, there were about twenty of them who kept repeating all together oh the poor thing, they were pitying her now, they were pitying the madwoman who'd been bringing us bad luck for years, the gendarme was dealing with the driver, sample of his blood at the chemist's, report, witnesses who hadn't seen a thing but they knew her, everybody, her sister lives in the Argentine with so it seems an actor but personally what I say, so on and so forth, gives you something to talk about, it's always in July that calamities happen to us, drownings, fires and accidents.

Or that she wasn't killed outright.

Or that the lorry simply passed her, and that she got to school at twenty to nine.

Madame Ducreux at her window was keeping one eye on little Alfred who was playing in the yard and with the other was sweeping the bedroom, as she was edging the broom behind the armchair she suddenly saw little Louis ten years earlier, the child was hiding, she was pretending to look for him, she suddenly found him and said oh the naughty little rascal you gave me such a fright and pulled him out from behind the chair and kissed him on the mouth, it's all very well to say they've had three since, it was all very well for her to say it to herself, the good mood she'd been in that morning vanished, the old sadness took its place but Ducreux was calling his wife to come into the shop, the girl couldn't cope, it was half-past eleven, all the ladies were fingering the bread in spite of it being forbidden and during this time little Alfred had wandered off, the mother like a madwoman left them all standing, she went and grabbed hold of the child in the yard, he had barely moved, he was making mud pies near the water-tank, come on d'you hear me we're going home, it's time for your soup or whatever.

While the ladies who were fingering the bread saw old Lorpailleur on her bike coming back from school, isn't it ten years since her mother died, dragging her mourning out like that, dragging her dead around with her, you can't tell me she isn't a bit mad.

There'd been a lot of talk about the disappearance of the Ducreuxs' little boy, people had imagined everything there was to imagine, a kidnapping neither more nor less, but it's all very well, you never really get over it, is it normal to have your child strangled, what was behind it, what sort of people did the Ducreuxs mix with, no it's not normal.

Which would have meant that as soon as the customer had gone out again I would have gone back to Verveine's.

And Verveine seeing me back again wanted to change the subject and asked after all my family, questions which I answered patiently, my nieces, my sister in the Argentine, an old retired cousin who used to work with the railways, I could have invented some more since the conversation inevitably had to come round again given its point of departure i.e. crazy old Lorpailleur.

He had known her mother well, a Voiret from Hottencourt, the oldest of eight children all brought up by her as the mother died after the last one, she was a Bianle from Crachon, my mother knew her well, she remembered seeing her fall one day writhing and foaming at the mouth, whereupon I immediately said aren't these things hereditary, nothing surprising if the grand-daughter suffers from the same complaint, when she fell the other day several people assured me that she was foaming at the mouth, to which he immediately replied I tell you she wasn't, I saw her with my own eyes, she was knocked down by a lorry, no trace of epilepsy in that, Mademoiselle Lorpailleur has a very strong constitution, I can't understand why you should get so excited about these old maids' tales, do you think we believe them, what are you getting at, I should be interested to know, looking at me over his glasses, extremely interested to know.

The kids in a circle round the victim.

Verveine who had seen her fall rushes over to her and gets Blimbraz to help him carry the injured woman to his chemist's shop.

Mademoiselle Cruze his sister who was cleaning her windows gets off her stool and starts scurrying about trying to make herself useful.

Five minutes after the accident the doctor came up with his bag, he said take her to the chemist's, and there, in the presence of Verveine, Mademoiselle Cruze and Madame Monneau, he examined the victim and said a slightly bruised shoulder, nothing serious, give her a stimulant, while old Lorpailleur was writhing on the divan and moaning as if she were at death's door, all the same I'm telling you, not the slightest trace of foaming at the mouth in all this, ask my sister if you like or Madame Monneau, do you doubt my word, in any case epilepsy just for your information is no less than . . .

The Ducreuxs' little boy, perhaps after all.

The Ducreuxs' little boy may not have been kidnapped.

But Verveine was carrying on about that business that happened ten years ago, he considered it his duty so he said to try and reconstitute the tragedy, is it normal that we never knew anything about it, how do we know whether the parents themselves didn't hush it up, in league with the police, the examining magistrates, so on and so forth, which would explain why they never talk about it, only yesterday Madame Ducreux came in for some aspirins with her little Frédéric, a lovely little boy, it was on the tip of my tongue to say isn't he like Louis, it was Louis wasn't it, I didn't say it but there was something about her look which told me that she understood why I was embarrassed, not that that was the first time I'd seen little Frédéric isn't it, but I don't know what it was that particular day that made him look so like the poor little boy who had his throat cut, maybe his red pullover or my own mood how should I know, patience is the only thing that ever gets you anywhere and by dint of crosschecking and imagination, oh yes you finally get there, truth will out in the blinding light of day.

As for Mademoiselle Lorpailleur's bruises I don't know if I can tell you, said Madame Monneau, just imagine she got them the day before, she fell off a chair when she was cleaning her windows and dislocated her shoulder, Cruze can't tell you anything about it, it happened at Crachon at her sister-in-law's, in my opinion she just quite simply let herself fall off her bike when she saw the lorry coming, either because she was afraid or because she thought it would be to her advantage, that's what I'd be more inclined to look into, she's such a mischief-maker, getting us to believe the lorry had run her over, what could the driver say, even so it's a bit much that there wasn't a living soul in the street at that hour to be a witness, Mademoiselle Cruze didn't see a thing whatever she may say, she was going into the baker's, you can't see the bend from there unless you've got eyes in your behind, excuse my language.[7]

ANALYSIS BY TONY DUVERT

The book begins with an assertion that calls forth a context immediately: "If old Lorpailleur is mad I can't help it."

The proposition "old Lorpailleur is mad" would be self-sufficient if it were a declarative of the type "the Marquise went out at five o'clock." But its inclusion in a conditional displaces the assertion to a "I can't help it." That phrase is a marker that:

> the person who says "I" is not responsible for the thing said, which is an exterior, endured fact; that the Lorpailleur woman's madness is a hypothesis, deducted from something that must be said.

Add to that that "old Lorpailleur" is enough to refer the reader back to an entire context of fictions, sites, and characters, which weigh upon the book to come from the outset and greatly weakens interest in the potential anecdote: everything is known in advance.

We can see to what degree this one phrase constitutes a generative, dynamic element; and we can assume that the novel's "exposition" comes to an end here. Everything else will flow from it, tributary from the initial assertion.

First tell why "old Lorpailleur is mad." It's because the teacher-novelist may have insinuated that the narrator was involved in a murder case, the murder of the "Ducreux's little boy." Information adopted, or so it seems, for its fecundity; on the one hand it shifts curiosity toward a new narrative axis; on the other it justifies the irritated tone of the first phrase: or let's say rather that this irritated tone engendered a development that exploits it.

It is evidently the spoken impression given by the beginning that now engenders an interlocutor, in the simple repetition of the initial phrase intact, save one incidental phrase: "If old Lorpailleur is mad *I said to Verveine* 'I can't help it.' "

Interlocutor = conversation. Here it is that we find it necessary to retain the narrator's *"idée fixe"* of having the Lorpailleur woman locked up. The discourse also assimilates to itself the answer of the druggist, Verveine. We pick up in it references to Mademoiselle Lorpailleur's family, "a sister in the Argentine, all the rest dead and buried."

The conversation makes its own setting, the druggist's shop. That was almost inevitable since up to now the association of the first phrase's satellites has taken place by proximity and extention. The centrifugal movement is going to accentuate itself, the "I" taking up the anecdote of the Ducreux affair again to encircle it even more closely in circumstances: the act, the victim, the witnesses, the parents, etc. All these details, special elements of the variations to come, must be noted: "the little Ducreux boy, four years old, was found strangled in Ferrets woods." That took place "a good ten years ago," in July, "a bad month in our parts"; a month in which took place, in 1873, another murder, "a fellow named Serinet shot dead by his brother-in-law." The witnesses (of the Ducreux affair) saw "the little boy going out of the yard at about ten in the morning." There was, and is this most important item, Mademoiselle Cruze, "cleaning the panes of her windows. The parents of the little dead boy are bakers. They have had three children since, little Laure, little Frédéric, little Alfred, all very nice."

An interesting connection reintroduces the initial interlocutor, Verveine, and its context, Lorpailleur's madness: "It's all very well to say they've had three children since . . . these things mark you for life, said Verveine." Often, we will thus see a remark we would first thing attributable to the narrator taken over afterwards by a third party serving simply as a connection between two themes, and following a fairly regularly coupling, speaker A remark A, speaker B remark B, etc.

So here's the first subject of conversation again, the seed or the root of *The Libera Me Domine*, old Lorpailleur who, "lost her mother years ago," is taken up again (there will be several examples of this) and extention of the small core of pieces of information accompanying the entrance of a proper name (here, with the name Lorpailleur, it was, "the rest dead and buried"). The school teacher is "still in mourning . . . on her bike going toward the school at half past eight."

The Lorpailleur woman on a bicycle, with her mourning crêpe which "will get caught in a gust of wind and sticks to her face round a bend just when a lorry's coming," is immediately the object of a short, aggressive version of the story: the narrator sees her "killed outright, lying there, on the road."

Each of the elements stated to this point: Lorpailleur's madness, Lorpailleur's accident, the Ducreux affair, the Ducreux family, will be, from now on, the core of diverse developments that will alternate and influence each other.

We are present at a first example of these overlappings or permutations whose use is going to be constant. We see Miss Cruze doing her windows, as stated in the Ducreux affair, but this time she catches sight of the Lorpailleur woman on a bicycle, and not the little victim. In the same sentence, also the first example of the numerous series of metamorphoses which will be so important throughout *The Libera Me Domine*, immediately after having seen old Lorpailleur on the bike, Mademoiselle Cruze sees, as in the first version, a child "go out of the yard." But now it's "little Alfred," (we still don't know the name of the dead child, but we know that Alfred is one of the three others). These two cases are miniscule. Nevertheless, they mark the first "slippage" of the discourse. From here on the fiction builds itself not by developments in the strict sense of the word so much as by reciprocal and deformed borrowings from one paragraph to the other.

Return of the narration, still in the tone irritation-aggression, to the vision of the teacher falling off the bike. But here she falls without the help of the truck: "she falls off she lies there screaming and kicking, . . . she's foaming at the mouth, it's obvious she was mad said Madame Monneau." Here we have a combination as we see, of the two statements: old Lorpailleur is crazy—I imagine old Lorpailleur falling off a bike, in a unique and convincing scene of an epileptic fit, the whole thing assumed a posteriori by a new speaker.

And at once, by association, the same scene: "she was lying in the road, the kids in a circle at a distance" but we come back to the run-down-by-a-truck version. The truck driver is there, and the aggression narrative is a complete success: "the doctor . . . leaning over the dead woman, feeling her pulse, listened to her pulse, and certified that she was dead." A fleeting reappearance follows of the information "her sister lives in the Argentine" augmented by: "with, it seems, an actor." The couple of foreigners, the sister plus Mr. X, born from a piece of gossip about an invented incident, plays an important role in what follows.

We have had a clear-cut, continuous episode of fiction, the Lorpailleur woman's accident on the road. Quite naturally, this too-clear-cut scene calls forth a first "*or*" which reverses it and introduces something else, "that the truck simply went by her, she would have gotten to school at eight-forty."

That time reference gives rise to a new quotation-development: "Madame Ducreux was keeping one eye on little Alfred who was playing in the yard." Let's recall that in the first version Mademoiselle Cruze caught sight of Alfred around ten in the morning; the second time, she saw little Alfred around eight-thirty. This time, the same Alfred is seen by Madame Ducreux at eleven-thirty; in all three cases, the children are coming out of the courtyard.

In this particular case, it would be impossible to say if this sort of repetition is, strictly speaking, a metamorphosis of what's stated initially or an embryonic development by analogy. We are dealing with banal, everyday scenes that as a matter of fact could very well repeat themselves this way, including real variants—*if*, that is, we were in a stable time flow, (the chronology of a *récit*, and not the floating time of a word that fabricates something happening in terms of a few "*idées fixes*")—and *if* each of these repetitions were not presented by the narrator as a unique phenomenon independent of its homologues.

In any case, Madame Ducreux sees her Alfred then she "suddenly saw Little Louis ten years before while edging her broom behind the armchair." Louis is the little dead boy.

Here the first stage of a repetition scene: "Ducreux [her husband, the baker] was calling his wife to come into the shop, the girl couldn't cope, it was half-past eleven, all the ladies were fingering the bread," and the extension of another scene already put in place: "little Alfred had wandered off, the mother like a madwoman left them all standing, she went and grabbed hold of the child in the yard, he had barely moved, he was making mud pies near the water tank."

The following paragraph, a very characteristic one, consists simply of a delightful quotation of five scattered elements previously stated: "While the ladies who were fingering the bread saw old Lorpailleur on her bike coming back from school, isn't it ten years since her mother died, dragging her mourning out like that, dragging her dead around with her, you can't tell me she isn't a bit mad."

By association the Ducreux affair reappears, enriched: "people imagined everything there was to imagine, a kidnapping neither more nor less," to which is added a pretty reflection that introduces a suspicion that will become very keenly felt "is it normal to have your child strangled, what was behind it, what sort of people did the Ducreux family mix with, no it's not normal." It is important to point out that the shifts from indirect to direct style are very frequent, as in other cases, the shifts from the conditional to the indicative, changes that make the *récit* swing in a perpetual roll from the imagined, or the reported, to the real, to the present. It is as if in a fog of words a few were suddenly grabbed onto, held, considered, revivified, coming to deflect by their sudden factitiousness the flow of a fiction which did not seem to foresee them.

The procedure makes the most of a new articulation: "Which

would have meant that as soon as the customer had gone out again I would have gone back to Verveine's pharmacy. And Verveine seeing me come back again wanted to change the subject. The antecedent of this, "which would have meant," is no doubt the reflection: "it's not normal to have your child strangled" (so I am going to "go back" to what I was talking about to continue discussing the thing).

Conversation with the druggist is the book's first context. The "sister in the Argentine" reappears in the discourse: but she is attributed to the speaker himself, "an old retired cousin who worked for the railways" and states specifically that he "could have invented some more" (relatives to satisfy the druggist's curiosity). An assertion strong enough so that we suspect everything from here on, that is, so that we add the hint *lie* to what already bore the warning *subjective report*. In particular, if there is a sister in the Argentine she's of no use since two people can claim her. We cannot recognize to whom she legitimately belongs. That's the inconvenience of the process: by having an attribute passed too often from one person to another, we detach that attribute from any possible subject: isolated, floating, it wanders in the text until someone recovers it; and such will be the case of this sister in the Argentine, as we will see later.

We do know that Verveine remains the common factor in the mixed Lorpailleur-Ducreux affair. We are going to be present at a slow slippage from one to the other, starting with the Lorpailleur woman and her madness. The speaker declares that his mother remembered having seen the Lorpailleur woman's grandmother "fall one day writhing and foaming at the mouth." Of course, she saw that because shortly before the text has "decided" that Miss Lorpailleur has had an epileptic fit. We establish heredity. But according to Verveine it wasn't *that* but, purely and simply, an accident. An affirmation that permits tipping the discourse toward the initial version of the story, the Lorpailleur woman knocked down by a truck. We see there once again "the kids in a circle round the victim," and "Mademoiselle Cruze was cleaning her windows." Only the druggist has said that the school teacher "had a very strong constitution." That declaration obviously weighs on the new version of the scene: the Lorpailleur woman will therefore only have a "slightly bruised shoulder"—since the narration, save a break with an "or," is modeled closely on its immediate context.

From here on in we have already reached a state of the narrative that, even while remaining in relation to the implications of the expositional phrase, is henceforth tributary of creations deduced from the cells this first phrase has engendered, and from the interaction, submitted to attractions by proximity, that these creations have either with each other or with one or another of their formative elements.

Then follows a continuation of the conversation with Verveine, which has moved over to the Ducreux affair; in which it is said that "the Ducreux's little boy may not have been kidnapped," a negation of a supposition put out earlier; that his brother, Frédéric "looks a lot like him"; and at last, and most importantly, people talk about the dead child as a "little boy whose throat was cut" (previously, he was strangled).

A weak connection ("as for . . .") leads back to the Lorpailleur woman, the bruises (which came at the conclusion of the last version of the accident) are now supposed to be due, according to "Madame Monneau," to a fall: "she fell from a chair when she was washing windows and dislocated her shoulder"—combination of Verveine's assertion (dislocated shoulder) and of the posture and occupation in which Miss Cruze has appeared each time so far. But that doesn't stop the text from adding on to the story with the contradictory affirmation: "in my opinion she just quite simply let herself fall off her bike when she saw the lorry coming, either because she was afraid or, she thought it would be to her *advantage*, . . . she's such a mischief-maker." It is quite obvious that the version of the story turning around the idea (if not the fact) of a fall, could fill it in with circumstances as to its causes and consequences that could open onto an infinite number of possible variants. The variants that are adopted obey the text already written and, although contradictory, they all refer to a known version of the event. Here the repetition is prolonged by the revelation of a motivation ("she is such a mischief-maker"), that in fact, reverses the origin of what's been stated. Let us remember, then, that we started out at the beginning of the text with old Lorpailleur on a bike and in mourning (this fanatical mourning was presented as a proof of her eccentricity) a woman whom the narrator hoped would be run down by a truck with no regrets. Then he saw her dead, and finally only hurt. But now, Lorpailleur *herself* becomes responsible for the imaginary scene. She's the one who supposedly made people believe through sheer mischief ("all that to have the driver tossed in jail"), that the truck ran her down. It's the last stage of the displacement of this fiction, which is here assumed by the person who, at the beginning, was its victim.[8]

The text of *The Libera Me Domine* continues to wheel about several centers of attention, like gulls in flight. The tension between telling a story and the nagging doubt that there may be no story to tell causes one word to give rise to another. As Duvert puts it:

> A lively technique of confusion, including interference, and slips of the tongue, organizes this complex material with great fluidity . . . And this fighting the romanesque within the romanesque condemns the narrative to a perpetual conflict (which is all-engrossing) between the demands of cancelled-out conventions and the disturbing procedures growing out of them.[9]

The voice does not put objects, people, and memories in their expected niches. Instead, it turns things upside down or inside out, as banality chokes poetry, and present and past meld into a hybrid, hypothetical future in which nothing is left but the speaking voice.

The speaker's jumbled clichés give rise to startling, often hilarious effects. His juxtaposition of verbal automatisms restores to words the freshness that habitual usage has taken away. He alludes to the "a posteriori needs of old maids," for example, and dismisses allegations about the "advances" of a homosexual priest by commenting blandly that "our children are in good hands." Levels of speech overlap like the speaker's anecdotes or the sense of outside and inside. Proper and improper usage dance together in unintended puns, recalling the bizarre unity of the time sequence. Even the French God of History tumbles from grace, its pedestal sapped by malapropisms and misspeech. Nothing escapes. Not even "the War," whose epic events survive only in the muddled memories of the very old and the fantasies of the very young and are celebrated in a senile academician's commemorative Bastille day speech, a hilarious mishmash of "the bleeding heart of France," "the Red Cross filling hospitals in Belgium to slow the German advance," a hazy impression of generals and prime ministers rushing about to save the country in taxis and dirigible balloons and the heroic and ageless Marshal Pétain, straight from the Dreyfus case, who saves the day at the Chemin des Dames.

RECURRING MELODY (PASSACAILLE)

As in *Monsieur Levert*, the opening sentence of *Recurring Melody* (*Passacaille*, 1969) sets a tone. The tension between syntax and sensibility, inside and outside, reflection and observation, gradually fixes the range and rhythms of its responses in the following pages. The book begins:

> Le calme. Le gris. De remous aucun.
>
> The calm. The gray. Nothing stirring.

Two sentences of a single, unqualified noun followed by an abrupt negation create the impression that the author is moving off dead center. The text continues:

> Quelque chose doit être cassé dans la mécanique mais rien ne transparaît. La pendule est sur la cheminée; les aiguilles marquent l'heure, . . .
>
> Something must be broken in the mechanism but nothing shows. The clock is on the mantel; the hands mark the hour . . . (*Recurring Melody*, p. 7).

The phrases then lengthen after the first negation, as if disregarding it. The first verb falls in the doubting mode, but the second makes an unconditional factual statement about passing time.

> Quelqu'un dans la pièce froide viendrait d'entrer, la maison était fermée, c'était l'hiver.
>
> Someone in the cold room may/will have just entered, the house was closed, it was winter. (p. 7).

The prose tips again toward uncertainty and mystery. When commas replace periods the precise designation carried by the nouns blurs, and the verbs slide into a conjectural tense.

After doubling back to a variant of the source phrase from which it grows, paragraphs three and four of the text sketch in the conjunction of setting, moment, and atmosphere in paragraphs three and four, eventually bringing Mortin into the scene.

> Le gris. Le calme. Se serait assis devant la table. Transi de froid, jusqu'à la tombée de la nuit.
> C'était l'hiver, le jardin mort, la cour herbue. Il n'y aurait personne pendant des mois, tout est en ordre.

> The gray. The calm. May/will have sat down in front of the table. Chilled through and through, until nightfall.
> It was winter, the garden dead, the grassy courtyard. There may/will have been no one for months, everything is in order. (p. 7)

The sketching in or "furnishing" movement continues as the voice describes what lies outside the house. But the recurring negations and the failing light sustain the initial impression of tentativeness and menace.

> La route qui conduit jusque-là côtoie des champs ou il n'y avait rien. Des corbeaux s'envolent ou des pies, on voit mal, la nuit va tomber.

> The road that leads there runs by fields where there was nothing. Crows take flight or magpies, you can't see well, night is falling. (p. 7)

The subject of time comes up again in the sixth paragraph, when Pinget focuses on Mortin in the room staring fixedly at the broken clock.

> La pendule sur la cheminée est en marbre noir, cadran cerclé d'or et chiffres romains.

> The clock on the mantel is of black marble, its face framed with gold and with Roman numerals. (p. 8)

Once again, the speaker's statements about time and the clock stand out by reason of their directness. Almost everything else is cast in doubt or contradicted. Yet the sense of where we are in time becomes distorted almost immediately when the voice tries to stitch inside and outside together.

> L'homme assis à cette table quelques heures avant retrouvé mort sur le fumier n'aurait pas été seul, une sentinelle veillait, un paysan sûr qui n'avait pas aperçu que le défunt un jour gris, froid, se serait approché de la fente du volet et l'aurait vu distinctement détraquer la pendule puis rester prostré sur sa chaise, les coudes sur la table, la tête dans les mains.

> The man seated at that table several hours before found dead on the manure pile may/will not have been alone, a sentinel was watching, a dependable farmer who may/will not have noticed that the dead man a gray day, cold may/will have gone up to the slit of the shutter and may/will have distinctly seen him put the clock out of order then stay prostrated on his chair, with his elbows on the table, his head in his hands. (p. 8)

The "fixing" of the scene in time proves to be as hazardous a project as any other movement toward definition, for the passage roams back and forth in the undefined period before nightfall. Delimiting the approximate time of the discovery of the body (to say nothing of its identity!) proves to be impossible because of the lack of punctuation and precision. The reader can break the sentence describing the cadaver in two ways: "The man seated at that table a few hours before, found dead" . . . or "The man seated at that table, a few hours before found dead . . ."

The previously described impression of déjà vu occurs when echoes from earlier Pinget novels confuse matters further. The image of Mortin with his head in his hands rang down the curtain of *The Hypothesis*, and *The Libera Me Domine* ended with the same image. The same image will recur yet again in the last scene of *Paralchemy*.

The free-form progression of words elicits the first of Mortin's asides, or autocritical comments, whose function becomes more important as the story becomes increasingly jumbled:

> Comment se fier à ce murmure, l'oreille est en défaut.

> How can one trust this murmur, the ear is faulty. (p. 8)

The opening passage sets the pattern for an exploration of the self that imparts to this work a deepening note of exhaustion and disgust. As Pinget gets closer and closer to "the level of words" and their frequently frightening associations, the meanings of seemingly straight-forward terms continue to be vague or ambiguous, and their grouping in sentences and phrases continues to be suggestive. The syntax expresses a circular dialectic of affirmation and negation. Word sounds suggest a brooding state. The phrases and sentences beginning the text repeat and build, expanding from familiar to unfamiliar material like foreign-language drills introducing long series of suppositions. "Or that" introduces alternate jangling possibilities. Eventually, the same phrase will present the inescapable, ultimate alternative—death.

Words fail to describe or restrict the speaker because the voice is drawn to that in language which is equivocal. The scantiness of punctuation forces the reader who wishes to pace the monologue's flow to pay close attention to its sentence rhythms. Names and phrases recur, and habits of speech slowly establish themselves in the reader's ear. But the act of taming the world and making it one's own is never completed, for the text's rhythms are like echoes in a forest, muddling voices instead of clarifying them. Accumulating verbiage drowns the meaning of many sentences in a plenitude of possibilities equivalent to nothingness, and the opening focus of free association and the mania for definition produce a flood of verbal ellipses. The initial statement's thrust is first blunted then reversed by the piling up of words that Pinget uses as semiplastic objects probing a mental landscape through stories furtively advanced and quickly withdrawn. Punctuation and page layout become as important as durational notation in music, and the grouping of sentences illustrates the rhythms of exploration in graphic terms. As the speaking voice threads its way through a maze of remembered or invented experiences the text leads the reader's eye through and around blocks of type:

> Le calme. Le gris. De remous aucun. Quelque chose doit être cassé dans la mécanique mais rien ne transparaît. La pendule est sur la cheminée, les aiguilles marquent l'heure.
> Quelqu'un dans la pièce froide viendrait d'entrer, la maison était fermée, c'était l'hiver.

> Le gris. Le calme. Se serait assis devant la table. Transi de froid, jusqu'à la tombée de la nuit.
> C'était l'hiver, le jardin mort, la cour herbue. Il n'y aurait personne pendant des mois, tout est en ordre. (p. 7)

The fuzzy temporal focus reflects Mahu's old quarrel with the arbitrariness of chronological time. Mortin's clock does not work, and he eventually rips off its hands in frustration. *Recurring Melody* projects the time continuum of an individual consciousness instead of running by the metronome of clock time, and Pinget suggested a solution to the problem of depicting time, remarking that:

> The act of letting myself go without material established beforehand, with no goal other than discovery, is to choose to depend on the future. Or to make the time of the writing coincide with the time of the book. Whether I use the present or past I am in the future. I know nothing of what was before. Yet as I go forward, a certain past creates itself, anterior situations take solid shape. So the book digs its own foundations from page to page. The future evokes the past. That future disappears at the end of the last page leaving a past that is more sophisticated and mysterious than the past of the classical *récit*.[10]

In other words, the writer-narrators use a present tense that is already past at the end of the sentence. Viewed in the perspective of the creative process, the present tense of the final phrase has maintained its "presentness" for the time involved in writing the book. The voice suspends time, as in stop-action photography, freezing in place a girl about to sell bread; stopping in midflight a six-year-old's rush toward death; fixing forks at a dinner party when they are already half raised toward pursing mouths. It juggles time to focus attention on the inventive process, or moves back and forth in it to advance a story or a supposition. Then time passes. The bread gets sold. The child's legs scissor together. Hungry mouths close over forks. The voice lives in time and living and talking, passing stool and passing breath over the vocal chords; both involve moving toward death.

The voice also lives in a defined space. Nowhere else in his work does Pinget give so precise a feeling of a given moment and a given place as he does in this work. Like Beckett's *Film*, Pinget's *Recurring Melody* focuses on smaller and smaller settings, moving from the village, to the country farmhouse, and finally to a single room. The bottom of *Recurring Melody's* last page carries the inscription "Sirancy, 1968." Those familiar with Pinget's chronicle know that, in the author's imaginary landscape, the town of Sirancy lies somewhere between Fantoine and Agapa. Anyone who has visited Pinget's country house in Touraine will feel that Sirancy and the wind-blown farm are the same. Seasonal sensations and movements also permeate the flow of words, providing a basso continuo to their variations.

A chilling wind blows through *Recurring Melody*. In the dead of winter, Mortin returns surreptitiously to a frigid room in a cold house to face his torment and consolation, the blank page. Back he comes, fearfully and doggedly, to the creative starting point of nothingness—dreading the confusion he is unable to put in order and the silence that is threatening to engulf him. At the walls, pressures from within meet counterpressures from without. Inside, a table, a clock. Soon frustration and restlessness drive Mortin outside. An indistinguishable object lies on the manure pile at dusk. What could it be? The drunken postman passed out? A boy's mutilated body? A dead cow? A scarecrow? One never will learn for sure. Mortin feels his neighbors' curiosity and hostility pressing in from without. Outside and inside meet in precarious balance in the text as hearing and speaking establish Mortin's sense of mental geography.

> To try to seize that murmur between two hiccoughs he had first sharpened his hearing as long as his youth lasted, then the curve past, he lost it progressively to end up shortly before the time under discussion at a compact deafness, at internal pattering, at dizzy spells . . . but with the help of his will. . . . he reconstructed a sort of passacaglia. (pp. 35–36)

Pinget's voices thrive at the intersection of contraries, husking at the edge of laryngitis where speech probes the unspeakable, and spoonerisms and verbal incongruities abound. Nevertheless, the need for structure, pattern, and order makes itself felt. The words do not spring from an uncontrolled imagination but are filtered carefully, selected according to which lines they interrupt or push forward. In his preface to *The Libera Me Domine*, Pinget described the process as being:

> Almost automatic writing but fully conscious. That is, with immediate filtering of the possibles, of what could be developed and of which I force myself to develop a minimal part, in spite of my disgust for all development.

At first he wanted to call *Passacaille* by a different title, *Le Simulacre (The Simulacrum)*. He changed the title to *Passacaille* because during the period of the writing he relaxed by listening to recordings of Bach's fugues. Like Bach's music, the book also develops variations on a theme, and the fugal principle of repetition gives it rhythm and progression.[11] The prose operates much like that kind of modern music which is intended not to please its hearers but, rather, to tease the aural nerve—to *make* the audience listen closely. As we have seen, Pinget's recent texts have their own peculiar structures in which repeated verbal fragments, instead of linear exposition, serve as the ordering principle, and in which sound orders sense.

Although certain phrases return in a serial arrangement, the order and function of the choruslike fragments vary. Occasionally they fill a gap while Mortin's mind searches for what to say next, or they may seem to take on a life of their own, like the chorus of a popular song (read "phrases" for "images" in the following autocritical allusion):

> But the strangest was that obsession that brought you back to the same images which since they had been evoked at the space of several months in conversation of some and of others willed not to be forgotten, demanded their fill of flesh, in short became alive and a dummy no longer, . . . (p. 87)

These talismanic sounds take on different connotations until sheer force of repetition shows that all of *Recurring Melody* has grown out of the suggestive overtones of the leitmotif phrase, "The calm, the gray, nothing stirring," with which it begins.

LIVING VOICES

Repeated sounds provide the only familiar landmarks on pages crammed with stories going nowhere. Pinget intersperses them with muttered asides about the room, the countryside, or the difficulties of isolating the elusive tone and getting it down. Little by little it becomes clear that the pattern of repetition develops the text's autocritical reflection upon itself. The fragments tell a story of their own: the speaker's painfully won affirmation, "I speak, therefore I am," and its corollary, "I am what I speak." The implications of those discoveries will become clearer if the reader, as he reads, lifts the repeated phrases in *Recurring Melody* from the broken anecdotal materials around them, making a sort of subtext of muttered asides on the birth of the novel.

> The calm, the gray. Nothing stirring. Something must be broken in the machinery but nothing shows. The clock is on the mantel, the hands mark the hour. (p. 7)
> ... Something broken in the machinery. (p. 12)
> A few images that had to be amplified, rid of their cinders, darkened until the moment when having become interchangeable their profound difference would bring into view a world of aggressiveness and chaotic retreat, that was the task he had set himself at that very table, in that cold house haunted by years of insouciance, everything there took on the accent of nostalgia and some evenings of terror, phantasms of the night which leave nothing intact of memory's suggestions.
> ... Work of marginal notation. (p. 18)
> ... He had carefully mulled over that story of the dead body and gave his consent to it, hesitating still though about the hour and the child but it was of little importance, a manure pile what could be more suitable. (p. 24)
> ... What to do with these scraps. (p. 39)
> ... Work of marginal notation. (p. 42)
> ... As if the chronicle of these countless instants ... (p. 43)
> ... Because he had to make do with what he had, to hurry before the departure, to make the least instant of time count as if the little time granted ... (p. 44)
> ... What to do with these scraps. (p. 45)
> ... Turn, return, go back. (p. 49)
> ... Careful, you never know. (p. 59)
> ... Alchemist of nothings which insure his survival. (p. 59)
> ... Reduction of a vapor, appearance of a line. (p. 61)

. . . His existence hanging loose as it were. (p. 65)
. . . In the sempiternal morning of his mania. (p. 67)
. . . Phantasms of the night and yesterday and tomorrow. (p. 68)
. . . Images to rid of their cinders. Darkness deeply composed where each lapse will have its alibi. (p. 68)
. . . As if the chronicle of these countless instants. (p. 70)
. . . What to do with these scraps. (p. 83)
. . . What to do with these scraps. (p. 83)
. . . Phantasms of yesterday and tomorrow. From one year to the other these great in depth changes. Would sap the foundations of our edifice, that laborious heap of straw. (p. 84)
. . . Turn, return, go back. (p. 91)
. . . Plunged into his apocalypse at high interest. (p. 93)
. . . Stains of ink and graffiti. Other themes would come up from the nerves' disorder. Work of marginal notation. (p. 97)
. . . This murmur interrupted by silences and hiccoughs.
. . . Flawed source of information. (p. 99)
. . . Two mechanisms running at half speed. (p. 106)
. . . They're right to say of an annoyance that people won't talk about it in a hundred years. (p. 106)
. . . Interrupted by silences and hiccoughs. (p. 111)
. . . Now without calendar or passion . . . (p. 113)
. . . The hour when I mull over. (p. 116)
. . . Mechanisms running at half speed. (p. 116)
. . . Misery of this situation, the last one to prolong until death follows, forget all vanity, all concern for appearances, must rejoin little by little the paradise of the Japanese painting and inscribe myself at the summit of a mountain, fixed forever, or under a footbridge to watch the river's water run, three immutable little waves. (p. 116)
. . . That phrase.
Not yet found.
You understand, he said, not yet found.
Work of marginal notation. (p. 118)
. . . Death at the slightest failure of thought. (p. 118)
. . . Here without calendar. (p. 119)
. . . From one year to the other these great in depth changes. (p. 119)
>   Without a crack on the outside.
>   Turn, return, go back.
>   Height profoundly composed. (p. 121)

>   ... A half-word interval.
>   Images to rid of their cinders. (p. 122)
>   ... To silence the murmur. (p. 125)
>   ... Death at the slightest failure of thought. (p. 128)
>   I undersigned in the cold room, hemlock, clock put out of order, I undersigned in the swamp, goat or bird carcass, I undersigned at the turn of the road, in the master's garden, old woman of evil spells, sentinel of the dead, deviate, dummy, in a pick-up truck on that course turned aside by the evil eye, toy of that course turned aside by the evil eye, toy of that farce we call conscience, no one, I undersigned midnight in daylight, staggering under trouble, old screech-owl, magpie, or crow ... (p. 130)
>   ... His existence hanging loose as it were. (p. 132)
>   ... Until nightfall.
>   Seated at the table a few hours before found dead on the manure pile, a sentinel kept watch who had not noticed that the dead man a gray day, cold, must/will have approached the crack in the shutter and must/will have seen him distinctly put the clock out of order then remain prostrate on his chair, elbows on the table, his head in his hands. (p. 133)

Pinget's voices say almost nothing that we can understand, if "understanding" means extracting their substantive content and fitting it into a logically consistent whole. They consume anecdotal fragments like so many wood chips and burn themselves out like the star in Robert Frost's poem, which when entreated to "say something to us we can learn and when alone repeat," answers simply "I burn."[12] Interrupted stories trace the hesitations of a consciousness coming to grips with itself and the world. The said and the unsaid, the rushing over and coming back, reveal multiple layers of consciousness and outcroppings of feeling until, in the end, we have an aural portrait of *how* the speaker is rather than *what* he is. The words flow on. Voices glide from story to story, carried forward by their own momentum like the child's toy, the Slinky, a flexible coil whose downward motion, once launched, sends it arching irreversibly downstairs.

The voice eventually rubs raw the cords producing it, and speaking at such a pitch of intensity eventually brings on the antithesis of speech, silence. Words first swallow up each other, and then their source. In texts of this kind, writing the first page poses the most serious problem, since timbre, content, and syntax will all flow from the initial lines. Cutting off the narrative cannot be a simple matter either. Pinget silences each voice only after he has given it an identity that distinguishes it from all the others to be explored. His dislike of the recognizable and the predictable makes it distasteful for him to repeat a tone once he has found it. So he interrupts the voice with an expanse of white on the rest of the unfilled page. The speaker knows then that total self-expression means death, and that filling the page means emptying himself.

> . . . a deep mechanism has perhaps been set moving and it may sap the foundations of our edifice, that laborious piling of straw . . . (p. 84)

A jolt *may* lock the shifting kaleidoscope into a pattern that is fixed once and for all. But the Pingetian voice moves through sound and silence as a fish moves through water. The speaker mutters along toward self-destruction, conscious, like Beckett's *Unnameable*.

> . . . You must go on. I can't go on. You must go on. I'll go on. You must say words, as long as there are any, until they find me, until they say me, strange pain, strange sin, you must go on, perhaps it's done already, perhaps they have said me already, perhaps they have carried me to the threshold of my story, before the door that opens on my story, that would surprise me, if it opens, it will be I, it will be the silence, where I am, I don't know, I'll never know, in the silence you don't know, you must go on. I can't go on, I'll go on . . . [13]

To read Pinget's latest works is to witness a flirtation with verbal suicide, and these texts generate the kind of morbid curiosity that draws crowds when an unfortunate threatens to leap from a building to his death. Yet contact with these works also liberates and excites one in a positive and refreshing way. The self-eclipsing voice spangles the night of silence with strange and beautiful stars, like the finale of a fireworks display. It is therefore hardly surprising that Pinget no longer feels that beginning his career as a writer was the most arduous part of his task, but rather that the major difficulty lies in continuing it. As he observed in the preface to *The Libera Me Domine:*

> Why continue this rigorous, demanding spiritual exercise? To discover, in the end, an ungainly moral truth that is my own, but so deeply buried under contradictions that I have only art with which to go after it.

The reader who comes to grips with *The Libera Me Domine, Recurring Melody, Fable,* and *Voice* will find rewards commensurate with the great effort required. *The Libera Me Domine* records a long, murmured prayer, not unlike the prayer for the dead alluded to in the title. To be sure, the supplication receives no answer, but in bringing the voice to life Pinget calls into play an exhilarating liberty of language. The transcription of despair becomes an unexpectedly powerful agent of liberation. One might well exclaim with him, "*O Libera, libera nos a malo. Libera nos de libris*" ("O Prayer of Liberation, deliver us from evil. Deliver us from books"). For the novel emancipates the reader from a bookish conception of literature and life and frees the author from the shackles of conventionalized prose. Its composition enables Pinget to carry on his quest through adventures in sound and frees him to deal with the universal fear of death, loneliness, and sterility in a manner at once so personal and so honest that its depth excludes the slightest overtone of sentimentality. In short, the prose of *The Libera Me Domine* and *Recurring Melody* does indeed invite the reader to make "the discovery of an ungainly moral truth" through a frightening but beautiful act of courage.

7 Fabulae Fabularum

Fable (Fable), and *This Voice (Cette Voix)*

> Everything leads to the belief that there exists a certain point of the mind from which life and death, the real and the imaginary, the past and the future, the communicable and the uncommunicable, the high and the low cease being perceived in a contradictory fashion.—André Breton, *Second Manifesto of Surrealism*

> To compose a poem with the mechanism of the dream . . . one word which changes meaning along the way.
> —Jean Cocteau, *Attempt at Indirect Criticism*

> In the perspective of interest to us, everything doubles back on itself, and becomes intermingled. A given sign represents another or includes a third. Speech interpenetrates itself in all directions and the text is read in the same way.—Pinget, *Paralchimie*

At first, *Fable* would seem an unlikely choice for the title of a book by Robert Pinget. The word is usually applied to stories with a "moral," and Pinget, as we have seen, is usually not interested in either telling stories or teaching lessons. On the contrary, his quest follows a relativistic, elliptical path that is profoundly anti-Cartesian. Whereas Descartes saw an orderly world of cause and effect, Pinget sees the ebb and flow of unpredictable cycles.[1] Yet when Descartes referred to his *Discourse on Method* as a "fable," he was suggesting, by limiting himself to the word's most common meaning, that his system of deductive logic should be applied universally, as well as primarily inserting a somewhat disingenuous disclaimer to protect himself from possible charges of heresy.[2] Pinget uses the word in the contradictory fullness of its several meanings so as to describe simultaneously what his book is and what it is not. The dictionary defines "fable" as a short moralistic tale, often with animals or inanimate objects as characters; as a story not founded on fact; as a story about supernatural or extraordinary persons or incidents, a legend; as an untruth or falsehood;

as the plot of an epic, a dramatic poem, or a play; and as idle talk—among other meanings. All these meanings apply to some degree to Pinget's *Fable* (1971) and to *This Voice (Cette Voix)*, which followed it in 1975. Moreover, consistent with Pinget's depiction of writing as a "quest," *Fable* is also a *"fabula"* about the act of writing. Significantly, *"fabulare"* is the Latin root of the Spanish *"hablar"* ("to speak"), and Pinget's writer-narrators all attempt to exorcise, by the use of words, the deep solitude and sorrow that they have in common. *Fable* adds the subject of broken love as a variation on this recurring theme of fragmentation and loss.[3] The text unfolds as a litany of shattered happiness, a threnody on the anguish of separation in the months following a lover's quarrel. The empty country house, once shared in love, serves as both a special focal point and an *"aide-mémoire"* as the narrator shuttles back and forth between past and present and between dream and reality. Various sites around the building evoke joy or suffering, and the writer-narrator pauses before them to mourn and reflect, as in the ritual of the Stations of the Cross on Good Friday. Ostensibly, the purpose of the narrator's quest is to find the magic word or phrase that will make his happy memories live forever, or that will at least give him the strength to forge a lasting work of art from his suffering—to create "a new fable . . . gathering my energies one last time, it will be the best part of me . . . tell everything over again to renew everything." But the text warns explicitly that, just as perfect love cannot last in this world, neither will a happy ending nor an uplifting "moral" be in the offing: "The number two of all numbers [is] the least perfect" (p. 58).

The narrative deals, movingly, with the theme of fragmentation. Perfect union, even between lovers, is illusory. In the same way, communication between writer and reader must also remain imperfect, and the schism between the conflicting aspects of the narrator's personality will never be completely healed. Pinget develops the configuration of imperfect pairs through an extensive use of leitmotifs featuring flawed couples or ambivalent symbols. The book's aesthetic and moral values cut two ways: each memory brings pain as well as joy; love is hate's night brother; Holy Communion is explicitly linked to oral sex, salvation to cannibalism: purity and its opposite are but varying faces of a single entity.[4]

The word "passion," for example, in the following passage refers at once to Christ's crucifixion, to the final death agony, and to sexual desire.

> But another atmosphere, that of the tormented conscience where no image passes without being controlled, deformed in the direction of a possible salvation, old chimera, when candor triumphed on Easter mornings, the initiate finds himself at the age of passions once again deprived of a sense of discrimination.[5]

Considered from a thematic point of view, *Fable*'s most striking aspect is its ambivalence. So many stories are started and then dropped or run together that no single plot or person is ever clearly defined. Pinget has used the device of deliberate blurring previously, but never to such a degree. He shifts the lovers from one set of roles to another: torturer and victim, wanderer and stay-at-home, master and servant, angel and androgyne, exile and occupant. Three subjects—identity, authorship, and death—are considered at length and in depth, and a dual vision of each of them emerges. It is extremely difficult to pin down the identity of the voice that is speaking at any given moment. For example, the first person appears initially in the twenty-sixth sentence and some ninety-six times thereafter, but the identity of this floating "I" shifts frequently. The narrator is referred to first as Miaille and then as Miette. Both names connote fragmentation and suggest several possible puns (me-I, me-eye, *"miette"* = "scrap" or "crum"). Once again, the recurrence of a character's name hints at a link to earlier chapters on life in Fantoine and Agapa, for a spinster school teacher named Miette also appeared in *The Inquisitory*. Inexplicably, in *Fable*, Miette is a male writer. The close similarity in sound between Miaille and Miette and their function as alternating narrators leads to the inference that they may represent alter egos of a divided personality. An equally ambivalent image of the dignity of authorship emerges. At one point, the poet is depicted as a bard or seer, and yet Mlle. Lorpailleur, the self-proclaimed poetess laureate of Fantoine and Agapa, is treated with derision:

> ... She was scribbling her poem, old barcarole, old elegy unravelling in her brain ... quavering Pythoness, priestess of that denigration into which her misshapen soul was sinking. (p. 32)

The writer is therefore portrayed simultaneously as both noble Christ-like seeker of truth and bitchy gossip-monger. Christ himself appears in *Fable*, in a baffling paradox of Christian iconography, as both martyred savior and divine fool. By extension, the writer's text, *Fable* itself, is both Promethean and Narcissistic, with several allusions to the appropriate Greek myths.

> To change words from one place to
> the other, a sublime game.
> To inhabit each word spoken in order
> to give it its meaning.
> He was no longer the plaything, but
> the player, no longer the exile from
> a problematic land but was finding
> his home in every town at every
> moment under different skies . . . (p. 68)

Miaille stopped talking, listening to the words following each other in that endlessly repeated phrase, not one was missing, so that's what it meant to occupy the dwelling place a measured, concrete, mysterious formula, it is everywhere in the rooms, in the attics, in the barn . . . (p. 51)

. . . he was dabbling with the verses of a poem which he was struggling to hold together, getting up in the morning, scribbling all day, dumbfounded by the sumptuousness of the word like a child dazzled by a preening peacock . . . (p. 36)

Miette scrabbled around in his bag, passed his finger over his old papers and unfailingly took out the letter. Terms from an almanach. What sort of pompous ass could have dictated it. . . . When he woke [from his nap] the old fool opens his knapsack again, takes the letter out again and tediously goes back over the product of his mental collapse . . . (p. 95)

But Miaille wasn't listening to him, attentive to something else, the tone perhaps which recalled others like it, those destinies which we know by heart and are told in the same way, softly without bitterness, lying words but what does it matter, they come from the same desert and return there all the same, the former Eden, still perceptible but further and further away, it has disappeared from memories, only the voice betrays it here and there by an inflection, an accent an intake of breath . . . (p. 40)

The flashlight would still go back and forth over the writings from the knapsack, bills from cheap restaurants, post cards, hasty rendezvous, he would read there nothing more than a homily without end. (p. 68)

. . . he recognized [in the gypsy's story] his own life or wanted to, the former Eden disappeared from memories, all that jumbled mess to vomit . . . (p. 47)

In short, Christ may or may not have died in vain. Miaille/Miette may or may not have loved for nothing. Writing *Fable* may be an act of discovery or a waste of paper. Floating between past and present, dream and reality, love and hate, purity and depravity, doubt and faith, the comfort of home and the nightmare of the ruins of atomic war, the narrator has recourse only to—words. The elaborate fugue in *Recurring Melody* gives way to an open-ended refrain. The long story fragments of *The Libera Me Domine* have been compressed into flashes of images appearing in serial clusters. Like a child's song made up as it goes along, *Fable* presents a world of multiple possibilities. The truth behind its many riddles, if indeed there is any such "one" truth, is a matter of chance—a flip of the coin. Even man's physical well-being is a shifting amalgam of chemical compounds. Following the dominant pattern of the microcosm of his entire saga in the reduced dimensions of a single text, Pinget relies here (with great effectiveness) on the paradox of repetition and change existing side by side. That uneasy interrelationship communicates the ambivalence that is poetry—and life. In the multiple meanings attributable to the title, we have seen a compressed example of this technique. By setting the word "fable" in varying contexts, Pinget plucks it from the muddied stream of everyday usage and shows it to the reader as being as clean and undomesticated as a freshly washed pebble. The same principle of sameness and unexpected change is painstakingly applied to every aspect of *Fable*—its imagery, its word order, its structure, its sentences, its phrases, its key words—all resulting in an incantatory prose that is very little different from poetry.

1. Since temporal and spacial divisions have been suspended in *Fable*, the text unfolds in the form of clusters of images bursting in the narrator's imagination. He is first seen lying in a barn, projecting images from his mind's eye onto the "screen" of the rafters. The pages of the book also serve as screens, as Miaille/Miette uses the house as a pantagram summoning phantoms from the past and the future. "Impossible to formulate today and tomorrow, we are aleatory" (p. 67). The resulting images may be "realistic" (the house, the barn, the herb garden), "nostalgic" (the now-parted lovers), or "prophetic" (an attack by barbarians, a city in ruins). Pinget has turned from the yellowed photographs of *Someone* to the flow of impressions of the cinematographer.[6] The "film" of *Fable*'s images seems at first to have been spliced with reckless abandon, but a careful study of associated words and phrases reveals that Pinget has taken care to make his key images polyvalent by putting them in changing contexts. The "naturalistic" description of Mlle. Lorpailleur's Witches' Sabbath, and the straightforward description of the herb garden trigger memories of the lost past and anticipated death.

2. The most basic device for making words strange, restoring the magic worn away by familiarity, is simply to uproot them, to displace them from the niche normally selected by syntax and common usage. Such dislocations need not be radical or even extremely numerous. But when used sparingly in conjunction with "normal" patterns they make the text seem at once both unusual and familiar. In the first sentence of *Fable*, for example, Pinget makes two slight variations in the syntactical order of subject/verb/object. Instead of saying: "He stopped in front of an abandoned barn to pass the night, went in and scooped out a hollow in the hay, where he went to sleep," he writes: "To pass the night he stopped in front of an abandoned barn, went in and in the hay scooped out a hollow where he went to sleep." In this case, by displacing the words "to pass" and "in the hay" Pinget calls the reader's attention to them. Given Pinget's scatalogical trope, association of speech, defecation, and the act of "passing through" the experience of loss, the preposition of the word underscores its multiple meanings, and the displacement of "hay" adds a note of insistent specificity to the generative string of images and phrases that will follow.

To pass the night he stopped in front of an abandoned barn, went in and in the hay scooped out a hollow where he went to sleep, with his knapsack under his head.

But someone had seen him in the moonlight, a walker out late.

There are times of despair, first which alternate with others when the soul sets itself free but little by little the alternation doesn't take place any more and that's when the head rots.

Did he think about it before going to sleep or did he just count the beams in the rafters.

And that other one out late.

The town had dissolved under the effect of a cataclysm, only cinders were left.

The population in small groups was camping in the ruins or heading toward the fields.

This future to dissolve.

Someone called Miaille or another but it's not time yet.

Poppies in the morning were turning red in the oats.

So the night is passed then.

He sets out in the direction of this field which is flaming and says poppie for the children, bouquets which fade, years long ago, sweet and long ago.

He pulls some cheese from his knapsack and a bottle of wine.

Naked men girdled with leather come out of the river and head toward the dead body stretched out on the rocky beach. They cut him into pieces with the knives hanging at their belts and begin to devour him. Their chief has reserved the sex for himself which he swallows in one mouthful before tackling the groin.

Or those bunches of delphiniums when June begins to turn blond in the fields.

A small enclosure full of aromatic herbs.

He will not have gone to sleep right away, he will have counted the beams in the rafters hanging on them the images of the day, those poppies, those naked men, those ruins of the city.

The body on the beach was a young boy's with white skin and blue hair, beautiful as ivory and lapis lazuli.

But the men assaulted him again, cut him in pieces again, devoured everything but his head which they hung across the chief's saddle.

And still the groups of exiles who picnic, tin cans, greasy papers, pasty faces, they go off again then stop again then go off again.

This city which is still smoking.

> A house which was ours he says and here I am among the exiles to chew on dry bread and weep without stopping from one stop to the next, from one night to the other, until the day when that possession will be no more than a photo in my pocket between the passport and a post card.
> And to see nothing more.
> Barely to hear.
> Barely a dull, inarticulated complaint, to perceive scraps of it then to find them, then to find harmonies on that old string of an instrument ripped apart by the barbarians.
> Complaint, complaint again, the poppies fade and the photograph turns yellow in the pocket, it was put in there yesterday, centuries of landslides, shudders, mortal lacerations.
> This Miaille or other who found himself alone in the barn recognized afterward, he came back to it by instinct, there he is crying from morning to night cannot decide to leave the premises old cliché, time has done its work, making past what only yesterday was the unique present.
> He went around the barn again, the stable, the out buildings, still carrying his knapsack for fear that the other, the observer in the moonlight might come and take it from him.
> It contains neither wine or cheese but letters, letters, notes from an appointment book, laundry bills, bills from cheap restaurants, notes written in haste, walks around the out buildings, pulls a weed here, puts a stone in place there, mortal laceration, the sun mercilessly dissolves what remained of a tenderness in which no one recognizes himself anymore.
> A small enclosure full of aromatic herbs. (pp. 9–14)

In the passage just cited, Pinget's departures from the word order of ordinary usage has the characteristic effect of freeing particular words and phrases from their habitual associations and scattering them into a multiplicity of possible meanings. As a result, certain words acquire an aura of mystery over and beyond their limited "everyday" function of conveying meaning in a more or less one-to-one ratio between word and thing. The reader has the impression of entering a room in which familiar objects, slightly displaced, seem to take on a bizarre, slightly sinister life of their own.

Repetition brings a certain coherence and stability to the seemingly chaotic flow of images by providing linguistic reference points. ("To renew everything by saying everything again.") That this is so can be demonstrated by means of a computer-generated concordance that has been done jointly by the present author and Professor Esteban R. Egea in order to study Pinget's technique of repetition and variation objectively. The computer charts shifts of context and varying associative values by (a) listing in alphabetical order all the words appearing in *Fable* and (b) supplying a consecutive listing of clusters of words immediately preceding and following each word in the alphabetical list. The resulting printout reveals how often each word appears and in what permutations and combinations it does so. If the critic knows what to look for, the concordance can serve, then, as a sort of isolating camera that cuts through the text's complexity and shows how every single word or phrase functions from beginning to end. Obviously such an approach must be applied with some care. Because it ignores the author's labyrinthine arabesques, one may be tempted to remove key images from the complex matrix of the text and to reconstruct the very linear fable that Pinget strives so successfully to leave polyvalent. If the critic respects the author's intent, however, and uses the computer data to confirm suspicions emerging from thorough knowledge of his work, the concordance reveals a complicated set of documentable, suggestive, almost subliminal linkages in the apparently random cascade of images.

3. As we have seen, *Fable* develops like an extended prose saga, or like a poem with each stanza taking its point of departure from phrases or images already stated. Repetition produces overlapping from paragraph to paragraph, giving the impression, since a key image is associated with a number of themes, that the text could be expanded almost indefinitely. In the following example, the word "*clos*," "enclosure," links the garden to several themes—death and resurrection, past happiness, the ultimate blindness of death, and the menace of barbarism—simply by repeating the phrase in varying contexts. This technique produces considerable richness of overtone and suggestivity as the varying themes become intermingled through repetition of the key word.

CLOS = "ENCLOSURE," "CLOSED"
A small enclosure full of aromatic herbs. (p. 11)

A small enclosure full of aromatic herbs.
When June brought back the picnic table under the grape arbor. (p. 14)
... walking around the enclosure, aromatics of death ... (p. 15)
... a man walking naked with a spray of flowers in his hands one sees him approach the enclosure of aromatic herbs, he lays down the flowers which come back to life ... (p. 23)
... gardener of enclosures hidden from view, a lily blooms there, and stock flowers, jonquils perfumes of aromatic herbs ... (pp. 36–37)
And there they were both back to the days before the fall and they lived without fear ... raking the closed aromatic garden ... (p. 48)
... couldn't read the letter his eyes were closed forever ... (p. 61)
... he would herd the [pigs] back to the enclosure which would no longer shelter aromatics. (p. 63)

Pinget repeats many other such trigger words in order to set up complex thematic associations in the reader's mind. The infinitive *"dissoudre,"* "to dissolve," is associated with the blurring of chronological time, lost hope, and physical decay.[7] The color blue and the recurring image of delphiniums link purity and lust.[8] Used in connection with the lovers, *"bois,"* connotes mystery and pleasure; but when used in reference to Mlle. Lorpailleur, the same word takes on gross and vulgar associations.[9] Whereas "house" and "corner" are generally used to evoke the security of love, the word "city" becomes a leitmotif of desolation.[10] The lingering overtones achieved by repeating sounds also set up subtle puns, as in the grouping scattered through the text of *"se mirer,"* "to admire oneself," *"miro,"* "blind," and *"miroir,"* "mirror."[11]

... il se penche sur le côté, mouvement qu'il fait pour se mirer dans l'eau. (p. 114)
Il est miro depuis le coup de lame ... (p. 88)
Elle se penche ... sur le livre en guise de mirroir. (p. 93)
... un salon ... avec des mirroirs tout le tour ... (p. 115)

... he leans over the side, movement he makes to admire himself in the water. (p. 114)
He is blind since the razor slash ... (p. 88)

> She leans over . . . the book as if it were a mirror. (p. 93)
> . . . a livingroom . . . with mirrors all around . . . (p. 15)

Far from being a limiting or restrictive influence, as one might expect, Pinget's particular use of repetition is generative. When a word is placed frequently in a given context, that association remains in the mind at a subliminal level like the image left on the retina after the eye is closed. Through repetition, words take on simultaneous, multiple meanings. Thus "city" and "ruins" become so run together (like the repeated set, "Monday, Tuesday, Wednesday") that later in the text, when a rebuilt city is mentioned, the reader "sees" both the new city and the smoldering ruins. By means of this technique, associations that are mutually exclusive on the level of logic are made to come to life as the text unfolds.

4. When the curtain rises on the second act of *Waiting for Godot*, the set is the same as that of the first act except for one detail: a few blossoms have appeared on the scrawny tree. Similarly, as the action unfolds, it repeats much of what has happened before: Pozzo and Lucky return, Estragon and Vladamir consider going away or committing suicide, the messenger boy returns bearing the same message. But Beckett introduces subtle variations that undercut the impression of sameness: Pozzo is blind, Estragon is less passive, and unexpected puns or replies intrude on the familiar vaudevillelike dialogue. The second act reflects the first, but it reflects it imperfectly. The spectator seems to be in a dream in which he thinks he knows what will happen next but isn't quite sure.

Although Pinget uses repetition extensively in *Fable*, the book's most basic stylistic device could be best described as repetitive alternation, with word groups fulfilling the function that plot fragments did in Pinget's previous works. *Fable's* overall structure reflects this curious narrative strategy. Like *Waiting for Godot*, *Fable* is in two parts, the second of which is ostensibly a reflection, a reworking of the first (as in *Mahu or the Material*, *Monsieur Levert*, and *Baga*). In fact, however, the second part takes on a life of its own, adding new material, reinterpreting statements, and playing on words.[12] *Fable's* double structure reinforces the work's thematic ambivalence and the stylistic balancing act between the familiar and the unexpected. The impression that the book has a binary, symmetrical structure is an illusion, for a closer look at both parts reveals that they differ significantly in length, in choice of words, and in tone.

The first part of *Fable* contains 445 sentences (11,405 words), the second, 265 sentences (6,336 words). Part one is narrated by Miaille and is the richer in images. In part two, narrated by the blind Miette, sound associations play a greater role. The semantic field of each part varies as new words and images move into the text and are dropped or used less frequently.[13] Sentence and paragraph lengths also vary. The second part runs more to extremes, with a higher proportion of very short and very long paragraphs.[14] As the excursions into dream and fantasy grow longer and more abrupt it becomes increasingly clear that the two parts of the text overlap without fusing. The text moves convincingly toward a resolution about two thirds of the way through part one, when Miaille seems on the verge of discovering the key to the verbal magic that will make him whole.

> Suddenly everything appeared to him no longer as consecutive, painfully linked together right up to an unavoidable end, but an open-ended event, open dwelling places where he could go from one to the other, he is at home in each, his place will not be taken from him by the tribulations to come, the accident has finally triumphed.
>
> And the other is at home there too, serene as on the first day, he has been caught in the trap, he is the soul of each dwelling place. Several faces in the mirror identical to the one looking into them, unity has been regained.
>
> Here the fable would end but it is already trembling from having been stuck to a moral.
>
> To change words from their places, sublime game.
>
> To inhabit each thing said and give it its meaning.
>
> From that moment on, he was no longer the plaything but the player, no longer the exile from a problematical country but each time found his home town under different skies, buzzing with loved voices which it pleased him to locate and rejoin, his ear subtly trained. Rediscoveries and reminiscences.
>
> Wherever you will be, I will be. And this modest victory he was tempted to make a triumph.
>
> The flashlight was still going back and forth over the notes in the

knapsack, bills from cheap restaurants, post cards, hasty rendezvous, he would read no more there than an endless homily.

Never spoke that language. Something is slipping somewhere. (pp. 67-69)

But something becomes unstuck. The last third of part one continues the search for the magic word or formula and ends in failure. Part two takes up the quest from the same point of departure. It alters the material developed in part one, making the lack of a conclusion or a denouement the more keenly felt. At the sentence level, open-ended alternation is achieved by a peculiar use of conjunctions and linking words. Their grammatical function, that of limitation, falls away, and they generate repetition and exploration of alternate possibilities. As in the series of "or that's" in *The Libera Me Domine*, "The conjunctions," as Jean Roudaut observed, "do not exercise a function of liaison between statements but play a pivotal role in developments: *but* and *unless* introduce sequences in opposition; *or*, equally plausible contradictory developments; *when* does not specify a moment in time but alternates with another *when*, this one followed by the imperfect."[15] Pinget produces a similar effect on the structural level by making the two parts of *Fable* imperfect mirrors of each other. Structurally, as well as thematically, "the number two is the most imperfect of all"—and with a vengeance!

5. If repetition tends to reassure the reader and hold the text together, forming the narcissistic pole of *Fable*, alternation provides the shock of the new and unexpected forming *Fable's* protean pole. Alternation takes many forms. There are frequent shifts from general to specific usage, as in the bringing into and out of focus of "the naked men."

> "*HOMMES NUS*" = "*NAKED MEN*"
> Some naked men . . . (p. 10)
> those naked men . . . (p. 11)
> But the naked men . . . (p. 11)
> My eyes were glued to the naked men . . . (p. 56)[16]

Pinget also varies the tenses and moods of key verbs like "*refaire le tour*."

> "*REFAIRE LE TOUR*" = "*TO WALK AROUND AGAIN*"
> Il refaisait le tour de la grange . . . (p. 13)
> . . . il aurait refait le tour des bâtiments . . . (p. 28)
> C'est à l'heure de midi qu'il a refait le trajet de naguère . . . (p. 30)
> Refaisait le tour des bâtiments à la nuit tombée . . . (p. 47)
> Il referait le tour des bâtiments à la nuit tombée, mais sans hâte. (p. 59)[17]

He substitutes a new word into a series or set of phrases made familiar through frequent repetition by shifting objects mentioned, thus changing the place description in the recurring set "on the left," "on the right."

> "*PLUS LOIN SUR LA DROITE*" = "*FARTHER ALONG ON THE RIGHT*"
> Worn down to the string. Further along on the right, excavations for a bridge over a river. (p. 84)
> Worn down to the string. Further along on the left, an administration building. (p. 84)
> Worn down to the string. Further along on the right the old clock tower.
> Worn down to the string. Further along on the left the station . . . (p. 84)
> The same. Further along on the right, the terrace of a cheap restaurant. (p. 85)
> The same. Further along on the right. The same.
> The city has risen from the dead. (p. 85)

The overall effect of alternation is to make the reader feel that he too, like Miaille/Miette, is an exile, lost between the known and the unknown, dream and reality, old and new, expected and unexpected.

By playing off repetition and alternation, Pinget succeeds in communicating the anguished, shattered world of lost love. The apparently disconnected flow of violent images calls into question the possibility of imparting order either to words or to the past. As such, the text would appear to be "a story not founded on fact," "a foolish or ridiculous story," implying, by extension, that love is "a fiction invented to deceive." And yet, Pinget treats the passion of God-made-man with great tenderness and a wistful desire to believe. Far from failing, the book succeeds in the life-giving task proclaimed in the title. For a fable is not merely a *"fabula"* or a homily with a useful moral. Fables also express man's dignity as a maker of myths. In the *récit*, Narcissus—unchanging, and self-loving—confronts the vision of protean man. The magic of Pinget's shifting word associations, like the interwoven repetitions in Beckett's *Watt*, fuses the opposing Greek symbols around the myth of the scriptor, the writer seeking, through words, symbolic power over death. On this score, *Fable* succeeds nobly. As Jean Roudaut observed:

> Such is the paradox of the work that, established against death, it gets farther away from life, that built as a protection, it reveals its underlying obsession. That undertaken as a game, it becomes a torture and a punishment; it is absolutely necessary to continue, not to stop, to write, not to be interrupted. No ending is desirable. What is hidden by the work resists any inquisitory, what it dissembles and reveals tears apart. The work bears a growing wound in itself. Proposing no message, it does not dissimulate the thing haunting it behind any disguise, be it intellectual, passionate or historical. From the game of literature is born the evidence that alone among words death plays a nonequivocal role. Death organizes circumstantial interlinkings. Death is the only compass that nothing can disorient.[18]

THIS VOICE (CETTE VOIX)

Death, words and salvation remain the primary concerns of Pinget's latest novel, *This Voice* (1975). Indeed, thematically and structurally *Fable* and *This Voice* are cut from the same cloth and may be considered complementary to each other, just as the author's works in two parts repeat, contradict, and complete each other. With *This Voice* Pinget shifts his ground from "fable" to "legend." Once again he typically insists on giving the broadest possible latitude to the implications of the literary term used, for the legend unfolding as the pages accumulate is obviously intended to be taken simultaneously as "a nonhistorical or unverifiable story handed down by tradition from earlier times and popularly accepted as historical," as "a collection of stories about an admirable person," and as "a lesson to be read."[19] In fact, the author-narrator makes that point explicitly at frequent intervals.[20] The story that develops, with the usual Pingetian elaborations and emendations, turns around a tangled skein of violent events involving certain recurring characters, Mortin and his household (his nephew and maid), as well as a number of unnamed village women who prattle on about alleged sexual improprieties, food prices, and the village weather. As usual, however, the story's objective elements soon become unverifiable, and one is never sure whether the more melodramatic events involved (Mortin's murder or death by a convulsive attack, for example) actually happened to him or to one of his brothers; in fact, the book proposes so many versions of the central event that it becomes increasingly unlikely that the event ever happened at all. *This Voice* also resonates with bits and pieces of lore about the author's mythical land pieced out in the chronicle to this date. The Levert family, the enigmatic fable, the unfinished letter, the imaginary son or nephew, the reluctant witness, Francine de Bonne Mesure, and the villages of Fantoine and Agapa echo through its pages like familiar participants in an ongoing epic. In Pinget's hands, however, the epic is accompanied by a mock-heroic, self-denigrating commentary.[21]

Nevertheless, for all that is old or repeated, *This Voice* strikes a new tone in Pinget's chronicle and its novelty may best be described by pointing out the nuance of meaning separating legend from fable. Whereas fables deal with fanciful, fictitious material, often of pagan origin, in Christian culture the word *legend* was originally used to denote a story concerning the life of a saint, whence the moral injunction that it contains material that *ought* to be read. Turning a hundred and eighty degrees from the anguished, blasphemous prayers of the narrator in *Fable*, who so patently yearns to believe, *This Voice* turns to the light of Christ's Resurrection to illuminate the author's anguished quest, the exhaltation and despair of the interplay of words, and the relentless approach of the final silence.

The stylistic devices used to accentuate the impression of simultaneity and elliptical movement extend the techniques of repetition and alternation developed so effectively in *Fable*. Pinget originally thought of giving the work the title *Anamnesis (Anamnase)*, a specific allusion to the way in which the book's various components are run together and blur, much as do dreams or memories dredged up from the subconscious or the distant past. In a brief comment in the author's own hand distributed along with the book, Pinget describes the complex anamnesis undertaken in the following terms: "An

anamnesis, literally a movement back into memory is in psychoanalytical language, the fact of recalling the past through a medical interrogation." In this particular case, the desired anamnesis is triple:
(1) The narrator's;
(2) The scriptor's (relative to the work accomplished to date);
(3) The anamnesis formulated relative to the structure of the book that recomposes or decomposes itself *backwards* starting from the novel's midpoint. In other words, the themes are taken up once more in the inverse order of their formulation.

As in the other books of Pinget's most recent manner, words and phrases are repeated or alternated at irregular intervals so as to appear in suggestive permutations and combinations. A seemingly endless contradictory series of "but's," "or's," and "and's" nullifies any sense of linear progression. As Pinget points out, the episodes double back on each other at the midpoint in the text, as the scriptor shuffles rapidly through the pack of narrative "givens" like a cardplayer anxious to deal himself a winning hand. The game that Pinget is and has been playing, however, is solitaire *"Réussite,"* or "success." But the narrator does not succeed in bringing his tour de force to a successful conclusion. The object of his quest has not varied a jot from one end of Pinget's chronicle to the other. Saturated with words (like Maupassant), striving to discover a lost, elusive verbal harmony (like Chateaubriand), Pinget's narrator seeks tirelessly to discover the magic word or phrase that will justify his suffering and give meaning to his waning life.[22] The agonizing process of working backward through imagination and memory to an Edenic, unspoiled prior state falls short of its goal.[23] In this sense, the anamnesis fails thematically and structurally. Perfection in this world is but the stuff of fables. But *This Voice* also manages to evoke a level of experience at which the text may be considered a success. In addition to the meanings mentioned explicitly by Pinget, "anamnesis" also refers to "a prayer in a Eucharistic service, recalling the Passion, Resurrection and Ascension of Christ."[24]

Early on in *This Voice* the narrator—be he Mortin, Mortin's nephew, or Pinget—imagines that he is living in an empty coffin in the village cemetery. Spacially positioned between heaven above and the grave below, the narrator dangles his legs from the coffin and speculates on two alternatives: earth's fractious vexations and a meaningless death, and the possibility of redemption. In this fragment (which Pinget has considered extracting from *This Voice* and having printed separately under the title *The Man who Got Away* [*Le Rescapé*]), the narrator occupies the same place in regard to his past and future prospects as Pinget does to his work. He is over-burdened and exhausted by the volume of verbal dross; he has panned for gold with much care but accomplished little for all his pains. Yet just as there could be no Resurrection without Christ's death, so too the platitudes, clichés, and anecdotal chaff that ground the scriptor's prose in trivia necessarily form a part of the ideal text, dimly imagined. It is in accepting language and life at its humblest and least promising that the door to a possible redemption is unexpectedly opened. The same surprise holds true at the level of language. As silence approaches, the legend of Christ's passion and redemption provides a covering metaphor that embraces both the emptiness and the magic of the Word in a single paradoxical trope. Christ may well have lived and died in vain, as the narrator cries out in *Fable*. And the chronicle of Fantoine and Agapa may well be as useless a jumble of letters as a toddler's alphabet blocks. But perhaps it is necessary to face those possibilities squarely and express them directly through language before the miracle of redemption can be accomplished.

> All that's needed is a phrase to transcribe
> And that proves that phrase whose meanders
> and repentences avoid a straight line unless it's
> suspicious of it.
> The love of what has been said comes back to you
> without warning.
> And so it goes.
> From far and near a recall a friendly greeting
> I am no longer afraid of nightmares.
> To the new fable let's wait until it becomes
> embodied as days pass.
> Because to say and say again are two different
> things entirely the material is expensive a little patience
> pulease.
> The lilies of the great sleep
> At last given back into poetry.
> A verbena in the garden.

All regrets stifled task accepted to recompose
against the anguish from whatever quarter it comes
this unforgotten dream in order to finally leave it
far behind old ceiling covered with birds and
flowers in the taste of the old days and to
progress toward the inaccessible without guide
posts without erasures without notes of any
kind impossible to grasp but there in which
to believe on pain of never dying.[25]

part four

Taking Stock

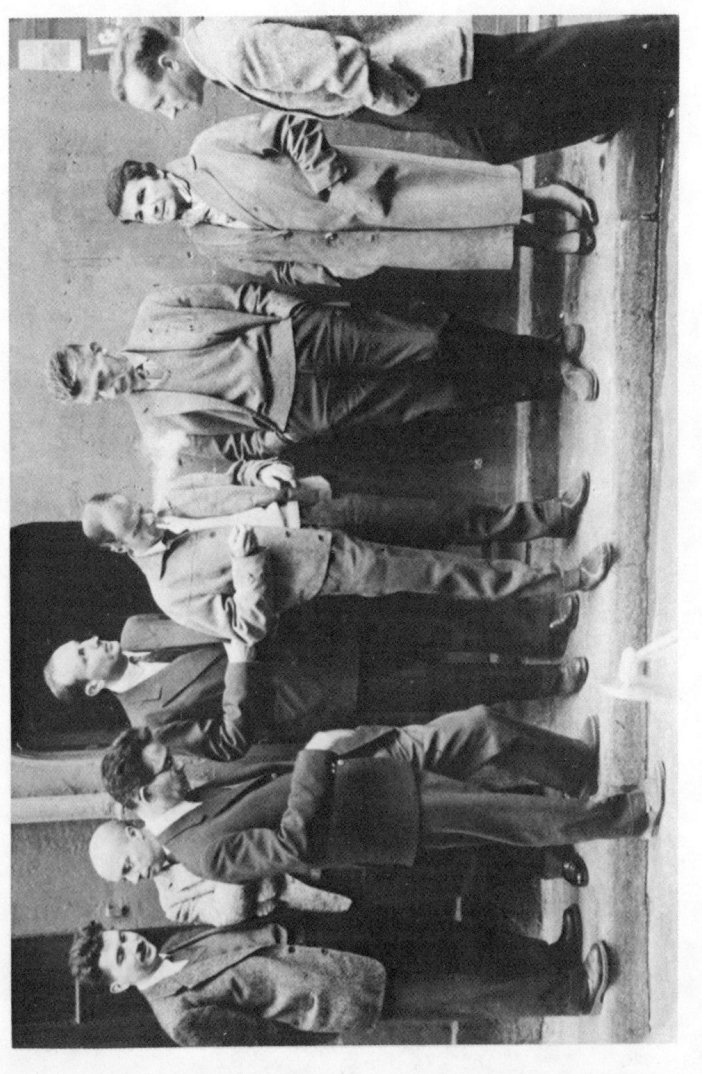

Midnight Novelists, from left to right: Alain Robbe-Grillet, Claude Simon, Claude Mauriac, Jérôme Lindon (publisher), Robert Pinget, Samuel Beckett, Nathalie Sarraute, Claude Ollier. *(Photo courtesy of Les Editions de Minuit)*

8 Pinget, Beckett, and Robbe-Grillet

écureils-bougies

> We accept the fact that what is *literary* (the word has become perjorative) functions like a grid or screen set with bits of different colored glass that fracture our field of vision into tiny assimilable facts.—Robbe-Grillet, *For a New Novel* (translated by Richard Howard)

Creativity's cross currents fascinate Robert Pinget more than the finished writings that emerge from them. Rather than define the central contours of his mock-heroic chronicle, he fills in its corners with details. The composition of each of his books follows the same pattern. Each one brings to life anecdotes that are interesting enough to be placed on the printed page, and yet Pinget aborts all the children of his imaginings well before full term. Eventually, growth leads only to death. His stories acquire credibility and coherence the more their original spontaneity is denied. Because he refuses to elaborate, Pinget is forced back again and again to his point of departure. His fiction is no Stendhalian reflection of the traffic on life's highway; rather, it sets up shop at the intersection of possibilities, where past and present, and conscious and unconscious, intersect, and where words and sounds collide.

Pinget's relentless amputation of the anecdotal forces the reader to consider the author's compulsion to write. The very struggle to fill the page eclipses the success or failure of the inquiry that sets narrative in motion, and Pinget's fiction remains as fluid as the unfinished treatise for which the philosopher Joubert accumulated notes all his life. The ever-expanding chronicle fulfills Maurice Blanchot's prediction in *Le Livre à venir (The Book of the Future)*, to cite a more contemporary analogy:

> [The book of the future should be] a work whose subject is completely different from what it seems, it ought not to bring itself to a conclusion or be able to begin, a work which is, as it were, in default in terms of itself, at a distance from what it expresses and for what it expresses, it flourishes in that distance, deposits itself in it, preserves itself in it and finally disappears in it.[1]

Such observations give the critic pause, however impatient he may be to establish lines of influence or to formulate definitive interpretations. Intentional ambiguities and silences make the saga of Fantoine and Agapa incomplete. So do its missing future chapters. No doubt the as-yet-unwritten last word of the last line will not change that condition or state of mind. But it would be foolhardy to attempt to evaluate its author's place in French fiction precisely before he has finished or abandoned his task. Such an attempt could well trigger a cycle of hypotheses, contradictions, and rectifications similar to M. Levert's drafts!

Unfortunately, the technique of advancing one step forward by taking two steps back lends itself less gracefully to criticism than to fiction. But no work of art exists in a vacuum, and Robert Pinget's novels are profoundly related to our age of dialectical confrontation. They probe the ambient turmoil, anxieties, and relativity of the times. Naturally enough, linkages to other contemporary writers are discernible in Pinget's work—cautionary warnings about premature evaluation notwithstanding. Robbe-Grillet wrote, touching upon a concern that Pinget explores in his work:

> The significations of the world around us are no more than partial, provisional, even contradictory and always contested. How could the work of art claim to illustrate a signification known in advance, whatever it might be? The modern novel, as we said at the start, is an exploration, but an exploration which itself creates its own significations, as it proceeds. Does reality have a meaning? The contemporary artist cannot answer this question: he knows nothing about it. All he can say is that this reality will perhaps have a meaning after he has existed, that is, once the work is brought to its conclusion.
>
> Why regard this as a form of pessimism? In any case, it is the contrary of a renunciation. We no longer believe in the fixed significations, the ready-made meanings which afforded man the old divine order and subsequently the rationalist order of the nineteenth century, but we project onto man all our hopes: it is the forms man creates which can attach meanings to the world.[2]

Germaine Brée and a number of other discerning critics see Pinget as an "experimenter" and have associated him, as such, with the "new novelists" who question the conventions and the clichés of traditional fiction. The "new-novel" group defies French tradition in another way, one that has no bearing upon literary form or technique per se. These writers' shared attitudes unite them without restricting their freedom of action. By refusing to sit at the knee of a "Master," and by exercising restraint in the promulgation of dogma, they have avoided the parochialism that has plagued French literary schools from La Pléiade in the sixteenth century to the Symbolists at the beginning of the twentieth. Schisms, anathemas, and papal decrees remain foreign to their movement, which is consistently more akin to Unitarian tolerance than to Catholic orthodoxy. A photograph of the group gathered in the street in front of the office of their publisher, Les Editions de Minuit, shows a loosely joined circle of free spirits, each author seemingly happy to have had an opportunity to discuss literature in stimulating and congenial company over a pleasant lunch, but each seemingly about to break away and return to the solitude of his own desk, where the serious business of *individual* literary creation will be done. Frozen momentarily in one of the sinuous, continuing motions of a dance, they have nothing of the guerrilla band about them. Even so, the theories they share do represent a more or less consistently revolutionary approach to the novel and make it possible to discuss them as a "school." They all accept, for example, rejection of previously accepted conventions as the necessary first step in searching for new forms (or in highlighting that search), and literary parody therefore plays an important role in much of their work. As Jean-Luc Seylaz observed, more than a decade ago:

> It appears perfectly obvious from here on that Pinget does not worry about or refuses to write traditional novels because the expression of the truth (of his truth) is incompatible with a certain order, a choice, and also a lie of the traditional novel. Just as it is also obvious that the use of the fantastic, which is so frequent in his first works, springs from a polemical intent. As much or more than a positive manifestation of the freedom of the mind and the fertility of a world, as in the work of the Surrealists, [this technique] is in fact a way of denouncing . . . the arbitrariness that reigns in our opinions and in the criteria of traditional literature by playing up an arbitrariness of another kind.[3]

Just as a brisk spring cleaning frees a house of the musty encumbrances of the past and makes it almost seem to breathe, tossing worn-out literary heirlooms on the scrap heap can liberate the artist. Neither act should be written off by the observer as necessarily petulant, sterile, or destructive. Pinget's novels up to *Monsieur Levert* inventory the contents of the house of fiction, take a turn about its vantage points, test the furniture, and gleefully consign great piles of it to the flea market. The surrealist period of clear-eyed and fanciful evaluation makes room for constructive experiments to come. Sweeping away attitudes and techniques imposes itself on any intelligent artist in an age when scientists are discovering more and more every day how precious little we know about our world, and that the continuing process of learning about it begins with eliminating erroneous preconceptions—and new conceptions, too, as these are tested and found wanting. Pinget seeks to reestablish aesthetic norms only after he has cleaned house by means of a Cartesian rejection of everything that he knows only at second hand, whether as the product of habit or of instruction. His narrators know neither where to begin their stories, nor how to tell them, nor, finally, what a "story" is. Their search for answers to these riddles links them to the protagonists of Claude Simon, Nathalie Sarraute, and the other "new novelists."

Reviewers have identified Pinget with the others among the new-novelist group for reasons other than their shared rejection of "accepted" conventions. Affirmations growing out of that rejection by Pinget and certain themes and techniques in his chronicle parallel similar features of Beckett's and Robbe-Grillet's novels. Their texts, like Pinget's, also shanghai the reader on inward-turning voyages of discovery in what Bernard Dort has described as the tendency of these texts to become "their own subject and object, guiding principle and end result, cause and truth." A preoccupation with the penultimate rather than the ultimate dogs the letter drafts, journal entries, and interior monologues of Beckett's and Robbe-Grillet's "creations" (one would hesitate to call them "characters"). Their narratives, like Pinget's, draw the reader into a search that falls short of its goal and joins the novelist, the reader, and the protagonist in a fraternity of frustration. According to Roland Barthes, an encourager and early apologist of Robbe-Grillet:

> The attempt of Robbe-Grillet (and some of his contemporaries, Cayrol and Pinget, for example, although in a quite different mode), aims to establish the surface novel: interiority is put in parentheses, objects, spaces and the circulation of man from one to the others are upgraded to the rank of subjects. The novel becomes the direct experience of man's touching where he lives, without permitting man to lean upon a psychology, a metaphysic or a psychoanalytical construct to come to grips with the objective milieu which he is discovering.[4]

Sadistic beatings and hair-raising chases fill the pages of the collection called *"La Série Noire"* (*"The Black Series,"* a prominent French dime-thriller collection). Would it not then be reasonable to expect to find thrillers published by Les Editions de Minuit ("The Midnight Press")? The detective story does, in fact, fascinate the "new novelists." They have parodied it and turned its conventions inside out in order both to expose its shopworn mechanism and to express their own conception of literature. The spark between Robbe-Grillet and Agatha Christie would seem at first glance to crackle between opposite poles. The linear pattern of Miss Christie's narration squeezes the story in shape as tightly as the corset of a blousy Victorian matron. Miss Christie "asks" questions the answers to which she knows before she begins to write. She leads the detective and the reader (if he is lucky) to discover the killer through a deductive process of intellectual strip-tease. The unmasking of the guilty party carries the conviction of inevitability comparable to the final step in a geometrical proof. The mystery-story writer applies the most pedestrian aspects of the Cartesian method to the activities of discovery and narration. Systematic doubt furrows the detective's brow—but only momentarily. Logic leads him down a familiar, linear path to the revelation of an absolute certainty. Questioning the efficacy of the conscious mind serves to increase the protagonist's confidence in it. The contrast between the thriller and the "new novel" could hardly be more striking. The mystery story dismisses the illogical and the inexplicable as illusions or aberrations; the new novel elevates them to the status of a privileged way of learning. Pinget's protagonists lose themselves in labyrinthine elaborations as the progression from one hypothesis to the next calls into question and even denies the very process that underlies it. Reading *The Inquisitory*, we realize very soon that the direction of the line of questioning slips away from the tenacious interrogator, from his mendacious victim, and, indeed, from the author himself. Questions engender answers that beget questions that elicit other answers. The process accumulates more and more possibilities instead of reducing their number or establishing one of them as more credible than the others. The manuscript of *Clope to the Dossier* ends in chaos and is, quite possibly, jettisoned into a well. The detective in Robbe-Grillet's *The Erasers (Les Gommes)* never realizes that his careful plodding from one point to the next has led him in a circle, and that the noose that he has laboriously been preparing for the murderer is actually tightening slowly around his own neck.

The new novelists have grafted luxuriant and incongruous fruit onto the venerable but tired tree of the mystery story. Focusing the narrative on the quest in and for itself reduces the genre to the novel in its purest form, sheer quest. The discovery of the criminal fades into the background; the reconstruction leading to that discovery counts for much more.

> ... the aim of the true mystery story is to go up in smoke, in the apotheosis of the explanation found at last by the detective. It dissolves in its own success: the criminal is exposed. You know what he's done and how he did it ... If Butor refuses that success for himself, he does not do so from masochism but by necessity. The basic intention [is] to show the larger creative act in process of working itself out behind the piece of fiction elaborated.[5]

The detective story and the new novel complement each other in this regard. In *Le Voyeur (The Voyeur)*, puzzling over whether a mutilation and rape actually took place entices the reader to consider certain more basic questions that are posed. In *Someone*, the search for some lost notes serves as a pretext for a far more widely ranging quest. Pinget's interest in the detective story arises out of his desire to strip the novel to its essentials. The successfully disintegrating inquiries express a thwarted search for a transcendent order. In Robbe-Grillet's *The Erasers*, Wallas tries to solve a crime. In Butor's *Passing Time (L'Emploi du temps)*, Jacques Revel seeks to project penny-dreadful clichés onto the red stained glass and drab streets of Bleston. In Pinget's *Monsieur Levert*, Levert's halting reconstruction of a memory pays his—Pinget's and Levert's—dues in the new novelists' brotherhood of searchers.

If the term "new novelist" includes all writers published by Les Editions de Minuit who reject the old, who experiment with the new, and who frequently tinker with the mystery story, then Robert Pinget certainly qualifies as a member. As we have noted, reviewers were quick to compare his work to the narratives of other new novelists, and he has never denied certain broad affinities between his fiction and theirs. But Bruce Morrissette, in a review of *The Inquisitory*, alertly recognized early on the error of lumping all the new novelists together:

> Here is a surprising book. An astonishing book by a writer whose works although "atypical" compared to those of Robbe-Grillet or other novelists placed in his so-called school, fit nevertheless into the framework of the New Novel.[6]

The implications of Morrissette's remark merit as much attention as the statement itself, for the qualifying words "atypical," "nevertheless," and "so-called school" point to dangers that the critic must bear in mind.

A glance at the "so-called" new novels need not be as perceptive as Mr. Morrissette's excellent study of Robbe-Grillet to reveal that the differences among the authors in the group count for at least as much as the attitudes they hold in common. Initially, critics, reviewers, and book dealers seized upon the term "new novel" in order to arouse the public's curiosity about works that are difficult to read and therefore hard to sell. The term provides a sort of literary umbrella, not a precise definition, that distinguishes the innovators from authors who believe that nothing has superseded the nineteenth-century world view, and from those who concern themselves primarily with furthering social and political goals. It fails to convey, however, the diversity that flourishes within the group. Suggesting one or two reasons why Pinget can be considered a "new novelist" does not, therefore, define his individuality. Pinget himself went so far as to say, in a 1962 interview:

> The label [new novelist] means nothing to me. I cannot imagine what connection could exist between, for example, Robbe-Grillet and myself. Since we all appealed to the taste of our publisher, Jérôme Lindon, one is forced to believe that there is some connection. But what?[7]

What indeed? Ticking off the techniques of Robbe-Grillet, the new novelist most unlike Pinget, and Beckett, the writer closest to him, may help us to obtain, through a process of literary triangulation, a more precise fix on our elusive target.

Pinget and Robbe-Grillet have shown their respect for each other, both personally and professionally, on many occasions. Robbe-Grillet reacted enthusiastically to *Mahu or the Material*, and he helped persuade Pinget to leave Gallimard for Les Editions de Minuit. He supported *The Inquisitory* and *Someone* vigorously in the competition for the Prix Femina, and he helped restore certain understandable but regrettable cuts to the second edition of *Graal Flibuste*. The impulse behind Robbe-Grillet's generous efforts is easily understandable. Passages from *For a New Novel* and a review of *Mahu or the Material* show how clearly he understood the similarities between Pinget's work and his own.

Then (as now) the theme of the quest and the portrayal of the search interested both novelists. The reader of *The Erasers* discovers little by little, as does the reader of Pinget's chronicle, that the attack on the linear way of experiencing reality, not the investigation of a crime, constitutes the novel's real subject. The mental process arising out of the detective's inquiry releases patterns of association that dip and dart about like Mahu's ramblings. The policeman's attempt to follow the conventional logic spoofed in the opening pages of *The Inquisitory* leads him further and further from the truth until, eventually, he himself shoots the victim whose murder he is trying to solve or prevent. The investigation escapes from his control, recalling the roller-coaster plunges of Mahu's stories. Pinget and Robbe-Grillet mock conditioned responses and suggest alternatives through the failures of Wallas and Mahu. Robbe-Grillet heightens the irony of the murder by suggesting that Wallas has unwittingly killed the father for whom he has been searching. Pinget similarly inverts the Ulysses/Telemachus motif in *Monsieur Levert* and *Dead Letter*, where (as in James Joyce's *Ulysses*) the father searches for the son. In *The Voyeur*, Robbe-Grillet describes a frantic attempt to account for a period of elapsed time when he presents a violent act from the criminal's point of view. The dogged single-mindedness of Mathias recalls the cemetery scene in *Monsieur Levert*, in which the narrator tries to "remake a memory for himself." Mathias cannot repress what he has either done or imagined he has done. He strives to build a smooth alibi, a protective wall, a "perfect story without chinks on the exterior," as the narrator of *Recurring Melody* would say. But three new cracks appear for every one he patches. Conflicting hypotheses confuse his account of himself, and his self-defense, for all the good it will do him, might just as well join Clope's manuscript at the bottom of a well.

Ambiguity "resides in the very consciousness of the characters," as Morrissette put it in his study, *The Novels of Robbe-Grillet*. "No exterior 'solution' can highlight the [novel's] framework but [only] the verisimilitude of the states of consciousness evoked, outside of an objective plot." The faceless projections that take the place of what we normally accept as characters in *Jealousy (La Jalousie)* flicker behind the same paradoxical screen of anonymity and familiarity that keeps us at a distance from the inhabitants of Fantoine and Agapa. The descriptions of the blue villa in *La Maison de Rendez-vous* create an atmosphere as opaque as the evocation of the Château de Broy in *The Inquisitory*.

Although Pinget and Robbe-Grillet use distinctly different techniques, Robbe-Grillet's *In the Labyrinth* brings him closest to his associate's characteristic themes and techniques because two simultaneous quests give this *récit* its basic structure. Robbe-Grillet zeroes in on a writer alone in a scantily furnished room and depicts his Mortin-like struggle to peg a story around a wounded soldier's odyssey in an alien city. The novel-within-the-novel articulates a dilemma that Pinget will not resolve. Like M. Levert, the protagonist of *In the Labyrinth* finds the task of drawing a coherent tale out of the chaos of the imagination far more difficult than he had expected it to be. As Mahu, John Porridge, and the narrator of *Graal Flibuste* could have warned him, the conflict between the Dionysian urge for full expression and the Apollonian quest for order produces an incoherence that gradually brings linear exposition to a complete halt: the time sequence blurs; words and phrases acquire multiple values on varying narrative levels touching upon the story, the story about the story, and the story about the story about the story; the purposeful journey turns into a random excursion whose limits are framed by rows of gray city blocks, instead of Graal Flibuste's magic portal. Gradually, the writer loses himself in the labyrinthine suppositions suggested by the novel's title. *In the Labyrinth* leaves the reader with much the same impression of disorientation that we find in M. Levert's description of the flower beds in front of the post office and the formal garden scenes in *Last Year in Marienbad*.

Despite the parallels just cited, however, neither fact nor a close reading of the texts justifies the notion that Pinget or Robbe-Grillet have influenced each other directly. Pinget had never read anything by Robbe-Grillet before completing *Mahu or the Material*, and both men have, in fact, taken antithetical public positions toward their craft. Furthermore, since the techniques and emphases of most of their novels set them quite clearly apart, an outline of their differences must counterbalance the enumeration of their shared preoccupations, if one wishes to situate Pinget's chronicle within the broad range of the "new novelists."

Robbe-Grillet's stance toward his work has been Janus-like from the outset. He obviously relishes the prerogatives of the critic and has footnoted and explained the evolution of his fiction in numerous articles, prefaces, and public lectures, taking pains to elucidate the phenomenological presuppositions that underlie his practice of expressing all impressions, conscious and unconscious, at the same threshold of reality. In short, he has clarified and advanced his theories by commenting upon his work as well as by creating it. The form of his early novels reflects this dual author-critic role. In each case, the text contains at its core a linear plot that the reader, if he is careful and patient enough, can piece together to make some kind of "sense." *The Voyeur* and *Jealousy* deal in blocks of experience comparable to Rorschach ink blots. "You" may well not see in them what "I" see, but we will both see *something*, if we look hard enough, because Robbe-Grillet gives us a standard against which to measure and interpret the protagonist's mental processes. For example, comparing the distortions that Mathias projects on the world and the vision of a "normal" viewer makes it possible for one to reconstruct his "crime," real or imagined, or at least to understand the root of his obsessions. Robbe-Grillet makes us aware of the mystery beneath the surface of the investigation that Wallas conducts by including and accumulating observations that do not fit the detective's hypothesis. And the author's autocritical statements establish the same kind of reference points for his fiction as a whole. He conceives his task as a self-explaining, occasionally didactic search for an aesthetic, a search that the writer-critic clarifies as he moves from one book or one theoretical premise to the next. His novels and his reflections on them give his work as a whole the forward thrust of an ongoing purposeful voyage of discovery.

The Inquisitory and *Clope to the Dossier* also invite the reader to extract a "story" from garbled insinuations and innuendos, but Pinget, reversing Robbe-Grillet's procedure, systematically sabotages the reader's every attempt to do so. What is more, until quite recently he has refrained, for several reasons, from making *any* explanatory statements about his work. The man's modesty and love of privacy equal his boldness as an artist. Besides, his pointing out past successes or failures, or his fixing future goals, could well threaten the very source of his art. Too many confessional interviews might interrupt the rhythm of "yes or no answer," the unconscious, incessant self-questioning that brings his imaginary world to life. A too-thorough analysis of precisely how the creative process functions might channel it into artistically unproductive monologues in little magazines. As things stand, Pinget's rare pronouncements on the problems and trials of writing have a limpid, Delphic quality. He has the gift of treating complex matters in deceptively simple terms. But he prefers to leave monographs to the critics, and is more likely to insert personal comments on his fiction into the novels themselves, where each volume affirms the new by challenging the old; each new book is a fresh departure toward a destination that continues to change en route, adding a new voice to the swelling fugue of tones where no previously heard timbre is repeated.

Whereas Robbe-Grillet's world has at its center images that serve the function of pieces in a puzzle, Pinget's province remains as kaleidoscopic as the verbal associations that set his narratives into motion. The differing emphases accorded to sound and sight also make the work of each author quite distinct. Robbe-Grillet is the principal exponent of what we may call the "school of the eye"; Pinget concentrates on the impressions that vibrate in the outer and inner ears. While the perceptions of Mathias change as his eyes flick from one object to another, the responses of John Porridge, as he labors over his text, are triggered by words and sounds. Pinget follows the echoes of words willy-nilly, delighting in the interplay of the sounds of syllables and sentences that tumble from his pen. For Mahu, and the later avatars:

> the character is born and dies, approaches and withdraws as soon as you lend him a name, he exists only by the sum of his syllables. . . . He starts to write; immediately he asks the fortuitous words that he just traced what he should say [next]. They suggest a path to him, he backs off and prefers to disobey them by disobeying himself . . .[8]

A look at the literary antecedents of both novelists also helps one to put their fictions into perspective. If surrealism had not existed, the "new novelists" would have had to invent it. Their "playing off" of apparently disparate elements has grown out of the basic surrealist strategy of creativity through juxtaposition. Pinget has been known to construct and develop a highly logical line of argument in the first fifty minutes of a lecture, only to suggest in the last ten that the opposite of what he has just said may well also be true—a putting into practice of the Hegelian dialectic that Breton so admired in the first surrealist manifesto. The wild goose chase in *Graal Flibuste* juxtaposes three sets of antithetical forces in the kind of suspension that the surrealists prized so highly. Pinget frequently undermines the foundation of the linear voyage as he reconstructs it, snorting at the limits of cause-and-effect narration by distorting its image in the mirror of parody. Consequently, his narratives portray the imperative necessity of the artist's quest as well as his awareness of the impossibility of accomplishing it. As sense and nonsense collide, the jolting impact of the collision somehow frees the mind from laziness and conditioned passivity, as in the shock of surrealist "black humor" *(comédie noire):*

> If surrealism tends to work toward total disintegration, it is not in order to end at pure nothingness, but for the sake of advancing toward the point which is the synthesis in act of all antimonies.[9]

The new novelists continue to use shock tactics of this kind, but the limited success of their predecessors' experiments has made them more skeptical of the impending inevitability of a transcending synthesis. Nor have they formulated a political program as

Breton's followers did. Nevertheless, their experiments advance the deepest aims of the surrealist revolution by breaking down the barrier between poetry and banality. As Roger Shattuck remarked in his introduction to Maurice Nadeau's *History of Surrealism*, men usually perceive experience in one of two ways:

> On the one hand, a deep-seated continuity appears to link all things and all events and to lend them a significance that provides our wonder . . . On the other hand, we frequently reach the point at which the routine, falsity and injustice of life inflict on us a feeling of senselessness; things happen without any explanation beyond mechanical temporal sequence. In this vision of the world, no meaning attaches to events and things and any effort at insight or sympathy ends in despair . . . Most of us are disposed to regard one of these two directions as the true one, just as in any reciprocal action, like that of a piston or eyes reading a page, or a comb arranging hair, one movement does the work and the return movement prepares a new stroke.[10]

The new novelists draw upon surrealism not only to make felt with equal intensity the movements of construction and destruction, of forward and circular motion; they convey the impression that both contribute to the same process. Robbe-Grillet and Pinget owe more specific debts to Breton's group. Dada painting explores the ambivalence between subjective and objective worlds. Surrealist descriptive technique blurs the limned contours of things, making them either permeable to the unconscious or utterly neutral and alien to it. In a sense, Dali's ominous objects prepared the public for Robbe-Grillet's totemistic world of things. Pinget tipped his hat to the surrealists by lecturing in America on Max Jacob. His choice of subject was significant, for the two are literary brothers in their use of dislocation of language, probing of cliché, mingling of jargons, as well as the derision of linear logic, memory and conventionality.

> Mme. Lemercier's piano has its own story. About twenty years ago, a certain employee of the Public Works Department arrived at the Guichin's place with a piano. It was a piano he took from town to town as fortune changed his domicile, a family piano, an inherited piano, a formidable piece of furniture which one held in great esteem, but hesitated to touch.[11]

The wayward, whimsical clavier from Jacob's *Le Roi de la Boétie* (*The King of Boétia*) would fit quite comfortably beside the ambulatory steeples, arrogant cucumbers, and apocryphal road signs encountered in Pinget's early works, those of his first "manner."

Robbe-Grillet and Pinget draw upon different elements of the surrealist experiment, the one interesting himself primarily in sight, the other in sound. Each has incorporated the aspects of Breton's movement that suit his particular preoccupations. Robbe-Grillet delights in describing what his characters see, not what they know that they "should" see. The optical illusions and visual distortions of surrealist imagery anticipated his technique. Breton described the shock of seeing an apparently guillotined man in a building. In fact, the fellow was simply leaning out of a window. In an optical illusion, the glass seemed momentarily to have severed his torso from the rest of his body. In a similar vein, the imagery of *The Voyeur* hints at parts of the body that arouse Mathias sexually. Though they are never actually described, the reader "sees" them through the recurring patterns and configurations that mark the protagonist's unconscious—circles left by glass bottoms on a table, boat moorings at dockside, loops of string. The suggestivity or utter flatness of things impresses the reader of Robbe-Grillet with the fact that objects can be either vessels full of meaning or completely empty, a phenomenon that recalls the viewer's reaction to one of Marcel Duchamp's "found objects" *(objets trouvés)*.

Pinget, on the other hand, draws upon the discoveries of Breton and the others in the domain of sound. Artaud's description of his approach to language, stated in a prefatory note to *The Surrealist Revolution* (1925), applies quite closely to the verbal associations from which life in Fantoine and Agapa springs and flourishes.

> Dissecting the words we love, without taking care to follow either etymology or agreed on signification, we discover their most hidden virtues and the secret language, canalized by associations of sound, form and ideas. Then language is transformed into an oracle, and we have in it (however tenuous it may be) a thread to guide us in the Babel of our minds.

The surrealists used to play a parlor game called "Le Cadavre exquis" ("The Exquisite Corpse"). It would have amused the retired boarders in *Someone* and fascinated its narrator.[12] Each player writes a word on a piece of paper folded so that no one can read what has been written previously. Unfolding the paper reveals a fresh sentence—not a linear unit of speech communicating purpose or cause and effect, but a random linkage of words and sounds such as, for example, the classic sentence that first resulted from this procedure "The exquisite corpse will drink the new wine" (*"Le cadavre exquis boira le vin nouveau"*). This sort of aleatory prose is not so far afield from the parade of Pinget's words. Like the poet described so long ago by Plato, the Pingetian narrator often teeters on the brink of surrendering completely to the transcription of sounds as the surrealists did when speaking through the device of automatic writing like "drowned men in the open air."

> For all good poets, epic as well as lyric, compose their beautiful poems not by art, but because they are inspired and possessed. And as the Corybantian revellers when they dance are not in their right mind, so the lyric poets are not in their right mind when they are composing their beautiful strains: but when falling under the power of music and metre they are inspired and possessed.[13]

Pinget has described this possession fancifully as a fatal "verbal madness." Total silence, the absence of verbal association, constitutes the other extreme limit within which Pinget operates. He has stated that the surrealist experiments with automatic writing have helped him chart the perilous course between proliferation and the void. Thus the narrator of *Someone* pretends to hunt for a piece of paper while actually intending to set in motion a process of incantatory writing approaching automatism. Yet Pinget relies heavily on the conscious to screen what emerges. In his preface to *The Libera Me Domine*, Pinget wrote of the process of creation that he experiences:

> I am completely conscious of getting the mechanism in motion; I turn on the faucet of the subconscious or let's say of feeling, but it is a voluntary process, almost automatic writing but using the entire consciousness, that is to say, with immediate filtering of the possibles.

The voice in *Someone* hopes to stumble upon a word association that will turn the insignificant upside down, pivot the emptiness of routine, and open the door to an Ali-Baba treasure trove of transcendent purpose; and in doing so he makes an aside that underscores the differing approaches of Pinget and Robbe-Grillet:

> I just made an unintentional play on words, a very feeble one, granted, but involuntary. I often think about that, involuntary plays on words. Perhaps not plays on words but relationships, things that resemble each other, that are very close and you don't know it, no one knows it, and you bring them out like that and a world, an entire universe is revealed to us, gulfs, hells. I'm not taking a very good time to talk about it . . . but you can do all you can to forget it and to think only of the gulfs opened by chance, not gulfs, things you didn't know about that suddenly start to move before our eyes or rather before our ears, but the ears start to see and they see so well that all of life is within reach, all our poor life as infectuous larva which gives us such a hard time is there uncovered, you can take it in the palm of your hand, it was a little bird, nothing at all, how could we have made such a fuss over it. Difficult to talk about that, very difficult. But I notice that it's always words that reveal this kind of thing to me, always involuntary associations, couplings or comparisons, always that. That's why I say that certain things, I just said it, I don't remember what any more, are perhaps only a question of words. (pp. 177–78).

This is not to say that objects and visual elements are lacking in Pinget's fiction. Verbal play often pushes off against specific, imagistic descriptions, and Pinget's narrators frequently interrupt the flow of their hypotheses with lists of the objects around them. Our discussion of *The Inquisitory* has touched on how the world of Fantoine and Agapa often seems to resemble a huge lumber-room crammed with cast-off furniture and hand-me-down works of art—the miscellaneous bric-a-brac of an outgrown culture. Pinget's running catalogs, instead of establishing a link between his work and Robbe-Grillet's, (as one might expect), accentuate their differences. In the chronicle of Fantoine and Agapa, the pleasure of detailed description for its own sake, or a character's desire to catch his breath, motivates the ticking off of objects. Robbe-Grillet's still life of a tomato in *The Erasers (Les Gommes)* serves a quite different purpose: he uses it to express the frustrated wish to describe things "as if I were not there" (as Baudelaire put it). Pinget's objects bewilder the reader because of the rapidity with which he exposes us to them. Robbe-Grillet's frighten and hypnotize because of their alienness, their neutrality. M. Levert uses talismanic objects to conjure up his son, or as full stops in the text to punctuate the articulation of his despair. Thus Pinget describes things repeatedly until they exist as functions of a consciousness tortured by its inability to express itself. The house façade in *Monsieur Levert*, the castle rooms in *The Inquisitory*, and the laundry shed in *Clope to the Dossier* all serve this purpose. Pinget avoids geometrical still lifes in the Robbe-Grillet manner. The differing treatment of objects in the works of the two novelists has even led some critics to suspect Pinget of spoofing Robbe-Grillet's style, as Raymond Queneau did in the following passage from *Blue Flowers (Les Fleurs Bleus)*:

> Behind the counter the owner, inactive, listens to the comments . . . he is wearing a square half-round, oval cloth cap decorated with white ovals. The background is black . . .

Reviewers have gone so far as to suggest that the passages in *The Inquisitory* in which the old servant furnishes the château from memory mock the tedium of Robbe-Grillet's "school of the eye." One even called Pinget's summa "a high-flying prank, a parodic put-on of the techniques of the New Novel," while another interpreted it as "the derision, the destruction of the new novel from within."

Anyone having a full grasp of Pinget's work or a personal acquaintance with the man must know that the idea of Pinget's deliberately making fun of Robbe-Grillet is malicious and unfounded. Pinget is not the sort of writer who makes sport of friends and esteemed colleagues. His considerable talents as a parodist are directed against nineteenth-century conventions that he considers unproductive. To direct them against his fellow "new novelists" would be to dissipate energy to no purpose. Pinget's lists of rooms and their furnishings do not simply take up space, nor can they be simply dismissed as satirical gewgaws. They enable the old man to throw his pursuer off the track and thus to double *The Inquisitory* back upon itself. They form the raw material for the world that the servant draws from the void and move Pinget off dead center. Indeed, the lists and recapitulations of lists express both the necessity and the futility of the creative enterprise itself. Commenting on his evolving technique in *Someone*, Pinget's narrator writes:

> But I don't want to give myself over to inventories any more. I did it before, conscientiously, patiently! In my other exposés to help me to concentrate, hoping *that* would clear out my subconscious, that it would open paths for me toward the essential. Big joke. No damn good. Objects aren't any help when you're aiming at the soul. You might think right at first that they help us find our place, or concentrate. Like hell. You get caught up in the game, you fiddle around with the description, you lick your chops, but in the end you're just as stupid as you were before. (pp. 22–23)

The bitterness of this passage about the cataloguing of objects reflects Pinget's mockery of his own methods; it is not directed at the work of another.

If Robbe-Grillet deliberately squints in order to write "on the level of things," Pinget cocks his ear to the subtlest overtones of language. He listens to echoes whose translation and transcription stretch verbal norms to their limits. It is not surprising, then, that the respective orientations of the two novelists have caused their work to develop in opposite directions—and not only with respect to the printed word. Robbe-Grillet's preoccupation with visual perception has found expression, for example, in the cinema, an interest shared and developed by the surrealists. As Michel Carrouges noted:

> Poetry's great task is not the architecture of the classics, nor the music of the romantics, not the elegant dissonances of cubism, not the pure explosive play of dadaism, but this film projecting from the sunken worlds. In the fabric of earlier poetry, we have sometimes caught flashes of the sparks struck from these worlds and which confer on it a power of charm and incantation; surrealism though is not content with these poetic mines, it wants from them the precious metal in its pure state.[14]

Several directors have proposed making films of Pinget's novels, but he has rejected their overtures—at least so far. To give Sophie Narre a face would be to destroy her, for she is not a person, or even a "character" in the usual sense of the word. She exists as the projection of an inner voice—and so she should remain. Filming Pinget's novels might well stabilize the shifting, protean topography of Pinget's province once and for all. He has offered maplike descriptions before, but only to change them, for Pinget's province is one in which roads are torn up before their completion, a land in which cartography is useless. Perhaps only a cinematic technique in which sound and image contradicted each other would be suitable, and even then the visual element would doubtless come out a poor second. The fact is, Pinget has progressively affirmed, in each of his succeeding books, the primacy of the *aural*.

> Fantoine and Agapa is a world that does not exist yet. A world I have never seen and will never see. To freeze it in an image would be to strip it of all reality. Once frozen it would fly off into the void. The towns float on the whim of words. No image [of it] takes shape in my eyes. It's their continual metamorphosis that participates in their essence. The same is true for the characters. Yet they must remain to support, if not themselves, at least by the presence of their names the language and the tone of the books to come. They exist not as defined but as in the process of definition.[15]

Robbe-Grillet, the *"voyant"* (and sometimes the *"voyeur"*), has probed the possibilities of the subconscious visions of his surrealist predecessors by adding mirror after mirror to his chamber of sadomasochistic curiosities and horrors. Pinget, the sorcerer of words, has chosen to elaborate Henri Michaud's fanciful verbal flights in spoken fugues. Both experiments enrich and complete the "new novel," but the "school of the eye" and the "school of the ear" lead their adepts in quite different directions. Of the dichotomy between the two realms of surrealist research, Carrouges observed:

> There is, in effect, a wide difference between the two kinds of automatism. Visual images are immediately reincorporated into the awareness as soon as they are perceived, while word groups remain sibylline, that is, they do not immediately surrender their image-content to the consciousness, thus allowing the flow toward the consciousness to be maintained.[16]

In much the same way, juxtaposing Pinget's and Robbe-Grillet's novels serves, in the main, to highlight the individuality of each. They are as different as the two kinds of automation referred to by Carrouges.

Comparing the chronicler of Fantoine and Agapa and Samuel Beckett enables one to assess Pinget's place among the "new novelists" from a different perspective, and also to lay to rest the canard that Pinget is, in some way or other, Beckett's disciple. The occasional collaborations of Pinget and Beckett moved in both directions: each has helped the other, in an association of equals. Pinget transposed *All That Fall (Tous ceux qui tombent)* into French for the Irish expatriate, and Beckett translated *La Manivelle* (literally, "The Crank") into English as *The Old Tune*.

The work of Samuel Beckett dominated the literary landscape of the sixties like the monolithic transmitter from another planet in Stanley Kubrick's *2001*. Hermetic, obscure, profoundly significant, Beckett's work still has the critics milling about in awe, like Kubrick's cavemen circling the alien artifact in his film. It is easy to understand why Pinget was at first admired as a follower of Beckett, and why such an evaluation by reviewers who have not studied the work of either author carefully would rankle Pinget, for there has in fact been no "influence" of one upon the other. Pinget had never even read any of Beckett's writing prior to finishing his *Mahu or the Material*, the work that first attracted Beckett's attention to Pinget. Nevertheless, the analogies between the fiction of the two authors, who did in fact collaborate, are numerous and, in some respects, uncanny. For example, while Pinget was in the process of writing Mahu's narrative, Beckett, knowing nothing of Pinget, was stringing out Mahood's hypotheses in *L'Innommable (The Unnamable)*. Mahu and Mahood, neighbors on the roof of the palate, the simultaneous creations of two novelists who had never heard of each other, proved to be literary cousins in more than similarity of name. Olivier Todd perceptively saw the literary kinship when he stated of Pinget: "If he *must* be like anyone, he is more like Beckett than any other member of the group."[17] Without overlapping, the worlds of the two men indubitably touch at many points.

Nostalgia for shattered mental order dominates the voyage of Beckett's tramps. Beckett strives to express the purity of an ideal realm forever lost by accumulating cliches and by exhausting matter—hence the flood of words and the accompanying decomposition of flesh. Decay has a compostlike, life-giving force in Beckett's work, as his creatures' tortured monologues give words new tastes in our mouths, like Chinese century-eggs, which become edible only after a long period of rot. Beckett denies his protagonists the comfort of stories whose orderliness might quiet their torment, and his narrators, like Pinget's protagonists, compulsively continue spinning out their tales regardless of their absurdity. Beckett's voyage and Pinget's quest move from the city *(Malloy, Mahu or the Material)*, to the country *(Molone, Someone)*, and finally to the solitude of the ivory prison of the cranium *(The Unnamable, The Libera Me Domine, Recurring Melody)*. As Raymond Federman remarked, in his study of Beckett's *Journey to Chaos:*

> These wandering derelicts have been indeed expelled from the world of man and are now condemned to exist in the illusory world of fiction, whose rules are not necessarily rational. While trying to adapt to this unfamiliar and deceptive condition, they seek to capture memories of their past, sometimes to invent a past for themselves, to rationalize their irrational predicament, and even to plan a possible return to the world of men—that is, to the world of conventional fiction. They soon realize, however, that they no longer function as human beings, or as traditional heroes; they have become puppets superimposed on a realistic setting with which their absurd fictional existence is incompatible. . . . The further one progresses into Beckett's universe, the more independent the characters become, and the more irresponsible, since they are given control of their own fictitious existences and are no longer subjected to reality and realism. As they achieve the status of creator-heroes, speaking for themselves in the first person, these outcasts turn against the creator who originally forced them into fiction. Yet even though they appear to control the world in which they exist, they cannot escape the hidden creator who drives them on, shapes them into further illusions, tortures them into further miseries, all the while watching from the corner of the eye "la main qui écrit, toute brouillée par—par le contraire de l'éloignement" *(Textes pour rien,* p. 161).[18]

The narrowing of perspective in Beckett's and Pinget's works pits verbal associations at the very apex of their respective styles. Beckett's derelicts string syllables and sentences together in order to build (like M. Levert) an airy barricade against death or to salvage their lives from emptiness (like the old-timer in *The Old Tune*). The narrator of one of Beckett's *Stories and Texts for Nothing (Nouvelles et textes pour rien)* mutters:

> I suppose it is one, if you like, if you really like. I don't say no this evening. You have to have them, it seems, once the word exists, don't need a story, a story isn't 'de rigueur,' nothing but a life, that's where I was wrong, one of the places, having wanted a story for myself when life alone suffices.[19]

In Pinget's and Beckett's works, language's function reflects its slap-dash quirkiness. Flexible and inadequate associations propel Beckett's nihilistic odyssey and bring it up short, reminding the reader of the impossibility of the speaker's quest. Language's irreducible ambiguity forms the basis of the "characters' " very being and endows their flounderings with a tragicomic sense of urgency. Thus Vladimir, Estragon, and *The Inquisitory*'s old servant hang over the abyss of silence on a thread of words.

Pinget and Beckett both describe the creative act as a continuing process of innovation, a repeatedly frustrated search in which language plays a vital role. Beckett, like Pinget, denies in the same breath what he has just asserted. His narratives totter along on stilts of affirmation and negation, and the summary that the central character of *The Unnameable* gives his monologue would apply equally well to Pinget's latest novels:

> What do you expect, they don't know either, who they are, where they are, what they are doing, or why things go so badly, so abominably badly. So they build scaffolds of hypotheses which collapse on top of each other, it's human, a lobster would not be capable of as much.[20]

Comparison of the recurring structural patterns of the two novelists can be carried a step further: their elaboration of suppositions accelerates the material and intellectual deterioration that their protagonists would seek to forget or avoid, and in both cases, the protagonists' physical contortions mime acute verbal and mental convulsions. When their means of locomotion break down, Beckett's characters slow to a crawl, their legs stiffen and atrophy, eliminating linear physical mobility. Like the narrator of *Someone*, they forget what they are seeking, and like this same narrator and the travellers in *Graal Flibuste*, they renew their objective as they approach it. In the end, the final paralysis of *The Libera Me Domine* and *Recurring Melody* sets in. The stories that the characters murmur "sotto voce" to keep up their courage peter out, repeat themselves, or swallow themselves whole, leaving the crooning voices as frighteningly alone as Clope. Molloy's Cartesian exposition on how to carry sixteen pebbles in his pockets so he can suck them in rotation leads to the same blank impasse as Levert's meticulous manipulations of the past. Both Pinget and Beckett deal with:

> series of objects or conversational building blocks, permutations of linguistic elements or combinations of possibles that, obeying the rules of algebra or exhausting the resources of logic, make up a huge game of hide-and-seek or loser-take-all between the person and the real in which the person flounders.[21]

Like the chapters of Pinget's chronicle, Beckett's monologues bog down. The syllables of the names of Beckett's narrators echo from one novel to the next, producing the impression of previous acquaintance that Pinget achieves by continuing to change the description of his imaginary province. Both Pinget and Beckett sketch an expressionistic landscape that is, paradoxically, disturbingly "other" and convincingly "real" at the same time. Molloy and Brindon's master try to tame the countryside through which they are wandering by naming its prominent features, but to no avail. Molloy's blasphemous appellations serve only to betray his fear, and the traveller's Michelin guide to the land of Graal Flibuste leads him and the reader nowhere. Place names recur, however, and their fragile links of continuity make Pinget's and Beckett's *récits* episodes in a journey that eventually calls into question both the episodes and the "reality" that shapes them. As Bernard Pingaud remarks in his afterword to *Molloy:*

> To read *Molloy*, or *Malone*, or the *Unnamable*, is to read the same book; but it is also to read no book at all, for the voice began speaking before, it will continue later: there is no reason why it

should be silent, and the words which we pick up are only fragments of an immense discourse, in the last analysis without an object . . . [22]

The presence of the speaker gradually overshadows all other concerns, and the depiction of the dilemma of the creative act gains in starkness and power.

We have suggested that the contrast between the works of Pinget and Robbe-Grillet is a matter of qualitative differences. What sets Pinget's novels apart from Beckett's is a matter of emphasis. Both novelists share an interest in language and the desire to stretch it and experiment with it. Whereas Beckett's narratives break the more obviously with the past, the saga of Fantoine and Agapa faces in two directions. While Pinget accompanies his attempt to reduce the novel to its essence with a running commentary on the very conventions that he is in the process of modifying or rejecting, Beckett's prose carries less of this reflective, often-fascinating subconversation with the reader. Don Quixote's shadow hovers over Pinget's mock-epic novels, as his narrators strive to:

> copy the old *in order* to install the new, to imitate worn out forms, not to declare their everlasting value, but to give them the most scrupulous examination possible, to weigh them against the rights, fragile, contested and contestable of the new which he is in the process of creating.[23]

Consequently, Pinget's characters frequently glance back at previously accepted modes of expression even as they try to find alternatives to them. Beckett's protagonists, on the other hand, stumble along in a world of fiction devoid of familiar literary landmarks.

Though the literary approaches of the two authors are not radically different, their differences have had significant impact on the popularity of their novels. Beckett's work has been showered with (probably unwelcome) attention; Pinget's has been relatively neglected until now. The reaction of his contemporaries furnishes a most unreliable indication of a writer's ultimate value, but in Pinget's case the incomprehension of normally perceptive reviewers is particularly worth noting, since it results from his treatment of the novel, the subject of this study. Pinget's paradoxical stance toward literary conventions seems to baffle many of his readers, and yet his very ambivalence in this regard constitutes one of his most valuable contributions to the novel. His fiction records a self-conscious search for an aesthetic and builds—thanks to the alternation between parody and invention, the banal and the romanesque—a precious bridge between old forms and new.

Critics have never doubted where to "place" Beckett on the literary horizon: his bold experiments have put him in the forefront of the avant garde, among the *"franc-tireurs"* ("the snipers" or "free-lancers"). Although Pinget's narrators use the first person, the protagonists of Beckett's more recent texts do not. A distinct tone always emerges from the static of Pinget's tangled stories, a tone differing from the timbre of previous speakers and from that of speakers to come, as in the succession of impressionistic audial sketches in *Around Mortin*. Beckett's novels, in contrast, depict the painfully meticulous refinement of the author's search for a single authentic voice, a voice that is the same from novel to novel, though its garrulousness is punctuated by increasingly long and agonizing pauses. As his prose has moved from the elaboration of a complex love triangle *(Murphy)* to disconnected shreds of coherent discourse *(Nouvelles et textes pour rien)*, Beckett has pushed communication to the very edge of silence. Beckett's rigorous method gives his novels a certain intensity that Pinget's early fiction may seem to lack. But Pinget does not set out to develop varying tones out of boredom. Nor does Beckett's speliological descent into the inner ear deter Pinget from plumbing the depths of Beckett's audial world in his own way, and it would seem a fair assessment to state that if Beckett's austere *continuo* builds suspense, Pinget's *oratorio*, in charting a similar quest, achieves a singing wistfulness of words.

As Beckett's novels deal almost exclusively with discovering new modes of expression, he devotes less time and space than Pinget to caricaturing and exploding outmoded forms. Beckett's characteristic distortion through irony is so obvious that his satiric intention is almost unmistakable. In contrast, Pinget works in a haze of ambiguity. Wrecked, never-written novels litter his books. Less oblique than Pinget, Beckett confronts the reader directly with his narrator's efforts to give significance to experience by wrestling with words.

Pinget prefers to tantalize the reader with misleading hints of a linear plot. Pinget has described his books as:

> an amalgam of stories that get tangled up in each other and confuse each other, an amalgam from which at first a sort of middle level truth comes out that the reader has trouble localizing but that does not upset him too much. The reader's mind latches onto several key words involuntarily; words like "forest," "house," "murder," "rape," not suspecting that I am leading him somewhere else by the trick of making him think that he recognizes situations that he already knows. At first, *Graal Flibuste* seems to be a disorderly fantasy, *M Levert* an unexplained but real drama, *Recurring Melody* a slightly tedious but acceptable obsession. This level of median psychology permits me to insinuate between the lines things I prefer not to formulate clearly. And anyway, why should the reader benefit from a clarity that the author does not have at his command [when] at work?[24]

Pinget chooses, then, to let the reader realize, little by little, that the novel does not really concern itself with the articulation of a coherent story but is directed toward the creative searching that the inquiry sets in motion. As we have seen, recurring characters and place names extend Pinget's strategy from novel to novel. He evokes a world that is strange and yet somehow familiar by maintaining a fine degree of continuity and by constantly adding new material. The cumulative enumeration of his imaginary province serves as an elaborate lure, for in his fiction, Pinget repeats just enough to encourage the reader who hopes to get a clearer notion of the layout of his world to keep turning the pages. As the reader does so, "facts" that seemed hard and fast transform themselves into rubbery suppositions, and preliminary observations on which he based subsequent conclusions buckle under the weight of accumulating contradictions. Finally, the pseudo-chronicle's false bottom collapses, and the reader finds himself in the world of poetry—the world in which objective truth counts for far less than the *quest* for truth.

9 Conclusion

> The house of fiction has in short not one window but a million—a number of windows not to be reckoned rather; every one of which has been pierced, or is still pierceable in its vast front by the need of individual vision. . . . They are but windows at the best, mere holes in a dead wall, disconnected; perched aloft; they are not hinged doors opening straight upon life.—Henry James, *Preface to Portrait of a Lady*

> We were all crouched in a small room against the comforting back wall, awaiting the millennium which had been gathering impetus since Adam and Eve. Up there was a universe, and down here would be a small strip of man come and gone, created, taught, redeemed, and gathered up in a bright twinkling, like a sprinkling of confetti torn from colored papers, tossed from windows, and swept from the streets by morning.
> The Darwinian revolution knocked out the back wall, revealing eerie lighted landscapes as far back as we can see. Almost at once, Albert Einstein and astronomers with reflector telescopes and radio telescopes knocked out the other walls and the ceiling, leaving us sunlit, exposed, and drifting—leaving us puckers, albeit evolving puckers, on the inbound curve of spacetime.—Anne Dillard, "Innocence In The Gallapagos," *Harper's* (May, 1975)

Marshall Mcluhan has endorsed a notion that the magazine *House Beautiful* has (and had) been preaching for years—that a man sees his house as an extension of himself. Henry James' artists inhabit a world of philosophically finite, prescribed phenomena. They gaze out at a single garden from the house of fiction they inhabit together. Their observations of activity in the garden may differ, but only because the windows are of different sizes and the angle of observation varies. In the Jamesian scheme of things, novelists may react to reality in many ways, but their broad experience of life is shared. Some writers are more perceptive than others and see the garden in greater detail and with greater precision than others. But to look out and see a unicorn munching on a rose, like the man in James Thurber's fable, would clearly have put the Victorian novelist beyond the pale as credible spectator of the real world.

In *The Inquisitory*, Pinget, like Henry James, uses a dwelling as a metaphor for the act of perception. Before erecting the Château de Broy, however, Pinget had gleefully torn up the Victorian novel's floor of reasoned discourse, dismantled its gables of authorial omniscience, and smashed its gingerbread trim of plot. The Château de Broy's corridors afford the reader glimpses into closed-off chambers of perception: the walls twist and curve, masking hidden stairways; the floors and ceilings give way, embracing the everyday and the imaginary. Thus learning is presented as a cyclical, ever-new, and ongoing activity.

The experience that James would communicate must pass through the same filtering agents that Pinget struggles to remove. Sense impressions go first through the censor of the conscious mind and then flow out through a screen of conventionalized forms as a "work of art." For Pinget, there are as many gardens as there are spectators, and so his work strives to interpose a minimum number of walls between reader and writer. Working at the outer limits of rationality, Pinget refuses to speak through a closed window. He tries rather to break through, to make the lines of words on the page as permeable as the castle walls, so that the reader will not simply understand his vision but will participate in its articulation.

Pinget's vision is not the only vision, of course, and his particular narrative approach does not invalidate the more traditional attitude toward the relationship of author and reader. But he is a remarkably honest, unflinching explorer of his own skeptical view of life, which he conveys through written commentary as fragmented and inconsecutive as his own version of life's non sequiturs. The wit, the flashes of recognition, the essential consistency (despite all the whimsical aberrations) of his wanderings in language all serve to make him a serious and meaningful innovator in the world of fiction in our fluid, indeed antirational, late twentieth century.

Pinget's fiction mirrors change and flux—change from the surrealist tales to the satiric *"récits"* and the fuguelike recent works, flux in the return of familiar voices. What will come next from his pen?

CONCLUSION

The solitary act of facing the blank page having become almost too much to bear, Pinget has recently turned again to theater with renewed interest. Playwriting means weaving more than one voice into dialogue. Writing itself, however, remains a daily activity, a need keenly felt by Pinget. Whatever is to come, Pinget's work will surely advance a double quest: a voyaging toward the unknown and a searching for self-expression.

And the author, like the narrator of *Someone,* is less alone than he thinks. The technique of shifting from realistic description to poetic experimentation makes the relationship between Pinget and his reader uncommonly subtle and complex. Like a skilled wrestler, Pinget turns to his own purpose the thrust of his reader's conditioned responses to the novel. He entices him into his world with the hint of a conventional story. Then he shifts with the rapidity of a well-executed switching maneuver, and the reader finds himself upside down. What is more, through the patterned response of his expectations, the reader has participated in the process in spite of himself. Stephen Bann, when writing of Pinget's work, dusted off the learned word "anagogical," which a dictionary defines as "having a spiritual meaning or sense referring to heavenly life, relating to or arising from the striving of inner psychic forces toward progressive or lofty ideals, relating to the psychotherapeutic interpretation of dreams and with emphasis on anagogic striving." In Pinget's case, all three meanings apply, for as Mr. Bann remarked:

> Pinget differs from Beckett in being concerned with a much fuller range of anagogical effects. At one level his works could be regarded as a series of essays in the implications of authorship. He differs from Beckett in presenting in his work not only the solipsistic personality of the author, but also the full range of human relationships open to him by virtue of his relationship to his audience.[1]

Unfortunately for Pinget, too many of his readers have failed to understand the purpose behind his elaborate parodies, and too many reviewers have missed the point of his having satirized their stereotyped, rigid manner of thinking, reading, and searching. Until now, the author's joke has backfired to such an extent that some critics have praised his chronicle for the wrong reasons. A discouraging number of readers have blandly accepted Pinget's chronicle at face value. Reviewers have praised the "neorealistic" portrayal of provincial life in *The Inquisitory* and the photographic accuracy of detail in the description of the boarding house in *Someone*. Such critics have complained about the "contradictions," which they cannot understand since they refuse to accept, or are unable to recognize or understand, Pinget's objectives—which is to say, the works themselves. Perhaps the present study will serve to clarify things for them.

As we have seen, Pinget's fiction has often been neglected, despite Robbe-Grillet's and Beckett's praise, because it seems to hesitate between accepting and rejecting traditional conventions. But *The Libera Me Domine, Recurring Melody, Fable,* and *This Voice* give ample proof that, after having carefully cleared the ground, Pinget has found a new and innovative idiom. His work is only now beginning to find its public. One may hope that his continuing quest will attract the attention it deserves. Much remains to be done—more close word-by-word studies such as Duvert's analysis of the opening of *The Libera Me Domine*, for example, and further exploration of Pinget's affinities to Max Jacob, the surrealists, and Queneau. If the present introduction to his work helps to encourage such projects, it will have served its principal purpose.

Paradoxically, the very ambivalence that has kept Pinget's work from reaching a wide audience constitutes one of his chronicle's most rewarding features. Pinget's novels *must* interest the adventurous general reader, the critic, and the literary historian precisely because he uses the "well-made" novel as a point of departure toward something new. The most dynamic and interesting currents of contemporary French fiction run through Pinget's turbulent prose. His work incorporates and juxtaposes the rejection of a well-established tradition of expression and the groping search for a new mode of communication. And it does so with both arresting urgency and keen wit. French writers tend to work very tightly within their own literary heritage. Turning his back on the past is therefore an anguishing decision for a French writer, and this bold act of renunciation gives Pinget's novels an atmosphere of tension. On the more individual level, French novelists often circle in on their target in concentric circles like an onion. They zero in on the secret garden of their own reality or their own expressivity with dread and anticipation. Anticipation of the flowers they may find. Dread that the garden door will

CONCLUSION

open onto nothing. The anguish of Pinget's latest works indicates clearly that Pinget has thrown himself into the game, unreservedly, risking all.

But Pinget's quest is unlikely to end in failure, for it shows how the novel flows on, renewing itself by challenging limits. Pinget's mock epic, with each component a fleeting moment in a broader, shifting perception, gives tonic proof that the novel remains vital. For life entails change, and only that which is alive can die.

AFTERWORD

Several of Pinget's recent and ongoing projects have been completed at this writing, and they are certainly worth mentioning, if only in passing. *Dictation (Dictée)* a sixteen-page radio play, was performed on the French National Radio under the direction of Georges Peyrou on July 10, 1975. In this work Pinget once again uses the radio medium with great success to continue his amusing yet troubling distortion of words and phrases. The play begins with a boss dictating to his secretary a somewhat garbled story about an old man who has been assaulted and robbed. When her employer gives her the signal by impatiently snapping his fingers, the secretary reads back bits and pieces of his monologue. In no time at all an antiphonal series of exposition and repetition has been set in motion recalling the variations and repeats that characterize *Fable* and *This Voice*. The alleged "investigation" soon becomes bogged down in a quagmire of clichés and non sequiturs and unfolds as a nonsensical syllogism without a conclusion. The nameless employer takes comfort in the "paradise of endless repetition" that protects him from silence, and by extension, from death. But the secretary tires of going over the same ground and storms out, slamming the door behind her. In a clever closing touch, the fragility of language as a magic charm against death is exposed when the employer's final words repeat themselves as on a broken record. In other words, the conversation that the listener was envisaging as "live" is in fact the nonlive recording of a dictation session. In this short piece Pinget conveys the sporadic nature of verbal communication with an effective economy of means.

With *The Month of August (Le Mois d' août)*, which appeared in *Minuit* in March, 1975, Pinget circles back over familiar ground while maintaining the stylistic experimentation with repetition and words as sound that characterize his most recent manner. Although not yet available in English translation, this short piece would serve as an excellent introduction to his work, combining as it does, the old and the new.

In this forty-page meditation, redolent of summer smells and sounds in the countryside, a Mr. Dream (M. Songe) allows his mind to wander as he waters his vegetable garden, a task whose major purpose seems to be to trigger a circular swirl of daydreams. Faced with the necessity of making a major change in his life, Mr. Dream finds himself caught in memories that end in the impasse of the self caught in a certain place and time and yet wandering through an association of words and images. The landscapes around Fantoine and Agapa, Crachon and Sirancy are filled in a little further, as August highlights their natural beauty and attracts tourists to their mountains and beaches. Mr. Chinze has retired long ago and Miaille continues to eke out a living. Mr. Dream spends his time writing a letter to his absent niece, Siso, jotting down impressions in his exercise book, or carrying on a running battle with his maid, Sosie.

As the name "Sosie" ("Twin") also suggests the juggling of syllables between Sosie and Siso, the two women are presented as blurred images in the dreamer's eye and might as well be indistinguishable. They merely provide the narrator with a wall against which he bounces a ball of words. The ensuing monologue moves along briskly from one subject to another, using a high percentage of short sentences and one-sentence paragraphs. The tone recalls the friendly, relaxed asides of the anonymous narrator of *Someone*, but the presence of the countryside makes itself felt even more fully. Pinget succeeds in communicating a sense of nature without recourse to lyrical descriptions or exhaustive catalogs. The land of Fantoine and Agapa comes across not as a pastoral, Rousseauesque utopia but as a mysterious kingdom, ineffably beautiful, unspeakably gross, inutterably "other"—as strange and as familiar as the old woman from the sanatorium for the blind who parades by the house each day with her hair in curlers, preparing herself for the coiffure that neither she nor her fellow sufferers will ever see.

Throughout his meditation out loud Mr. Dream seeks to escape ("To get out of one impasse one must take another"), only to discover, as so many of Pinget's narrators have before him, that if a dramatic exit does exist, it can be nowhere other than in words themselves. And although the miraculous transformation has not yet taken place as the text draws to a close, it is obvious that the search will continue through the elusive and yet life-giving medium of language.

Three radio plays—*"The Man Who Returned from the Dead"* (*"Le Rescapé,"* alternate title, *"Le Chrysanthème"*), *"Dictation"* (*"La Dictée"*), and *"Crazy Notion"* (*"Lubie"*)—await publication by Minuit. Experimenting in yet another medium, Pinget has completed two thirds of a film scenario entitled *"Travel Far" ("Voyager Loin")* in which characteristically whimsical voyagers set off in a broken-down taxi (compare the tired jitney in *Baga*).

True to his métier, Pinget is at work on another novel, which he described in a recent interview with this writer as follows:

> I am currently working on a novel and would like to make it the conclusion of my work from the point of view of technique and ideology.
>
> It happens in fact that that work spread out over some thirty years follows a meaningful progression that I've become aware of as it unfolded. It would be a matter of fixing its objective, which will not go along without scrupulous attention as the knowns of the unconscious, like those of the conscious, ask to be interpreted and channeled, considering the very extensive field that they explore or try to explore.

And so, the novelist's quest goes on.

NOTES

Introduction

1. Robert Pinget, *Baga* (Paris: Les Editions de Minuit, 1958), pp. 66–67.
2. Olivier de Magny, "Robert Pinget ou le palimpseste", Postface to *Graal Flibuste* (Paris: Union Genérale d'Editions, Le Monde en 10/18, 1963).
3. Early in the twentieth century André Gide went to some pains to make a distinction between the novel *(le roman)* and the narrative *(le récit)*.
    "It wasn't only a question of tone and style. In 1911 Gide stopped using the term 'novels' that he had given to *The Immoralist* and *Straight Is the Gate*. The text of the dedicatory letter from *Lafcadio's Adventures* to Jacques Copeau is well-known in this regard:
    " 'Why am I entitling this book a *sotie?* And why *récits* for the three preceding ones? It is to make it clear that they are not novels properly speaking . . .
    " '*Récits* and *soties* . . . it seems to me that until now I have written only *ironic* (or critical books if you wish), and this latest is no doubt one of them.' "
    See Claude Martin. *André Gide. La Symphonie pastorale* (Paris: *Les Lettres modernes*, 1970, p. xxii).
    Since Gide, French criticism makes a distinction between the *roman*, which presents a global, syncretic overview of life through many characters, and the *récit*, which describes life ironically through the restricted vision of a single character. The distinction tends to blur somewhat in Pinget's work for reasons that will be self-evident. But generally the shorter pieces like *Clope to the Dossier* and *Fable* would best qualify as *récits* and longer works like *The Inquisitory* or *Someone* as novels. In any case, in order to avoid confusion that might arise in English between the use of "narrative" as both a noun and an adjective, the French term *récit* will be used when appropriate.
4. Works by Pinget in English translation (both extant and in progress) include the following titles available in the British Isles:
    Mahu or the Material [*Mahu ou le matériau*], trans. Alan Sheridan-Smith. London: John Calder, 1967.
    Baga [*Baga*], trans. J. Stevenson. London: John Calder, 1967.
    No Answer. [*Le Fiston*], trans. Richard Coe. London: John Calder, 1976; American distribution by Grove Press under the title *Monsieur Levert*, translation by Richard Howard.
    The Inquisitory [*L'Inquisitoire*], trans. Donald Watson. London: Calder

& Boyars 1966. American distribution through Grove Press, New York.

The Libera Me Domine [*Le Libera*], trans. Barbara Wright. London: John Calder, 1972.

La Manivelle [*The Old Tune*]. Bilingual edition of *La Manivelle* with English version by Samuel Beckett on interfacing pages. Paris: Les Editions de Minuit, 1960.

The Old Tune [*La Manivelle*]. Bilingual edition of *La Manivelle* with English trans. by Samuel Beckett on interfacing pages. London: Calder & Boyars, New Writers Series, no. 2, 1964.

Plays Vol. I. *The Old Tune* [*La Manivelle*] *Dead Letter* [*Lettre Morte*] *Clope* [*Clope au dossier*], trans. Barbara Bray. London: John Calder, 1964.

Plays Vol. II. *Architruc* [*Architruc*] *About Mortin* [*Autour de Mortin*] *The Hypothesis* [*L'Hypothèse*], trans. Barbara Bray. London: Calder & Boyars, 1967.

Recurring Melody. [*Passacaille*] and *Fable* [*Fable*] are at this writing slated to appear through Calder & Boyars.

5. Pinget texts currently available in the United States include: *L'Hypothèse* in Volume 2, *Le Théâtre des enfers* from the anthology, *Panorama du Théâtre*, ed. Jacques Benay and Reinhard Kuhn. New York: Appleton Century Crofts, 1967.

The Inquisitory [*L'Inquisitoire*], trans. Donald Watson. New York: Grove Press, 1966.

Monsieur Levert [*Le Fiston*], trans. Richard Howard. New York: Grove Press, 1961.

Somebody (excerpts) in *French Writing Today*, ed. Simon W. Taylor. New York: Grove Press, 1969.

Plays, Vol. 2. *Architruc, The Hypothesis* [*L'Hypothèse*], *In Connection with Mortin* [*Autour de Mortin*], trans. Barbara Bray, ed. Simon W. Tayor. *The Libera Me Domine*, translation Barbara Bray, is scheduled to appear through the Red Dust Press, New York.

In this study of Pinget, I have used available English translations of the texts accessible to me, indicating their source in the notes. Where no translations were available to me, I have used my own. In this regard, I am deeply indebted to Calder & Boyars for letting me use my own translations of *Baga* and for authorization to quote from the Bray translation of *The Hypothesis* [*L'Hypothèse*] and the Sheridan-Smith translation of *Mahu or the Material* [*Mahu ou le Matériau*]; to Grove Press for permission to use the Watson translation of *The Inquisitory* [*L'Inquisitoire*] and the Howard translation of *Monsieur Levert* [*Le Fiston*]; to The Red Dust Press for permission to quote from the Wright translation of

Le Libera, and to Les Editions de Minuit to use my translations of the remaining Pinget texts which have not yet appeared in English, i.e. *Between Fantoine And Agapa* [*Entre Fantoine et Agapa*], *The Fox And the Compass* [*Le Renard et la boussole*], *Graal Flibuste*, *Clope to the Dossier* [*Clope au dossier*] *Paralchemy* [*Paralchimie*], *Someone* [*Quelqu'un*], *Recurring Melody* [*Passacaille*], *Fable*, *Identity* [*Identité*] and *This Voice* [*Cette Voix*].

6. Pierre Fisson, "Pierre Fisson mène l'enquête sur le roman," *Le Figaro Littéraire*, 858 (Sept. 29, 1962), p. 3.
7. For further elucidation of division into cycles see Jean Roudaut, "Robert Pinget et la boussole," *Critique*, Paris, no. 303/304 (September 1972), pp. 730–31:

"It would be possible to divide Pinget's work into 'cycles':—the 'mystical' cycle with *The Fox And the Compass, Graal Flibuste, Baga*, those novels apparently remain the farthest removed from the daily routine of the inhabitants of Fantoine and Agapa (but even *Séraphitus Séraphita* and *Louis Lambert* participate in the *Comédie humaine*, however obliquely). In the voyage narratives, the story of a King searching for his empire, each is about conquering a center, a habitable place where the being might coincide with itself. And that [theme] which appears beginning with the very first books will be the subject of the latest one to date, *Fable*. The 'realistic' cycle would include *Monsieur Levert, Clope to the Dossier, The Inquisitory, Someone*, and *The Libera Me Domine*. The use of the adjective 'realistic' is no more justified really than that of 'mystical,' for the notion of an objective and autonomous reality becomes dissolved in the cycle. Images and phantasms are the narrative's only material. *Recurring Melody* and *Fable* seem to me to be the first elements of a new 'mythological' cycle. It is a cycle in which interplay along with the essential material of the primordial images of the mob, of murder and castration and desire the 'or that . . . , or that' structure used in *The Libera Me Domine*. We have entered a chamber of mirrors.

"These three pseudo-cycles are far from being mutually independent of each other. If the characters move about, the narrative systems also shift from one novel to the other. The technique of questioning as the source of discourse does not exist exclusively in *The Inquisitory*, nor is amplification to be found only in *The Libera Me Domine*, or repetition only in *Fable*. The novels give value to previously used narrative elements one after the other, as if it were necessary at a certain moment to prove them out, to give them a try, or to let them peter out into nothing. In Pinget's work there is a sort of transposition at the level of narrative modes, a transposition of the moral temptations of *Don Quixote* (the book which, along with the Bible, is the most closely related to Pinget's work). Instead of being classified by themes, the novels could well be classed according to the rhetorical devices used."

Chapter 1

1. Tony Duvert. "La Parole et la fiction," *Critique*, 252 (May, 1968), p. 447.
2. N. J. Berrill, *Man's Emerging Mind* (New York: Dodd, Mead, 1955).
3. " . . . the great Danish physicist Niels Bohr found in the quantum theory when it was developed thirty years ago this remarkable trait: it is consistent with describing an atomic system, only much less completely than we can describe large-scale objects. We have a certain choice as to which traits of the atomic system we wish to study and measure and which to let go; but we have not the option of doing them all . . . there are mutually exclusive ways of using our words, our minds, our souls, any one of which is open to us, but which cannot be combined." J. R. Oppenheimer, quoted in W. H. Auden's *A Certain World* (New York: Viking Press, 1970), pp. 322–23.
4. Except where specified, translations into English will be my own. (See Introduction, Footnote #4). Word play often shoulders aside literal meanings in Pinget's work, so rather wide latitude has been taken in some of the transpositions from French to English. Wherever verbal ambiguity makes translations particularly treacherous, English and French will run (hopefully in harness) side-by-side.
5. Robert Pinget, *Entre Fantoine et Agapa* (Paris: Les Editions de Minuit, 1966), p. 7. The original edition of *Between Fantoine and Agapa (Entre Fantoine et Agapa)* published by La Tour du Feu in 1951 contains some fragments later deleted, notably a mock film scenario. When revising the book for the 1966 edition Pinget wisely scrapped it. The 1966 Editions de Minuit edition may be considered as definitive and all references will be made to it.
6. Ibid., p. 7.
7. Lewis Carroll, *Through the Looking Glass* (New York: Peter Pauper Press, 1930), p. 30.
8. *Entre Fantoine et Agapa*, p. 30.
9. Ibid., p. 34.
10. Ibid., p. 35.
11. Ibid., pp. 23–25.
12. Ibid., p. 94.
13. Ibid., p. 10. This statement may be a parodic allusion to Sartre's treatment of multiple consciousness in *The Reprieve*.

14. Ibid., p. 105.
15. Alain Robbe-Grillet, "*Mahu ou le matériau, Le Renard et la boussole,*" *Critique* (January, 1954), pp. 82–85.
16. Alain Bosquet, "Robert Pinget, *Mahu ou le matériau,*" *Preuves* (September, 1957), p. 85.
17. Robert Pinget, *Mahu ou le matériau* (Paris, Les Editions de Minuit, reissue of original edition of Robert Laffont, 1952), p. 43. *Mahu ou le matériau* exists in only one edition, the original printing by Laffont. When Pinget began publishing with Les Editions de Minuit, that publisher simply put an Editions de Minuit cover on the unsold copies of Laffont's edition.
18. Ibid., p. 115.
19. Ibid., p. 187.
20. Ibid., p. 117.
21. Ibid., pp. 211–12.
22. Robert Pinget, *Le Renard et la boussole* (Paris: Les Editions de Minuit, 1971), pp. 92–93. *The Fox and the Compass (Le Renard et la boussole),* published originally by Gallimard in 1955, was reissued in 1971 by Les Editions de Minuit. As with *Mahu or the Material,* Minuit simply bought out unsold copies and replaced the jacket. The pagination of the 1955 and 1971 texts is therefore the same.
23. Ibid., pp. 211–12.
24. Ibid., p. 220.
25. Ibid., p. 221.
26. Ibid., pp. 235–36.

Chapter Two

1. Olivier de Magny, "Robert Pinget ou le palimpseste," Postface to *Graal Flibuste* (Paris: Les Editions 10/18, 1963), pp. 165–66.
2. See Bernard Dort's, "Fascination ou métamorphose," *Cahiers du Sud,* no. 338 (December 1956), pp. 133–37.
3. Robert Pinget, *Graal Flibuste,* edition intègrale (Paris: Les Editions de Minuit, 1966), p. 161. As in the other early works, the genesis of *Graal Flibuste* is a bit complicated. There are three editions of the book. In the first (Paris: Les Editions de Minuit, 1956) and the second (Paris: Les Editions 10/18, 1958) several chapters were cut from Pinget's original manuscript. These initial cuts were eventually restored to the third edition, "l'edition intègrale," at the author's request backed by Alain Robbe-Grillet in his role as editor (Paris: Les Editions de Minuit, 1966). The third edition is the definitive one.
4. Ibid., pp. 7–8.

5. "They had pushed refinement to the point of shoeing the cows [in the barn] in felt slippers so as to avoid hoof marks on the flagstone floor, as a native explained. [There was] a glass shelf in front of each stall where a goblet and a tooth-brush were placed. The dental hygiene of the cow has perceptible repercussions on her milk capacity." (Ibid., p. 35).
6. Ibid., p. 37.
7. Ibid., p. 73.
8. The traveller cites an "Ida's Mishaps" by a certain W. H. Sampeek ("ça me pique," "it's itching me") and a treatise on erotic dreams by one "S. Blanculz" ("blanc cul," "white arse").
9. Ibid., p. 57.
10. Marthe Robert, *L'Ancien et le nouveau* (Paris: Grasset, 1963, p. 126).
11. Jean-Jacques Pauvert, *La Jeunesse littéraire d'André Malraux* (Abbeyville: 1964).
12. *Graal Flibuste*, p. 33.
13. Ibid., pp. 45–46.
14. Ibid., pp. 118–19.
15. Ibid., pp. 154–55.
16. Ibid., pp. 230–31.
17. In the first editions of the book (Paris: Les Editions de Minuit, 1956) and (Paris: Les Editions 10/18, 1958) the voyage ends as the travellers gaze up at the arch. The Chinese-box-like final description opening onto new adventures was restored in the "edition intègrale" as well as the chapters: "Les Camprophages" [The Camphoreaters], "Les Poissons mous" [The Limp Fish], "Un Crime prémedité" [A Premeditated Crime], "La Montagne" [The Mountain], "Les Ecureils-bougies" [The Candlesquirrels], "Le Coeur poilu" [The Hairy Heart], "Le Petit Salon" [The Little Living Room], "Un Baptême" [A Baptism], "La Femme morte" [The Dead Woman], "Le Mystère Dunu" [The Dunu mystery], "La Dame de Chatruse" [The Lady from Chatruse], and "Le Château de Bonne Mésure" [The Castle of Bonne Mesure].
18. Edward Lear's way with words in "The Jumblies," a voyage poem, resembles the buoyant tone of the second stage of Pinget's narrator's experiment:

> They sailed to the Western Sea, they did—
> To a land all covered with trees:
> And they bought an owl, and a useful cart,
> And a pound of rice, and a cranberry-tart,
> And a hive of silvery bees;

> And they bought a pig, and some green jackdaws,
> And a lovely monkey with lollipop paws,
> And forty bottles of ring-bo-ree
> > And no end of Stilton cheese.
> Far and few, far and few,
> > Are the lands where the Jumblies live:
> Their heads are green, and their hands are blue;
> > And they went to sea in a sieve.

    Edward Lear, *Lear's Nonsense Books* (Boston: Roberts Brothers, 1888), p. 20.
19. *Graal Flibuste*, p. 40.
20. Ibid., p. 94.
21. Robert Pinget, *Baga* (Paris: Les Editions de Minuit, 1958), p. 7.
22. For discussion of the similarity between Pinget's and Jarry's clown-kings see: Roger Grenier, *Baga, La Table Ronde* (December, 1958); Alain Bosquet, "Pour quelques-uns" *Combat* (May, 1958); and Maurice Nadeau, "Romans de jeunes et jeunes romans" *France Observateur* (February, 1958).
23. Robert Pinget, *Baga*, p. 66.
24. Ibid., pp. 67–68.
25. Ibid., pp. 102–05.
26. Ibid., p. 119.
27. As in the case of Baga, an aura of equivocal and gross sexuality emanates from the queen's name. Conegrund is described as a sort of Earth Mother and her name is certainly a pun on the word "*con*" ("cunt"). There is also perhaps a veiled literary allusion to Candide's beloved Cunegonde, whom Voltaire's hero perceived as the finest flower of feminity and whom the reader recognizes as a low-class tart.
28. Olivier de Magny, "*Baga* par Robert Pinget," *Les Lettres Nouvelles* (October, 1958), pp. 452–53.

Chapter 3

1. Robert Pinget, *Monsieur Levert*, translated by Richard Howard, (New York: Grove Press, 1961), pp. 18–19. (The Richard Coe translation of the same text, distributed in Great Britain, is entitled *No Answer*.)
2. Ibid., p. 22.
3. Ibid., pp. 26–27.
4. Ibid., pp. 49–50.
5. Ibid., p. 52.

6. Ibid., pp. 52–53.
7. Ibid., p. 53.
8. Ibid., pp. 53–54.
9. Ibid., p. 55.
10. Ibid., pp. 7–8.
11. Robert Pinget, *Le Fiston* (Paris: Editions de Minuit, 1959), pp. 88–89.
12. Robert Pinget, *Monsieur Levert*, translated by Richard Howard (New York: Grove Press), p. 64.
13. Jean Roudaut. "Robert Pinget et la boussole," *Critique*, no. 303/304 (September, 1972), p. 748.
14. Ibid., p. 748.
15. *Monsieur Levert*, p. 94.
16. Ibid., p. 96.
17. Ibid., pp. 114–15.
18. Ibid., p. 115.
19. Ibid., pp. 121–22.
20. "And if we find so many dead bodies strewn throughout the pages (as along the beach in *Fable*) it is because the corpse as fictional material is used here as in an exorcism. The device operates a sort of stratagem . . . which the narrator makes use of to put off the moment of his own death. For even though the dead man's seat is reserved for him from the outset, the narrator resists occupying it throughout the book." For more extended Freudian interpretation of death and verbalization in Pinget's work from which this quotation is taken, see chapter 3 of Philippe Boyer's, *L'Ecarté(e)* (Paris: Seghers-Laffont, 1973).
21. Jean Roudaut. "Robert Pinget et la boussole," *Critique*, no. 303/304 (September 1972) p. 750.
22. *Monsieur Levert*, pp. 124–25.
23. Ibid., p. 55.
24. Samuel Beckett has done a skillful reworking into English of a radio play Pinget extracted from *Clope to the Dossier*. The Beckett text points up the difficulties of translating Pinget's work quite graphically by using interfacing pages with the French original on one side and the English version on the other: Robert Pinget, *La Manivelle ("The Old Tune"), pièce radiophonique avec texte anglais de Samuel Beckett* (Paris: Les Editions de Minuit, 1960). The Beckett translation alone is also available in the Calder & Boyars anthology of Pinget's theater.
25. Robert Pinget, *Clope au dossier* (Paris: Les Editions de Minuit, 1961), pp. 27–28.
26. Pinget later expanded this *"tour de force"* of tripped-up tongues and

sprained memories into the one-act play *La Manivelle*, translated into English as *The Old Tune* by Samuel Beckett.
27. *Clope au dossier*. p. 84.
28. Ibid., p. 100.
29. Ibid., pp. 102–04.
30. Ibid., p. 105.
31. Ibid., p. 124.
32. Ibid., pp. 125–26.
33. Ibid., pp. 131–32.
34. Philippe Boyer, *L'Ecarté(e)* (Paris: Seghers-Laffont, 1973), p. 141: "At the other extreme there is death from excessive pleasure which, in bringing to a close, at least for the moment, the desire to write, leaves behind the book as a sort of left-over. And in keeping with the metaphor of fiction, that is the death for which the narrator will pay the price. . . . 'No more time, no more time, no more time' (C.D. 135). Here is another final word. The time to do what? There isn't even enough time to say when the ground (or the page) slips away at the moment of pleasure."
35. *Clope au dossier*, pp. 134–35.
36. Jean Roudaut, "Robert Pinget et la boussole," *Critique*, no. 303/304 (September, 1972), p. 737.
37. *Clope au dossier*, p. 75.
38. Ibid., p. 16.
39. Ibid., p. 18.
40. Ibid., p. 128.
41. Bernard Pingaud, "Beckett, le précurseur," postface to Samuel Beckett's *Molloy* (Paris: Les Editions 10–18, 1963), p. 203.

Chapter 4

1. Germaine Brée, "The 'New' Novelists of France," *The Meanjin Quarterly* (September, 1963), p. 276.
2. For details about Pinget's hard luck in the French literary prize lottery of 1963 see: Raymond Las Vergnas, "Fleurs et couronnes," *Les Annales Conferencia* (January, 1963), pp. 24–25; George Schlocker, "Literary Harvest in France," *Books Abroad* (Spring 1963).
3. Jean Raymond, "De Robbe-Grillet à Pinget," *Cahiers du Sud* (January, 1963), pp. 290–93.
4. "If the book appears as a palimpseste, it is because images from the first books interfere with those of the latest one, and images from the

first pages with those of the last." Jean Roudaut. "Robert Pinget et la boussole," *Critique* (September, 1972), p. 735.
5. Tony Duvert, "La Parole et la fiction," *Critique* (May, 1968), pp. 447–48.
6. Robert Pinget, *The Inquisitory*, translated by Donald Watson (New York: Grove Press, 1966), pp. 247–48. The original French edition is: *L'Inquisitoire* (Paris: Les Éditions de Minuit, 1962). Passages in English are taken from the Watson translation distributed by Grove in the United States. The same translation is distributed in the British Isles by Calder & Boyars.
7. Ibid., p. 357.
8. Ibid., pp. 368–70.
9. Ibid., pp. 398–99.
10. "Gradually the text, aided by the reader's imagination, caused the answering voice to materialize. . . . He was mere emptiness, but now he begins to penetrate the book's substance, himself taking shape as it discloses what he reveals. . . . There is no one there except an answering voice that, with the reader's help, creates itself and its surroundings as it answers." Léon Roudiez, *French Fiction Today* (New Brunswick: Rutgers University Press, 1972), p. 187.
11. Robert Pinget, *Quelqu'un* (Paris: Les Éditions de Minuit, 1965), p. 17.
12. Denise Bourdet, "Robert Pinget," *Revue de Paris* (January, 1963), pp. 120–24.
13. Robert Pinget, *The Inquisitory*, p. 129.
14. Carl Bjurström, "De Cheminadour à Sirancy-la-Louve," *Critique*, 190 (March, 1963), pp. 195–202.
15. Commenting on the large number of inventory-like lists of furniture in *The Inquisitory*, Phillipe Boyer observed: "It is quite clear that [the questioner and his victim] each know just as much about the furniture in the living-room and that that is not what [the list] is all about. Not to know more about it but to exhaust all knowledge and in doing so to show that, far from exhausting it, one is inevitably faced with the following paradox: the more you know, the less you know. In other words, the more you know, the more you know you know nothing." Philippe Boyer, *L'Ecarté(e)* (Paris: Seghers-Laffont, 1973), p. 138.
16. Olivier de Magny, "Robert Pinget et le palimpseste," postface to *Graal Flibuste* (Paris: Les Editions 10/18, 1963), p. 174.
17. Robert Pinget, *Quelqu'un*, p. 13.
18. Ibid., pp. 190–91.
19. Ibid., p. 9.
20. "One can conceive that the narrator finally becomes sickened by the word which holds out his only guarantee of survival, speaking as one

vomits with an irresistible urge to get it over with. But resisting death is so exhausting that one eventually wishes for it." Philippe Boyer, *L'Ecarté(e)* (Paris: Seghers-Laffont, 1973), p. 143.
21. Robert Pinget, *Quelqu'un*, p. 73.
22. Ibid., p. 218.
23. Ibid., p. 28.
24. Ibid., p. 10.
25. Ibid., p. 170.
26. J. Plessen, "Prix Femina, Robert Pinget," *Het Franse Boek*, 1 (January, 1966), p. 17.
27. Dominique Rollin, "Un Rire de deux cent cinquante pages," *Le Nouvel Observateur* (November 15–21, 1965).
28. *Quelqu'un*, pp. 52 and 195.
29. Ibid., pp. 165–66.
30. Ibid., p. 214.
31. Ibid., pp. 219–20.
32. Ibid., p. 227.
33. Adolphe Grégoire, "*L'Inquisitoire*," *La Revue Nouvelle* (August, 1966), pp. 129–33.
34. *Quelqu'un*, p. 30.
35. For a detailed schematic outline of Pinget's cyclical use of recurring narrative elements see Claude Lieber, "Lecture de *Quelqu'un*," *Littérature*, 10 (Paris: 1972).
36. "What is common to all these works is the 'displacement' of the titles. They do not sum up, do not signify the contents; but seem to indicate what, precisely the book is not: *Baga* is the name of an all-powerful Minister, but what is spoken is monopolized by King Architruc; *Someone* does not designate the person speaking but the person who should listen." Jean Roudaut, "Robert Pinget et la boussole," *Critique*, no. 303/304 (September, 1972), p. 731.
37. *Quelqu'un*, pp. 22–23.
38. Ludovic Janvier, *Pour Samuel Beckett* (Paris: Les Editions de Minuit, 1966), p. 126.

Chapter 5

1. Jean Thibadeau, "Un théâtre de romanciers," *Critique* (September, 1960), pp. 676–82.
2. For a perceptive analysis of the theme of the couple in Pinget's theater see: Anne C. Murch, "Couples et réflets dans le théâtre de Robert Pinget," *Revue Romantique* 5 (1970), pp. 159–72.

3. Robert Pinget, *Ici et Ailleurs* suivi d' *Architruc* et *L'Hypothèse* (Paris: Les Editions de Minuit, 1961), p. 232.
4. The term "chronicle" used here and elsewhere refers to Pinget's entire serial output. As we have pointed out, the author's treatment of time is hardly chronological.
5. Robert Pinget, *Ici et Ailleurs.* . . . pp. 207–08.
6. Robert Pinget, *Identité* suivi d'*Abel et Bela* (Paris: Les Editions de Minuit, 1971), pp. 42–43.
7. Ibid., p. 15.
8. Ibid., p. 99.
9. Robert Pinget, *Paralchimie, Architruc, L'Hypothèse, Nuit* (Paris: Editions de Minuit, 1973), p. 11.
10. Ibid., pp. 56–57.
11. Ibid., p. 22.

Chapter 6

1. Robert Pinget, *Préface* (published as separate pamphlet accompanying *Le Libera*), (Paris: Les Editions de Minuit, 1967).
2. Ibid.
3. See Léon Roudiez, *French Fiction Today* (New Brunswick, N.J.: Rutgers University Press, 1972), p. 203.
4. Robert Pinget, *Préface* to *Le Libera*.
5. Robert Pinget, *The Libera Me Domine*, translated by Barbara Wright (London: Calder & Boyars, 1972; New York: Red Dust Press, 1976), pp. 136–37.
6. Tony Duvert, "La Parole et la fiction," *Critique* (May, 1968), p. 449.
7. Robert Pinget, *The Libera Me Domine*, trans. Barbara Wright, pp. 5–12.
8. Tony Duvert, "La Parole et la fiction," *Critique* (May, 1968), pp. 540–55.
9. Ibid., p. 546.
10. Robert Pinget, *Préface* to *Le Libera*.
11. "Actually, the description of the *passacaglia* (or the related *chaconne*) with its lack of complete tune, the theme consisting of a short succession of harmonics to be repeated over and over again without interruption, could apply to this book once linear narrative is substituted for tune and descriptive fragment for harmony." Léon Roudiez, *French Fiction Today* (New Brunswick, N.J.: Rutgers University Press, 1972), p. 202.
12. Robert Frost. "Choose Something Like a Star," from *Complete Poems* (New York: Holt, Reinhart & Winston, 1949), p. 575.
13. Samuel Beckett, *Three Novels* (New York: Grove Press, 1965), p. 414.

Chapter 7

1. Pinget is not the only "new novelist" to take a swipe at Cartesianism. Most likely, the long, hilarious search in Beckett's *Molloy* for a way to suck sixteen stones in succession is a broad parody of Descartes' method of logic.
2. "But in proposing this piece only as a story, a fable, in which among some examples that can be imitated one will perhaps also find others that it would be prudent not to follow, I hope it will be useful to some." René Descartes. *Discours de la méthode* (Paris: Les Editions 10/18, 1963), p. 27.
3. One of the most moving monologues in *Paralchimie* (pp. 56–57) seems to allude to a similar situation and the paralyzing feeling of helplessness and defeat.

    "And as one thing led to another, the conversation having been prolonged until very late, they were drinking near the hearth, glasses in hand, in that house which they'd gone to so much trouble to build and and then to furnish, to make habitable, both of them grown old between those four walls where they had shared the same existence for so many years with their rheumatisms and their paunches, their eyes no longer clear and wrinkles which make them look like Uncle Alfred, one suddenly says to his brother while gazing at the ceiling, do you think, all that to come to this, what did we have in mind, the other couldn't answer and for a long moment he will have seen a thousand shadows pass by on parade, a thousand shadows he couldn't even have named, was it disgust, grief or resignation, bits of phrases impossible to say going back to different times accumulated in his head and no longer having a voice to attribute them to, all forgotten, faded away, like an atonal murmur, discontinuous, fragmented, which insists inappropriately on the vanity of memory and the horror of time.

    (A pause)

    All they accomplished was ephemeral . . . "

    Robert Pinget. *Paralchimie* (Paris: Les Editions de Minuit, 1973), pp. 56–57.
4. "Proposes his merchandise.

    Opens his pants.

    The Lord will make it up to you.

    Takes out the blessed sacrament." (p. 35)

    ". . . it seems that all she eats is the eucharist . . ." (p. 45)

    ". . . He didn't even take the trouble to button himself up, the whole package was exposed to the sun and the people were chanting *o salutaris.*" (p. 57)

"He is there in front of the person kneeling, he shows him his circumcision and the other rushes over, he takes communion from the sacrament . . . and the praying one remained hung from the sex of the Lord imploring his mercy . . ." (pp. 42–43).

"That cross planted in the midst of hills.
The holy fruit was nailed to it." (p. 62)
Robert Pinget, *Fable*. (Paris: Les Editions de Minuit, 1971).
5. Ibid., p. 70.
6. Roger Shattuck, in *Proust's Binoculars* (New York: Random House, 1963), observed a somewhat similar device in Proust's imagery: "Optics furnishes a vocabulary that implies fixed units of observation and retention. When the testimony of our senses reaches the mind, it becomes an image. But—and here's both the rub and the way out—never one only: *many images*, in rapid and delayed and intermittent succession, and for the most part contradictory." (p. 22)
7. *"DISSOUDRE"* = *"TO DISSOLVE"*
Their future to dissolve. (p. 10)
The past to dissolve as well. (p. 12)
. . . bitter as the bile in the shadow of years to dissolve. (p. 16)
The intangible peace . . . To dissolve as well. (p. 17)
That hope to dissolve. (p. 21)
That past to dissolve . . . (p. 38)
That past to dissolve and the future as well . . . (p. 56)
That future to dissolve (p. 82)
. . . he will graft that finger joint to his carcass then will feel it dissolve. (p. 83)
This time measurement to dissolve. (p. 86)
This chronology to dissolve. (p. 112)
8. *"BLEU"* = *"BLUE"*
. . . a boy with white skin and blue hair . . . (p. 11)
. . . the Miaille of years past, blue-eyed with a blond beard . . . (p. 21)
. . . all the buds [of the delphinium] drinking in the night air, pale, pale blue. (p. 23)
He dunked his bread in his coffee . . . his eyes a pale blue . . . he looks like . . . (p. 64)
"DELPHINIUMS"

... the delphiniums are getting blue in the fields, unless it be his tears ... (p. 14)
... the delphiniums and the dead body make up one single spray of flowers barely visible in the moonlight. (p. 16)
... a man of flesh and blood walking naked with a spray of delphiniums in his hands (p. 23)
The city smoldering in ruins. The boy with the delphiniums. A destroyed passion ... (p. 25)
... the boy with the delphiniums jumped up ... (p. 64)

9. *"BOIS"* = *"WOODS"*
... il voyait sur la route passer deux promeneurs
... le bras de l'un sur le bras de l'autre ... ils disparurent dans le bois. (pp. 16–17)
... ils entraient dans le bois pour l'accouplement du soir ... (p. 18)
... longue extase répétée jusqu'au matin où se déprenaient leurs sexes dans la rosée. Sortent du bois ... (p. 18)
... passant par le bois où s'aimaient les personnages blancs ... (p. 30)
... ainsi qu'une bique égrène ses crottes, elle allait s'asseoir à l'orée du bois et de son réticule sortait un agenda où elle griffonnait son poème ... (pp. 31–32)
... ils pénétraient tous trois dans le bois ... et la vieille s'asseyant sur un tronc assistait aux ébats et aux accouplements comme à une messe étrange, embouchant de-ci de-là un membre roide ... (pp. 32–33)
... couchés dans le bois à regarder s'ébattre les archanges ... (p. 49), [Le Narcisse d'Epinal] se lève
... et va forniquer dans le bois ... (p. 53)
... ses simulacres, le clos, la cour, la grange, le petit bois ... (p. 60)
Et ils sont lourds [les noyés] ... et durs comme du bois. Vous croyez charger une poutre. Ou un gibet. (p. 62)

... he saw two men out for a walk pass by on the road ... arm in arm ... they disappeared into the woods. (pp. 16–17)
... they entered the woods for their nightly coupling ... (p. 18)
... long ecstacy repeated until dawn when their sexual organs parted from each other with the dew. They came out of the woods ... (p. 18)
... passing by the woods where the personages in white made love ... (p. 30)
... and like an old nanny goat dropping her dung in strings, she went to the clearing in the woods and took out her appointment book on which she scribbled her poem ... (pp. 31–32)

> . . . they went into the woods, all three . . . and the old woman sitting on a tree trunk watched their gambols and couplings as if [she were] at an unholy mass, popping into her mouth here and there a stiff member . . . (pp. 32–33)
>
> . . . lying in the woods watching the archangels frolic . . . (p. 49), [The Two-Bit Narcissus] gets up and goes off to fornicate in the woods . . . (p. 53)
>
> . . . his phantoms, the closed garden, the courtyard, the barn, the little woods (p. 56)
>
> And they are heavy [the dead bodies] and stiff as wood. You think you're picking up a beam. Or a scaffold. (p. 62)
>
> . . . to teach them [said Mlle. Lorpailleur] to teach those plutocrats from what wood our populations are heated . . . (p. 109)
>
> [Miette] is going to touch the walls . . . in order to absorb all that wood into himself . . . (p. 116)
>
> . . . leur apprendre [dit la Lorpailleur] à ces ploutocrates de quel bois nos populations se chauffent . . . (p. 109)
>
> [Miette] va tâter les murs . . . pour se pénétrer . . . de tout ce bois . . . (p. 116)

10. *"VILLE"* = *"CITY"*

    > The city had melted as a result of a cataclysm . . . (p. 10)
    >
    > These ruins of the city. The body on the beach . . . (p. 11)
    >
    > That city still smoking. (p. 12)
    >
    > And why that city, those ruins . . . (p. 14)
    >
    > . . . there would only be one room left in that city smoking under its ruins . . . (p. 19)
    >
    > . . . the collapse of the city and the cemeteries made in haste . . . (p. 20)
    >
    > The city smoking under its ruins. The boy with the delphiniums. (p. 25)
    >
    > But the city was still smoking under its ruins, the old nightmare . . . (p. 38)
    >
    > . . . and what is left of those beautiful desires, the city was smoking under its ruins and the penitent remained hung . . . (p. 42)
    >
    > As he arrived one day, coming from the city in ruins . . . (p. 50)
    >
    > . . . he might [one day] find his home city under different skies (p. 68)
    >
    > The city had melted as a result of a cataclysm. (p. 80)
    >
    > To know why the cataclysm or the city. (p. 83)
    >
    > The city has risen again. Cataclysm unexplained. (p. 85)

11. Robbe-Grillet uses a similar technique in *Projet pour une révolution à New*

York but the elements that he repeats are visual, for the most part, whereas Pinget works more often with sounds.

12. Mahu's inspired babbling contrasts with Latirail's feeble efforts at story telling. Architruc's fantasies become more outlandish in the second part of *Baga*, and Levert's drafts in part two of *Monsieur Levert* elaborate on the initial hypothesis without coming to any conclusions.

13. Frequency List of Recurring Key Words:

		PART I	PART II
coquelicot	"poppy"	9	1
ange	"angel"	13	0
grange	"barn"	10	5
lettre	"letter"	10	3
aveugle	"blind"	2	10
carrefour	"intersection"	2	7
cadavre	"cadaver"	8	1
exilé(s)	"exile(s)"	16	2
delphiniums	"delphiniums"	6	0
miroir	"mirror"	5	2
cavalier(s)	"horseman (men)"	4	1
sexe	"sexual organ"	9	2

14. STATISTICAL COMPARISON OF SENTENCE LENGTHS IN *FABLE*. SHORT SENTENCES.

	PART I	PART II
Sentences of 1 word	.44%	3.8%
2 words	1.1%	3.4%
3 words	3.8%	3.0%
4 words	6.2%	7.9%
5 words	6.7%	13.2%
6 words	6.06%	4.9%
7 words	3.1%	4.9%
Total # of Sentences. of 7 words or less	27.4%	41.1%

STATISTICAL COMPARISON OF SENTENCE LENGTHS. LONG SENTENCES.

	PART I	PART II
Sentences of 90–150 words	0.0	2.9%
Sentences of 150–236 words	0.0	4.5%

15. Jean Roudaut, "Robert Pinget et la boussole," *Critique*, no. 303/304, p. 742.

16. Other examples of general/specific alternation are:
    A. *"EXILÉS"* = *"EXILES"*

... the groups of exiles ... (p. 12) ... here I am among the exiles ... (p. 12) ... why those exiles ... (p. 14). Perhaps the image of the exiles on their funeral journey ... (p. 41) ... the prayer of exiles of all sorts ... (p. 42) ... now the boat is navigating toward the far-off shores where exiles of all sorts get together ... (p. 50) ... the vale of tears for exiles of all kinds ... (p. 60). Denounce the error of exiles of all kinds ... (p. 67). The exiles plough the seas ... (p. 72). Interrogating the exiles is worthless ... (p. 83). The exiles are swarming through my head, he says ... (p. 87)

B. *"MUSETTE" = "KNAPSACK"*

... he went to sleep with his knapsack under his head. (p. 9) He takes the cheese from his knapsack ... (p. 10) ... still carrying his knapsack ... (p. 13) In his knapsack (p. 17) ... the knapsack under my head ... (p. 30) Or the story of the knapsack's contents. (p. 31) ... my knapsack under my head ... (p. 51) He would open his knapsack ... (p. 53) ... the flashlight going back over the writings from the knapsack ... (p. 68) ... he fell asleep with his knapsack under his head. (p. 80) It is then that a kid fishing through the knapsack ... (p. 81) When he woke up, the old fool opens up his knapsack again ... (p. 95)

17. There is also considerable shifting of tense and mood in "se lever," "to get up."

SE LEVER

... il s'est levé et a couru dans l'eau éclaboussante ... (p. 24) Il se serait levé, aurait refait le tour des bâtiments ... (p. 28) Il s'est levé, il a repris la petite route ... (p. 39) ... il se levait le matin pour courir à l'étable ... (pp. 51–52) Et Miaille se levait, il serait le porcher ... (p. 63)

18. Jean Roudaut, "Robert Pinget et la boussole," *Critique*, no. 303/304, p. 749.

19. In a current dictionary *(The Random House Dictionary of the English Language)*, "legend" is variously defined as a nonhistorical or unverifiable story handed down by tradition from earlier times and popularly accepted as historical; a body of stories of this kind, especially as they relate to a particular people, group, or clan; an inscription, especially on a coat of arms, on a monument, under a picture, or the like; a table on a map, chart, or the like, listing and explaining the symbols used; a collection of stories about an admirable person; one who is the center of such stories; and a story on the life of a saint, especially one stressing the saint's miraculous or unrecorded deeds.

20. The phrase "Légende ce qui doit être lu" ("Legend, that which ought to be read" is taken up as a refrain at several points throughout. Robert Pinget, *Cette Voix*, (Paris: Les Editions de Minuit, 1975).
21. "But what were they about those notes of stories, tell me nuncle.
    Just stories yes a thousand stories.
    Then [the book] was for children.
    You're right Theo. I'm going to try to tell them but don't interrupt me or I'll lose the thread here we go there was the story of the café of illusions and the one about the unfortunates dragging their wretchedness about with them and the one about the castle and the one about the lilypond and the one about the path in the wood and the one about the tunnels that keep on being dug and being dug and the one about the cemetery and the one about the word that sticks in your throat and the one about the lost letter and the one about the nephews made to order and the one about the tribunal and the sentencing and the one about the king in disgrace and the one about killers everywhere and the one about the garden with nettles in it and the one about the knife and the one about the dead children and the one about sorrow and the one about rats and the one about the innocents and the one about trips to nowhere and the one about the city and the one about the crossroads and the one about sorrow and the one about the murderers and the one." Ibid. pp. 176–77.
22. "When we read, we so saturated with French writing that our entire body gives us the impression of being a paste made of words, do we ever find a line, a thought that is not familiar to us, or of which we haven't had at least a premonition?" Guy de Maupassant, Preface to *Pierre et Jean* (Paris: Albin Michel, 1972), p. 21. "Our heart is an incomplete instrument, a lyre with missing chords, an instrument on which we are forced to produce the accents of joy on the tone consecrated to sighs." Chateaubriand, *René* (Paris: Classiques Garnier, 1965), p. 212.
23. "An agreement is missing." Robert Pinget, *This Voice*, p. 7.
24. *The Random House Dictionary of the English Language*.
25. Robert Pinget, *This Voice*, pp. 229–30.

Chapter 8

1. Maurice Blanchot, *Le Livre à Venir* (Paris: Gallimard, 1959), pp. 69–70.
2. Alain Robbe-Grillet, *For a New Novel*, translated by Richard Howard (New York: Grove Press, 1965), p. 141.

3. Jean-Luc Seylaz, "Pinget tel qu'en lui-même," *Ecriture* I, no. 45 (Lausanne, Apr. 13, 1964), p. 121.
4. Roland Barthes, "La Littérature objective," *Critique*, 86–87 (August, 1954), p. 591.
5. Jean Pouillon, "Les Règles du jeu," *Les Temps Modernes*, 134 (April, 1957), pp. 1,591–98.
6. Bruce Morrissette, "Robert Pinget, *L'Inquisitoire*," *The French Review* (October, 1963), p. 121.
7. Peter Lennon, "Architruc," *The Manchester Guardian* (June 22, 1962).
8. Alain Bosquet, "Roman d'avant garde et antiroman," *Preuves*, 79 (September, 1957), p. 85.
9. Michel Carrouges, *André Breton and the Basic Concepts of Surrealism*, trans. Maura Prendergast (University: The University of Alabama Press, 1975), p. 71.
10. Roger Shattuck, "Introduction" to M. Nadeau's, *The History of Surrealism* (New York: Macmillan, 1965), pp. 18–20.
11. Max Jacob, *Le Roi de la Boétie* (Paris: 1921), p. 19.
12. Maurice Nadeau, *Histoire du surréalisme* (Paris: Editions du Seuil, 1945), pp. 277–78.
13. Michel Carrouges, *André Breton and the Basic Concepts of Surrealism*, trans. Maura Prendergast (University: The University of Alabama Press, 1972), p. 110
14. Ibid., pp. 126–27.
15. Robert Pinget, "Le Mécanisme de la création littéraire," Lecture, Williams College, Williamstown, Mass., April 21, 1970.
16. Michel Carrouges, *André Breton and the Basic Concepts of Surrealism*, trans. Maura Prendergast (University: The University of Alabama Press, 1974), p. 135.
17. Olivier Todd, "French Stylist," *Time and Tide* (Sept. 28, 1961), p. 1,612.
18. Raymond Federman, *Journey to Chaos, Samuel Beckett's Early Fiction* (Berkeley: University of California Press, 1965), pp. 21, 111.
19. Samuel Beckett, *Nouvelles et textes pour rien* (Paris: Les Editions de Minuit, 1958), pp. 156–57.
20. Samuel Beckett, *L'Innomable* (Paris: Les Editions de Minuit, 1953), p. 174.
21. Ludovic Janvier, *Pour Samuel Beckett* (Paris: Les Editions de Minuit, 1966), pp. 193–94.
22. Bernard Pingaud, "Beckett, le précurseur," Postface to *Molloy* (Paris: Editions 10/18, 1963), p. 299.
23. Marthe Robert, *L'Ancien et le nouveau* (Paris: Grasset 1963), p. 37.

24. Robert Pinget, "Le Mécanisme de la création littéraire," Lecture, Williams College, Apr. 21, 1970.

Chapter 9

1. Stephen Bann, "Reputations — XII: Robert Pinget," *The London Magazine*, 4:7 (October, 1964), p. 24.

BIBLIOGRAPHY

I. WORKS BY PINGET

A. NOVELS AND PLAYS:

Entre Fantoine et Agapa [*Between Fantoine and Agapa*]. Jarnac: Editions du Feu, 1951. Paris: Les Editions de Minuit, 1966.
Mahu ou le matériau [*Mahu or the Material*]. Paris: Robert Laffont, 1952. Paris: Les Editions de Minuit, 1957.
Le Renard et la boussole [*The Fox and the Compass*]. Paris: Gallimard, 1955. Paris: Les Editions de Minuit, 1971.
Graal Flibuste [*Graal Flibuste*]. Paris: Les Editions de Minuit, 1956. Paris: Editions 10/18, 1965. Edition intègrale. Paris: Les Editions de Minuit, 1966.
Baga [*Baga*]. Paris: Les Editions de Minuit, 1958.
Le Fiston [*Monsieur Levert*]. Paris: Les Editions de Minuit, 1959.
Lettre morte [*Dead Letter*]. Paris: Les Editions de Minuit, 1960.
La Manivelle [*The Old Tune*]. Paris: Les Editions de Minuit, 1960.
Clope au dossier [*Clope to the Dossier*]. Paris: Les Editions de Minuit, 1961.
Ici ou ailleurs [*Here or Elsewhere*]. Paris: Les Editions de Minuit, 1961.
L'Inquisitoire [*The Inquisitory*]. Paris: Les Editions de Minuit, 1961.
Autour de Mortin [*About Mortin*]. Paris: Les Editions de Minuit, 1965. Minuit, 1965.
Autour de Mortin. Ed. Anthony Cheal Pugh. London: Methuen, 1971.
Quelqu'un [*Someone*]. Paris: Les Editions de Minuit, 1965.
Le Libera [*The Libera me Domine*]. Paris: Les Editions de Minuit, 1967.
Passacaille [*Recurring Melody*]. Paris: Les Editions de Minuit, 1969.
Identité suivi d'Abel et Bela, Nuit [*Identity, followed by Abel and Bela, Night*]. Paris: Les Editions de Minuit, 1971.
Fable [*Fable*]. Paris: Les Editions de Minuit, 1971.
Paralchimie [*Paralchemy*]. Paris: Les Editions de Minuit, 1973.
Cette Voix [*This Voice*]. Paris: Les Editions de Minuit, 1975.

B. SHORT PIECES AND NARRATIVE FRAGMENTS:

"Le Mystère Dunu" ["The Dunu Mystery"], from *Graal Flibuste*. *Les Nouvelles Littéraires*, 1,867 (June 13, 1963), p. 6.
"Le Pique-nique" ["The Picnic"], from *Quelqu'un*. *Cahiers de la Compagnie Renaud-Barrault* (February, 1966), pp. 60–68.
"Mandala" ["The Mandala"], from *Paralchimie*. *Minuit*, no. 1, pp. 45–48.
"Amorces" ["Beginnings"]. *Minuit*, no. 4, pp. 26–29.
"Le Mois d'août" ["The Month of August"]. *Minuit*, no. 13, pp. 2–41.
"Pseudo-principes d'esthétique," in *Nouveau roman: Hier aujourd'hui*. Paris: Union Générale des Editions, 1972, pp. 311–24.

Interview III (from *Autour de Mortin*, Cahiers Renaud-Barrault (October, 1964), pp. 58–70.

"*Dictée*" ("Dictation"), published in its radio-play form in *Minuit* (May, 1976).

C. WORKS UNPUBLISHED AS OF SEPTEMBER 1978:

Le Réscapé. Radio play taken from *Cette Voix* and performed by Radio Stuttgart in late December, 1974, and Radio Bremen in early April, 1975. Projected French variant to be "*Le Chrysanthème*" ("*The Chrysanthemum*").

Le Bourreau. Radio play produced by France Culture in 1978 and by Radio Stuttgart in 1975; German title, "*Wer Spricht?*"

Micrologues. A series of short, surrealistic sketches based on wordplay. The series includes the following short pieces: "Le Mystère du trou de balle" ["The Bullethole Mystery"], "Conseils" ["Advice"], "Le Parapluie" ["The Umbrella"], "Le Cafard" ["The Blues"], "Le Temps" ["The Weather"], "Linguistique" ["Linguistics"], "Cocot" ["Cocot"], "Les Oignons" ["The Onions"], "Le Hasard" ["Luck"], "Le Professeur" ["The Professor"], "Secretaire-Bidon" ["The Fake Secretary"], "Vouvou Miam-Miam" ["Bow-wow Yum-yum"], and "Visite Guidée" ["The Guided Tour"]. An alternate projected title for the last of these works is "*M. Songe*" ("*Mr. Dream*").

La Lubie. Radio play *("The Crazy Notion")*.

Voyager Loin. Film scenario *("Travel Far")*.

D. WORKS BY PINGET CURRENTLY AVAILABLE IN ENGLISH TRANSLATION:

Mahu or the Material [*Mahu ou le matériau*]. Trans. Alan Sheridan-Smith. London: John Calder, 1967.

Baga [*Baga*]. Trans. J. Stevenson. London: John Calder, 1967.

No Answer [*Le Fiston*]. Trans. Richard Coe. London: John Calder, 1961.

Monsieur Levert [*Le Fiston*]. Trans. Richard Howard. New York: Grove Press, 1961.

The Inquisitory [*L'Inquisitoire*]. Trans. Donald Watson. London: Calder & Boyars, 1966. American distribution through Grove Press, New York.

The Libera Me Domine [*Le Libera*]. Trans. Barbara Wright. London: Calder & Boyars, 1972; New York: Red Dust Press, 1976.

La Manivelle [*The Old Tune*]. Bilingual edition of *La Manivelle* with English version by Samuel Beckett on interfacing pages. Paris: Les Editions de Minuit, 1960.

The Old Tune [*La Manivelle*]. Bilingual edition of *La Manivelle* with English translation by Samuel Beckett on interfacing pages. New Writers Series, no. 2. London: Calder & Boyars, 1964.

Plays, vol. I. *The Old Tune* [*La Manivelle*], *Dead Letter* [*Lettre Morte*], *Clope* [*Clope au dossier*]. Trans. Barbara Bray. London: John Calder, 1964. This translation is scheduled for American publication by The Red Dust Press, New York, 1977–78.

Plays, vol. II. *Architruc* [*Architruc*], *About Mortin* [*Autour de Mortin*], *The Hypothesis* [*L'Hypothèse*]. Trans. Barbara Bray. London: Calder & Boyars, 1967.

Somebody (excerpt from *Quelqu'un*) in *French Writing Today*. Edited by S. W. Taylor. New York: Grove Press, 1969.

"The Investigation" (section from *The Inquisitory*). Trans. Jean-Marc Vary. *The Meanjin Quarterly*, 22:3 (September 1963), pp. 249–68.

E. WORKS BY PINGET CURRENTLY [1977-1978] BEING TRANSLATED FOR FUTURE PUBLICATION:

Recurring Melody [*Passacaille*]. London: Calder & Boyars.
Fable [*Fable*]. London: Calder & Boyars.
Someone [*Quelqu'un*]. London: Calder & Boyars.
This Voice [*Cette Voix*]. London: Calder & Boyars.

II. *CRITICISM*

Abirached, Robert. "Le Nord et le sud" (review of *L'Inquisitoire*), *La Nouvelle Revue Française*, 20 (Dec. 1, 1962), pp. 1,069–72.

———. "*L'Inquisitoire*-Les Cartes du temps," *Etudes* (February, 1963), pp. 235–44.

———. "Carnet de théâtre," *Etudes*, 305:6 (June, 1960), pp. 404–07.

———. "Images d'enfer," *Le Nouvel Observateur*, 70 (Feb. 16–22, 1966), p. 40.

———. "Sur le roman moderne en France," *Le Français dans le monde*, 29, pp. 6–9.

Alberès, R. M. "Amer et farfelu" *(Baga)*, *Arts* (July 1, 1958).

———. "Le Coeur et l'esprit" *(L'Inquisitoire)* *Les Nouvelles Littéraires* (Oct. 18, 1962).

———. *Les Métamorphoses du Roman*. Paris: Albin-Michel, 1966.

———. "Cette nouvelle école littéraire . . . ," *A La Page*, 44 (February, 1968), pp. 213–21.

———. *Le Roman d'aujourd'hui. 1960–1970*. Paris: Albin-Michel, 1970.

———. *Littérature, horizon 2000*. Paris: Albin-Michel, 1974.

Albini, Maria B. "L'Altra Francia litteraria," *Il Ponte* (June, 1963), pp. 793–803.

Alter, Jean. "Robert Pinget: *Le Renard et la boussole*," *The French Review*, 46:5 (April, 1973), pp. 10,064–65.

Anex, Georges. "*L'Inquisitoire* de Robert Pinget," *La Gazette de Lauzanne* (Oct. 13, 1962).
———. "Robert Pinget, *Quelqu'un*," *La Gazette de Lauzanne* (Dec. 4, 1965), p. 18.
———. "Inventaire de la solitude," *(Quelqu'un* and *Autour de Mortin)*, *Journal de Genève* (Dec. 4–5, 1965).
———. "Moments littéraires, Robert Pinget, Prix Femina," *Journal de Lauzanne* (Dec. 4–5, 1965), p. 18.
———. "La Parole et le silence," *Le Journal de Genève* (June 7, 1969).
———. "Un Ton Inimitable" *(Cette Voix)*, *Le Journal de Genève* (Feb. 22, 1975).
Anonymous. "*Quelqu'un* de Robert Pinget," *Indications*, 23:7 (1966).
———. "All Trivia," *(No Answer)*, *The [London] Times Literary Supplement* (Oct. 20, 1961), p. 749.
———. "La Saison des prix. Au Femina, quatre dames vont se battre pour Pierre de Mandiargues," *Le Monde*, 5,864 (Nov. 23, 1963), p. 13.
———. "Robert Pinget: Mes racines, je les ai découvertes en travaillant," *Nice Matin* (Dec. 19, 1965).
———. "Une saison du T.N.P." (on the transposition of *Le Fiston* into *Lettre Morte*), *La Pensée Française* (August, 1960), pp. 68–70.
———. "Pinget Adapted by Beckett," *The Times* (London), 56,177 (Nov. 24, 1964), p. 15.
———. "Question and Answer," *(L'Inquisitoire)*, *The Times Literary Supplement* (Dec. 28, 1962).
———. "Hearts that Beat Under a New Novel Facade," *The Times Literary Supplement*, 3,329 (Dec. 16, 1965), p. 1,173.
———. "Robert Pinget, *Paralchimie*," *The Times* (Mar. 1, 1974).
———. "Zum Erscheinen des Romans '*Passacaglia*' von Robert Pinget" (opening passage of *Passacaille* and preface to *Le Libera* in German translation), *Sammlung Luchterhand Information Vorsehau*, 12 (January, 1970).
———. "Survival Kit" *(Passacaille)*, *The Times Literary Supplement*, (London), 3,520 (Aug. 14, 1969), p. 897.
———. "Blue blood and stocking," *The Observer*, 9,045, (Nov. 8, 1964), p. 22.
———. "Avant-garde Plays on French Official Stage," *The Times* (London), 56,584 (Mar. 19, 1966), p. 15.
———. "A partir du 28 février, Ionesco, Beckett et Pinget au Théâtre de France," *Le Monde*, 6,538 (Jan. 20, 1966), p. 12.
———. "Les bruits de la ville, Robert Pinget," *Le Nouvel Observateur*, 65 (Feb. 9–15, 1966), pp. 30–31.
———. "Les enfants s'amusent" *(Theater)*, *Le Nouvel Observateur*, 49 (Oct. 20–26, 1965), pp. 33–34.

———. "Goncourt et Renaudot le 22 novembre," *Le Monde* (Nov. 20, 1965), p. 12.

———. "Les Enfants chéris des éditeurs," *Le Nouvel Observateur*, 43 (Sept. 8–15, 1965), p. 23.

———. "Waves in a teacup," *The Times Literary Supplement* (London) (Oct. 13, 1961), pp. 712–13.

———. "L'Opinion des nouveaux romanciers," *La Quinzaine Littéraire*, 121 (July 1–15, 1971), p. 10.

———. *"Architruc et la Manivelle,"* Paris-Théâtre 187 (1962), pp. 61–3.

———. "Les Trois Livres qu'ils ont préférés en 1965," *Le Nouvel Observateur*, 59 (Dec. 29, 1965), p. 25.

———. "Quatre jeunes auteurs français," *Cahiers de la Compagnie Madeleine Renaud, Jean-Louis Barrault*, 46 (October, 1964).

———. "Enter a Plumber" *(Paralchimie)*, *The Times Literary Supplement* (London), 3,756 (Mar. 1, 1974), p. 214.

———. *Cette Voix*. *New French Books* (Summer, 1975), p. 535.

Aragones, J. E. " 'Tartufo' de Molière y tres autores de hoy," *(Architruc)*, *Estafeta Literaria*, 481 (Dec. 1, 1971), pp. 37–38.

Astier, Pierre A. G. *La Crise du roman français et le nouveau réalisme*. Paris: Debresse, 1968.

———. "Le nouveau roman: Analyse d'un renouvellement du genre romanesque, 1955–1960." *Dissertation Abstracts*, 24:4 (October, 1963) 1,609 (Brown University).

Audouard, Yvan. "Pièces détachées," *Le Canard Enchaîné* (Mar. 16, 1966), p. 7.

Aury, Dominique. *"Quelqu'un, Autour de Mortin,"* *La Nouvelle Revue Française* (Jan. 27, 1966), pp. 141–42.

Bachman, J. "Robert Pinget," *Die Tat*, (Oct. 25, 1969).

Bajini, Sandro. "Robert Pinget, *L'Inquisitoire*," *Il Verro* (December, 1962), pp. 112–14.

Baldick, Robert. "Letter from Paris," *Aspect*, 2 (March, 1963), pp. 54–55.

Bann, Stephen. "Robert Pinget," *The London Magazine*, 4:7 (Oct. 7, 1964), pp. 22–35.

———. *"Quelqu'un* by Robert Pinget: *La Maison de rendez-vous*, by Alain Robbe Grillet," *The London Magazine*, 6:2 (May, 1966), pp. 94–98.

———. "Robert Pinget: The End of a Modern Way," in *Directions in the Nouveau Roman*, 20-Century Studies (December, 1971), pp. 17–29.

———. "Novel Facade," *The Times Literary Supplement* (London), 3,332 (Jan. 6, 1966), p. 9.

Baqué, Françoise. "La Destruction; Robert Pinget, Samuel Beckett," in her book, *Le Nouveau Roman*. Montréal: Bordas, 1972, pp. 14–29.

_____. "Les inventaires inutiles: Robert Pinget," in *Le Nouveau Roman*. Montréal: Bordas, 1972, pp. 100–02.
_____. "L'Enquête policière," in *Le Nouveau Roman*. Paris, Montréal: Bordas, 1972, pp. 119–25.
Barjon, Louis. "*L'Inquisitoire*," *Etudes*, 316 (1963), pp. 235–40.
_____. "Les Prix littéraires," *(Quelqu'un)*, *Etudes*, 324 (January, 1966), pp. 72–7.
_____. "Art, formes et signes" *(Quelqu'un)*, *Etudes*, 324 (January, 1966), pp. 75–77.
Bars, Henry. "Des modes littéraires de la modernité," *Revue Générale Belge*, 8 (August, 1966), pp. 1–17.
Benedictus, David. "Architruc. Hypothesis," *Plays and Players*, 14:10 (July, 1967), pp. 42–43.
Bergonzi, Bernard. "A World of Things" *(No Answer)*, *The Spectator* (Sept. 29, 1961), p. 434.
Bernard, Marc. "Un raz de marée. Spectacle: Beckett–Pinget–Ionesco," *Les Nouvelles Littéraires*, 2,011 (Mar. 17, 1966), p. 13.
Berridge, Elizabeth. "Novelist of the New Woman," *The Daily Telegraph*, 34,807 (Mar. 23, 1967), p. 21.
Bishop, Thomas. "Life in the Labyrinth" *(The Inquisitory)*, *The Saturday Review* (Feb. 11, 1967), p. 41.
_____. "After That One Great Innovator," *The Nation*, 215:7 (Sept. 25, 1972), pp. 249–51.
_____. *L'Avant-garde théâtrale; French Theatre Since 1950* (Anthology) Ed. Thomas Bishop. Lexington: D. C. Heath, 1975.
Bjurstrom, Carl-Gustaf. "De Chaminadour à Sirancy-la-Louve," *(L'Inquisitoire)*, *Critique*, 190 (Mar. 19, 1963), pp. 195–202.
_____. "Pinget," *Bulletin de la librairie ancienne et moderne*, 35, pp. 264–76.
_____. "Robert Pinget," *Bonniers Litterära Magasin*, 35:4 (April, 1966), pp. 264–76.
Blanzat, Jean. "*Graal Flibuste* de Robert Pinget," *Le Figaro Littéraire* (Feb. 16, 1957).
Bleikasten, André. "Faulkner et le nouveau roman," *Les Langues Modernes*, 4 (July-August, 1966), pp. 54–64.
Bloch-Michel, Jean. "Quelqu'un ou personne?" *(L'Inquisitoire, Autour de Mortin, Quelqu'un)*, *Preuves*, 180 (February, 1966), pp. 79–80.
_____. "Los premios literarios de 1965," *Horizontes* 9:46 (Apr. 15, 1966), pp. 20–21.
Boideffre, Pierre. "Déclin ou résurrection du roman?" *(Quelqu'un)*, *Les Nouvelles Littéraires* (Mar. 4, 1974).

Bonal, G. "Le Libera," *Revue de Paris*, 75:5 (May, 1968), pp. 155–56.
Bonnefoy, Claude. "Les Partants de la rentrée," *Arts*, 1,013 (Sept. 15–21, 1965), pp. 7–8.
Borel, Jacques. "Petite introduction à l'*Ulysse* de Joyce," *Les Temps Modernes*, 260 (January, 1968), pp. 1,291–1,307.
Borsatti, Manuella. "Universul romanelor lui Pinget," *Analele Universitatii Bucuresti, Literaura Universale si comparata*, 20:2, pp. 117–23; with a résumé in French, "L'Univers des romans de Pinget," p. 124.
Bory, Jean-Louis. "Lettre Morte ou la tragédie dénaturée," *Bref, Théâtre National Populaire* (May, 1960).
———. "L'Ecole du regard au secours de l'école de l'oreille" *(L'Inquisitoire)*, *L'Express* (Nov. 1, 1962), pp. 29–30.
———. "Portrait de Robert Pinget," *Cahiers des Saisons*, 7 (Winter, 1962), pp. 189–91.
———. "La Politesse du désespoir" *(Autour de Mortin, Quelqu'un)*, *Le Nouvel Observateur*, 53 (Nov. 17–23, 1965), pp. 28–29.
———. "*Passacaille*," *Le Nouvel Observateur*, 254 (Sept. 22–28, 1969), p. 43.
Bosquet, Alain. "Deux techniques du récit; Georges Piroué, Robert Pinget" *(Clope au dossier)*, *Combat* (Mar. 23, 1961).
———. "Les Expériences de Robert Pinget" *(Architruc, L'Hypothèse, Ici et ailleurs)*, *Le Monde* (Dec. 2, 1961).
———. "Une passionnante expérience, *L'Inquisitoire* de Robert Pinget," *Le Monde* (Sept. 29, 1962).
———. "La Verité inaccessible," *(Le Libera)*, *Le Monde des Livres*, 7,181 (Feb. 29, 1968), p. 13.
———. "Robert Pinget *Mahu ou le matériau*," *Preuves* (September, 1957), p. 85.
Bowerman, Kate M. "A Thematic Analysis of *L'Inquisitoire* by Robert Pinget," *Dissertation Abstracts International*, 34:5 (November, 1973). Dissertation, University of North Carolina, Chapel Hill.
Bott, Françoise. "Monsieur tout-le-monde" *(Quelqu'un)*, *L'Express*, 751 (Nov. 8–14, 1965), pp. 95–96.
Boubat & Tournier. *Miroirs; autoportraits*. Paris: Denoël, 1973.
Bourdet, Denise. "Robert Pinget," *La Revue de Paris*, 70:1 (January, 1963), pp. 120–24.
Boyer, Philippe. "Robert Pinget, *Passacaille*," *Esprit*, 370 (April, 1968), pp. 760–62.
———. "*Le Libera*," *Esprit*, 35 (Apr. 4, 1968), pp. 760–62.
———. "Mezzo Voce," chapter in his book *L'Ecarté(e)*. Paris: Seghers-Laffont, 1973, pp. 113–45.

———. "Mezzo-voce," *Action Poétique*, 50 (1972), pp. 53–61.
———. "Robert Pinget, *Passacaille*," *Action Poétique*, 50, (1972).
Boyer, Régis. "Romans actuels, oeuvres de recherche" *(Graal Flibuste)*, *Le Français dans le monde*, 48 (April-May, 1967), pp. 6–14.
Bratschi, Georges. "*Quelqu'un* de Robert Pinget," *La Tribune de Genève* (Dec. 5, 1965).
Bray, Barbara. "Un Kaléidoscope de verité" *(Lettre Morte* and *Ici et ailleurs)*, *Cahiers Renaud-Barrault*, 53 (February, 1966), pp. 55–59.
———. "Paris Prizewinner" *(Quelqu'un)*, *The Sunday Times* (London), 7,438 (Dec. 5, 1965), p. 47.
Brée, Germaine. "The 'new' novel in France," *The American Society Legion of Honor Magazine*, 31:1 (1960), pp. 33–43.
Brenner, Jacques. *Journal de la vie littéraire, 1962–64*. Paris: Julliard, 1965.
Brooke-Rose, Christine. "Making It New" *(L'Inquisitoire)*, *The Observer*, 9,143 (Oct. 2, 1966), p. 26.
Broome, Peter. "A New Mode of Reading Pinget's *Passacaille*." *Nottingham French Studies*, 12:2 (October, 1973), pp. 86–99.
Buèges, Jean. "Un Célibataire timide a séduit les douze dames du Femina," *Paris Match*, 872 (Dec. 25, 1965), p. 93.
Burncoa, Charles. "*Le Renard et la boussole* par Robert Pinget," *Les Nouvelles Littéraires* (January, 1954), p. 3
Burns, Alan. "Everything and nothing," *(L'Inquisitoire)*, *Tribune*, 30:45 (Nov. 11, 1968), p. 14.
Cathelin, Jean. "Un Ecrivain insolite: Robert Pinget," *France Observateur* (Mar. 26, 1959).
Chabert, Pierre. "*Le Libera*," *Les Lettres nouvelles* (June, 1968), pp. 171–74.
Chalon, Jean. "Trente jurés, dix critiques . . . ," *Le Figaro Littéraire* (Dec. 15, 1962), p. 3.
Chambers, Ross. "*The World Around Mortin. A Reading of Robert Pinget's Autour de Mortin*." North Ryde: Macquaine University, *French Monographs*, 1:1 (July, 1973).
Chapsal, Madeleine. "Ça crève, ça crève," *L'Express* (Dec. 12, 1965).
———. "L'Inspiration n'existe pas," *La Quinzaine Littéraire*, 54 (July 16–31, 1968), pp. 8–9.
———. "La Drôlerie terrible de Robert Pinget" *(Passacaille)*, *L'Express*, 933 (May 26–June 1, 1969), pp. 75–76.
———. "Les Voix de Robert Pinget" *(Le Renard et la boussole, Fable, Identité)*, *L'Express*, 1,055 (Sept. 27–Oct. 3, 1971), pp. 47–8.
———. "Faux témoignages sous les tilleuls" *(Le Libera)*, *L'Express*, 54 (Feb. 10–18, 1968), pp. 37–38.
———. "Robert Pinget: Des Riens à la dérive" *(Cette Voix)*, *L'Express*

(Mar. 17, 1975).

Chavardes, Maurice. "Voix d'Outre Monde" *(Cette Voix)*, *Témoignage Chrétien* (Mar. 6, 1975).

Ciarletta, Nicla. "Tendenza del teatro d'oggi," *L'Approdo Letterario*, 23–24, pp. 157–60.

Cismaru, Alfred. "Robert Pinget, an introduction," *American Benedictine Review*, 19:2, pp. 203–10.

———. "Robert Pinget: *Passacaille*," *The French Review*, 44:1 (October, 1970), p. 183.

Corke, Hilary. "New novels," *The Listener*, 77:1,979 (Mar. 2, 1967), p. 301.

Corvin, Michel. *Le Théâtre nouveau en France*. Paris: Presses Universitaires de France, 1966.

Cramer, H. V. "Ein Mann wird befragt," *Die Zeit*, Hamburg (Dec. 10, 1965), pp. 23–24.

Dalmas, André. "Paradoxe du langage" *(Baga)*, *Le Tribune des Nations* (Nov. 4, 1958).

———. "La Façon de dire" *(Le Renard et la boussole, Fable)*, *La Quinzaine Littéraire*, 128 (Nov. 1–15, 1971), pp. 7–8.

———. "Quelque chose d'Existence" *(Cette Voix)*, *La Quinzaine Littéraire* (Mar. 16, 1975).

Decock, Jean. "*Identité* suivi de *Abel et Bela*," *The French Review*, 46:4, (March, 1973), pp. 863–65.

De Decker, Jacques. "Les fabulations de Robert Pinget" *(Fable, Identité) Le Soir* (Nov. 10, 1971).

Delacourt, Robert. "*Quelqu'un*," *Table Ronde*, 216–17 (February, 1966), pp. 199–200.

Dennis, Nigel. " 'Late Again,' He Groaned" *(L'Inquisitoire)*, *The New York Review of Books* (Mar. 23, 1967).

Desponds, André. "Sous l'habit sans éclat des jours d'oeuvre," *Zofinque*, Genève (Oct. 8, 1959). Also in *Les Critiques de Notre Temps et le Nouveau Roman*, Ed. R. Ouellet, Paris, Montréal, Garnier, 1972, pp. 113–17.

Dumayet, Pierre. "Robert Pinget, 'un roman n'est pas fait pour amuser,' " *Le Nouveau Candide* (Aug. 1, 1962).

Dussane. "Lettre Morte," *Mercure*, 339 (1960), pp. 317–19.

Dutourd, Jean. "Spectacle: Ionesco—Pinget—Beckett," in *Le Paradoxe du critique*. Paris: Flammarion, 1972, pp. 187–88.

Duvert, Tony. "La Parole et la fiction," *Critique*, 252 (May, 1968), pp. 443–61.

Endres, E. "Das Leben, ein Verhör" *(L'Inquisitoire), Der Monat,* 208 (January, 1966), pp. 70–72.

Erval, François. "Formentor Prizes 1964," *Atlas,* (July, 1964), pp. 50–51.

Escarpit, Robert. *"L'Inquisitoire* par Robert Pinget," *Le Canard Enchaîné* (Aug. 24, 1962).

Esslin, Martin. *The Theatre of the Absurd.* Harmondsworth, Middlesex: Penquin Books in association with Eyre & Spottiswoode, 1968.

Estang, Luc. *"Le Libera," Le Figaro Littéraire,* 1,139 (Feb. 12, 1968), pp. 20–21.

Farrall, Stephanie Nicole. "Avatars of Fabulation in 20th Century French Drama," *Dissertation Abstracts International,* 34:9 (March, 1974). Dissertation, Indiana University.

Ferris, Paul. "Puzzler on the Third" *(About Mortin), The Observer,* 8,973 (June 23, 1963), p. 35.

Finas, Lucette. *"Quelqu'un." Les Lettres Nouvelles* (March-April, 1966), pp. 169–72.

Fisson, Pierre. "Pierre Fisson mène l'enquête sur le roman," *Le Figaro Littéraire,* 858 (Sept. 29, 1962), p. 3.

Fletcher, John. "Littérature d'aujourd'hui," *(Clope au dossier, L'Inquisitoire), Bulletin de l'Université de Toulouse,* 5 (February, 1964), pp. 642–43.

Foissy, Guy. "La Manivelle et Robert Pinget," *Le Quotidien de Paris* (June 11, 1974).

Fritz, Walter Helmut. "Angelockt von der Leere," *Frankfurter Hefte,* 25 (1970), pp. 735–40.

Galey, Mathieu. "Deux timides" *(Clope au dossier). Arts* (Apr. 5, 1961).

_____. "Un redoublant et un repêché," *Arts,* 10 (Dec. 1–7, 1965), p. 12.

Gallagher, David. "New Fiction," *The Times* (London), (Feb. 23, 1967), p. 8.

G. G. "Ce Soir Chaîne III, Robert Pinget" (compte rendu d'un interview de Pinget de 20 minutes filmé à sa maison de comparne), *Le Figaro* (June 7, 1974).

Gaugeard, Jean. "Demeures de la parole" *(Le Libera), La Quinzine Littéraire,* 44 (Feb. 1–15, 1968), p. 5.

_____. "In Search of a tone" *(Le Libera), The Times Literary Supplement* (London), 3,451 (Apr. 18, 1968), p. 390.

Gautier, Jean-Jacques. "Les Auteurs nouveaux chez Molière" *(Architruc), Le Figaro,* (Jan. 24, 1971).

_____. *"Identité* de Robert Pinget," *Le Figaro,* 8,769 (Nov. 24, 1972), p. 28.

―――. "28 mars 1960 *Lettre Morte* de Robert Pinget; *La Dernière Bande* de Samuel Beckett" from *Deux Fauteuils d'Orchestre*. Paris: Flammarion, 1962, pp. 330–34.

Gay, Daniel. "Les Romans de Pinget, une expérience de l'écriture." Summary of Thesis Submitted to La Faculté des Lettres, The University of Fribourg, 1967, 3:4.

Géorlette, R. "Aspects du roman policier français contemporain," *La Fenêtre ouverte*, 55 (April, 1965), pp. 99–118.

Godard, Colette. "Avant-première" (interview), *Le Monde*, 8,092 (Jan. 19, 1971), p. 16.

―――. "Abel et Bela," *Atac Informations*, 49 (April, 1973).

Gramigna, Guiliano. "*L'Inquisitoria* di Robert Pinget," *La Fiera Letteraria*, 41:16 (Apr. 28, 1966), pp. 16–17.

Grégoire, Adolphe. "*Quelqu'un*," *La Revue Nouvelle*, 43 (1966), pp. 211–14.

―――. "*L'Inquisitoire* de Robert Pinget," *La Revue Nouvelle*, 38 (August, 1963), pp. 129–33.

Guissard, Lucien. "Quelques représentants du nouveau roman" *(Le Renard et la boussole, Fable), La Croix* (Feb. 28, 1972).

Heissenbüttel, H. "Protokoll eines Verhors" *(L'Inquisitoire), Frankfurter Allemeine Zeitung* (Feb. 6, 1966).

Henkels, Robert, Jr. "Robert Pinget. The Quest of the Novelist," *Dissertation Abstract*, 30:1 (July, 1969). Doctoral thesis, Brown University, 1968.

―――. "French Voices, *Le Libera*," *Novel*, 3:1 (Fall, 1969/70), pp. 89–90.

―――. "*L'Inquisitoire*," *The French Review*, 45:3 (February, 1972), pp. 707–09.

―――. "The New Novel. Self Analysis," *(Passacaille) Novel*, 5:3 (Spring, 1972), pp. 274–77.

―――. *Fable*, *The French Review*, 46:1 (October, 1972), pp. 232–33.

―――. "The House Metaphor in *L'Inquisitoire*," *Critique*, 14:3 (1973), pp. 100–08.

―――. "Présentation de thèse: 'Robert Pinget, The Novel as Quest,' " *Présence Francophone*, 6 (Spring, 1973), pp. 170–71.

―――. "Graal Flibuste's Curious Voyage," *Studies in the Twentieth Century*, 13 (Spring, 1974), pp. 117–24.

―――. "Graal Flibuste de Pinget: le voyage parodique vers un nouveau roman," *Présence Francophone*, 7 (Fall, 1973), pp. 117–24.

―――. "Robert Pinget, 1919–" *Présence Francophone*, no. 13, Spring, 1977.

_____. *Cette Voix. The French Review*, 59:4, pp. 641–42.
Herisse, Marc. "Une réussite difficile à renouveler" (*About Mortin* on television). *France Soir* (June 11, 1970).
Hilsbecher, Walter. "Ein Schritt über den 'Nouveau roman' hinaus," *Merkur*, 20 (May, 1966), pp. 486–89.
Huddersfield, J. J. B. "Robert Pinget" *(Cette Voix), Notre Temps* (Mar. 17, 1975).
Jurt, Joseph. "Robert Pingets variationen" *(Passacaille), Civitas* (July, 1970), pp. 964–65.
Kanters, Robert. "Métamorphoses du roman judiciare," *Le Figaro Littéraire* (Oct.27, 1962), p. 2.
Kayser, Lucien. "Un Paquet de Pages en Vrac" *(Fable), La Lettre et l'Esprit* (April, 1975).
Kellman, Steven G. "*Quelqu'un* in Pinget's Fiction," *Mosaic*, 5:3 (Spring, 1972), pp. 137–44. Also in *New Reviews of the European Novel*, Ed. R. G. Collins & Kennith McRobbie. Winnipeg: University of Manitoba, 1972, pp. 137–44.
Kesting, M. "Im Sturzbach der Visionen, Pinget's *Passacaglia*," in her *Auf der Suche nach Realität, Kritiche Schrifter zur modernen Literatur*. München: Piper, 1972, pp. 137–41.
Knapp, Bettina L. "Robert Pinget, *Le Libera*," *Books Abroad*, 42 (October, 1968), pp. 548–49.
_____. "An interview with Robert Pinget," *The French Review*, 42:4 (March, 1969), pp. 548–54. Reprinted in *Off-Stage Voices*. Troy, N.Y.: Whitson, 1975, pp. 71–77.
_____. "*Identité* suivi d'*Abel et Bela*," *Books Abroad*, 46 (1972), pp. 438–39.
_____. "Robert Pinget, *Paralchimie*," *Books Abroad* (May, 1974).
_____. "The Parisian Theatrical Scene: 1973–74," *Drama and Theatre*, 12:1 (Fall, 1974), pp. 11–14.
_____. "Fable," *Books Abroad*, 46 (1972), p. 438.
Kuhn, Reinhard. "Robert Pinget, *Quelqu'un*," *Novel*, 1:1 (Fall, 1967), pp. 93–95.
Lanotte, Jacques. "*Clope au dossier*," *Présence Francophone*, 1 (Fall, 1970), pp. 210–18.
_____. "*Passacaille*," *Lavende Talen*, 275 (February, 1971), pp. 123–27.
_____. "Pour aborder *Le Libera*," *Ecritures* 68 (Liège: Cahiers du cercle interfaculaire, de littérature de l'Université de Liège), 1968, pp. 50–52.
_____. "*Fable*, récit," *Marche Romane*, 21:1-2 (1971), pp. 103–05.
La Rochefoucauld, J. D. "*L'Inquisitoire* de Robert Pinget," *Arts*, 882 (Sept. 19–25, 1962), p. 3.

Laws, Frederick. "Dirty work at the border," *The Daily Telegraph*, 34,914 (July 27, 1967), p. 21.
Lennon, Peter. "Robert Pinget," *The Guardian*, (Nov. 30, 1965), p. 9.
Lenoir, Jean-Pierre. "The Season in Paris," *International Theatre Annual*, 5 (1961), pp. 84–102.
Le Sage, Laurent. *The French New Novel: An Introduction and a Sampler*. University Park: The Pennsylvania State University Press, 1962.
Lieber, Jean-Claude. "Structure du récit dans *L'Inquisitoire*," *Poétique*, 14 (1973), pp. 250–60.
_____. "Lecture de *Quelqu'un*," *Littérature*, 10 (May, 1973), pp. 65–76.
Lindon, Jérôme. "Littérature dégagée," *New Morality*, 2:2-3, pp. 105–114.
Linze, Jacques-Gérard. "Lectures de vacances et notes sur l'état du roman," *Revue Générale: Arts, Lettres et Sciences Humaines*, 8–9 (September, 1974), pp. 29–43.
Livingston, Beverly. "The 'New' Novels of Robert Pinget (1951–1971): A Study in Theme and Technique." Doctoral dissertation, The University of Chicago, 1974.
Long, Gale Harold. "The Novels of Robert Pinget: The Impossible Quest for Truth and Meaning of Self, 1951–1969," *Dissertation Abstracts International*, 33:4 (October, 1972), 1734A.
Magny, Olivier de. Ed. *Graal Flibuste suivi de Robert Pinget ou le palimpseste*. Paris: Union Générale d'Editions, Le Monde en 10/18, 1963.
_____. "Le théâtre de Pinget," *Cahiers de la compagnie Madeleine Renaud, Jean-Louis Barrault* (February, 1966), pp. 49–54.
_____. "Pinget," *Esprit*, 26:2 (1958), pp. 47–49.
Mansuy, Michel, Ed. *Positions et oppositions sur le roman contemporain*. Paris: Klincksieck, 1971.
Marcel, G. "La Difficulté d'être," *Les Nouvelles Littéraires* (Apr. 7, 1960), p. 10.
Maria, Roger. "Robert Pinget, Plus loin que ce qui est écrit" (televised interview), *L'Humanité* (June 8, 1974).
Marisel, André. "Robert Pinget" *(Cette Voix)*, *Esprit* (April, 1975).
Martinoir, Francine de. "Pinget ou les chantiers de la Parole," *Sud*, 5–6 (1971), pp. 21–25.
Massé, Joseph. "Un écrivain" *(Fable)*, *Gazette Medicale de France*, 78:37, pp. 6,863–64.
Mauriac, Claude. "*L'Inquisitoire*, Robert Pinget," *Le Figaro* (Oct. 24, 1962).
_____. "Le Mirroir éclaté" *(Fable)*, *Le Figaro* (Oct. 15, 1971).
_____. "Pinget," chapter from *L'Allitérature contemporaine* (Paris: Albin-Michel, 1969), pp. 267–73.

_____. "Robert Pinget, les oiseaux-mouches et les hannetons," *Le Figaro* (Mar. 8, 1975).

Mercier, Vivian. "With a Cast of Hundreds" *(L'Inquisitoire), The New York Times Book Review* (Feb. 19, 1967), pp. 4, 49.

_____. "James Joyce and the French new novel," *Tri-Quarterly* (Winter, 1967), pp. 205–19.

_____. "The Building Material," in *The New French Novel from Queneau to Pinget*. New York: Farrar, Straus & Giroux, 1971, pp. 363–415.

_____. "Write or be written," *The Nation*, 215:18, (Dec. 4, 1972), pp. 563–65.

Merivale, Patricia. "Waiting for Death. The Dialogue of the King and the Fool in the Modern Drama," *Comparative Literature in Canada*, 3:1 (Spring, 1971), p. 8.

Meyer, Fernand. "Pinget, le livre disseminé comme fiction, narration et objet," dans *Le Nouveau Roman, Hier, aujourd'hui*. Colloque au centre culturel international de Cérisy-la-Salle. Paris: Union Générale des Editions, 1972, 2, pp. 299–310, with a discussion, pp. 325–50.

Micha, René. "Une forme ouverte du langage" *(L'Inquisitoire) Les Temps Modernes*, 201 (February, 1963), pp. 1,484–90.

Michaelis, Rolf. "Ein Leben in Frage und Antwort" *(L'Inquisitoire), Frankfurter Allegemeine Zeitung, Litteraturblatt* (Nov. 6, 1965).

_____. "Totengebete und anders Gebrabbel," *Frankfurter Allegemeine Zeitung, Litteraturblatt* (Nov. 7, 1970).

_____. "Jemand gesucht," *Frankfurter Allegemeine Zeitung, Litteraturblatt* (Nov. 18, 1967).

Michel, Marcelle. "Autour de Mortin" (television version), *Le Monde* (June 5, 1970).

Mignon, Paul-Louis. "Robert Pinget," *Avant-Scène*, 469–70, (Apr. 1–15, 1971), p. 68.

Montalbetti, Jean. "15 ans de nouveau roman-enquête," *Magazine Littéraire*, 6, pp. 4–9.

Morot-Sir, Edouard. "The New Novel from Queneau to Pinget," *Romanic Review*, 43, pp. 314–16.

Morrissette, Bruce. "Robert Pinget, *L'Inquisitoire*," *The French Review* (October, 1962), pp. 121–22.

Mourlet, M. "Enquête—fiction" (adaptation of *Autour de Mortin* for television), *Les Nouvelles Littéraires* (June 4, 1970).

Murch, Anne C. "Couples et reflets dans le théâtre de Pinget," *Revue Romane*, 5:2 (October, 1970), pp. 159–72.

Nightingale, Benedict. "Handcuffs and Flowers," *New Statesman*, 85:2,181 (Jan. 5, 1973), pp. 28–29.

Nores, Dominique. "Pinget à Strasbourg," *La Quinzaine Littéraire*, 166 (June 16-30, 1973), pp. 34-35.

———. "Pinget," *Les Lettres Nouvelles*, 8:4 (June, 1960), pp. 146-48.

Nye, Robert. "M. Pinget's magic roundabout," *The Guardian*, 37,644 (July 21, 1967), p. 5.

———. "Nets and socks," *The Guardian*, 37,519 (Feb. 24, 1967), p. 7.

O'Flahertly, Kathleen. *The Novel in France, 1945-65*. Cork: Cork University Press, 1973.

Ollier, Claude. "Robert Pinget: *Le Fiston, Lettre morte,*" *La Nouvelle Nouvelle Revue française*, 14 (September, 1959), pp. 532-34.

Ouellet, Real. "Robert Pinget" in his edition of *Les Critiques de Notre Temps et le Nouveau Roman*. Paris, Montréal: Garnier, 1972, p. 108.

Ormesson, Jean d'. "La difficulté d'écrire," *Les Nouvelles Littéraires*, 2,307 (Dec. 10-16, 1971), p. 8.

Oster, Daniel. "Depuis la mort d'Ulysse" *(Cette Voix)*, *Les Nouvelles Littéraires* (Mar. 17, 1975).

Pasche, Jean. "Les Mots sont aussi des demeures," *Journal de Lausanne* (Aug. 9, 1968).

———. "Cet amour des phrases" *(Passacaille)*, *Feuille de Lausanne* (Aug. 27, 1969).

Pechar, Jiri. Chapter on Pinget in *Francouzsky "novy roman."* Prague: Ceskoslovensky Spisovatel, 1968.

Perrone-Moises, Leyla. "Robert Pinget," in *O novo romance frances*. Sao Paulo: Bunti, 1966.

Perros, Georges. "Robert Pinget: *Le Fiston,*" *La Nouvelle Nouvelle Revue Française*, 77 (May, 1959), pp. 915-17.

———. "Robert Pinget. *Quelqu'un,*" in *Papiers Collés II*. Paris: Gallimard, 1973, pp. 296-303.

———. "Pinget ou le matériau," *Critique*, 225 (1966), pp. 150-54.

Petit, Jacques. "Romanciers contemporains" *(Le Libera)*, *Le Français dans le monde*, 64 (April-May, 1969), pp. 48-50.

Piatier, Jacqueline. "Les Prix littéraires" *(Quelqu'un)*, *Le Monde*, 6,494 (Nov. 30, 1965), p. 22.

———. "Le nouveau roman," *Tendances*, 48 (August, 1967), pp. 385-408.

———. "Une belle prouesse du nouveau roman" *(Passacaille)*, *Le Monde*, 1,083 (July 17-23, 1969), p. 11.

Pingaud, Bernard. "*Le Fiston,*" *Les Lettres Nouvelles*, 1 (Mar. 4, 1959), pp. 14-15.

Pingaud, R. "Robert Pinget," in *Ecrivains d'aujourd'hui* (1960), pp. 409-13.

Poirot-Delpech, Bertrand. "Auteurs nouveaux à la Comédie Française," *Le Monde*, 8,093 (Jan. 20, 1971), p. 21.
———. "Au Soir le Soir Théâtre 1960–1970." Paris: Mercure de France, 1969.
———. "Verbe sans sujet" *(Cette Voix)*, *Le Monde* (June 8, 1975).
Plessen, J. "Prix Femina, Robert Pinget, *Quelqu'un*," *Het Franse Boek*, 36 (1966), pp. 16–19.
———. "*Quelqu'un*," *Revue de L'Université de Laval* (Québec), (1965), pp. 714–16.
Pollman, Leo P. "Robert Pinget" in *Der neue Roman in Frankreich und Lateinamerika*. Stuttgart: W. Kohlhammer Verlag, 1968.
Pos, Sonja. "Franse prijzen voor Robert Pinget . . . ," *Litterair Paspoort*, 192 (January, 1966), pp. 2–6.
Poulet, Jacques. "Un exercise réussi" *(Identité)*, *L'Humanité* (Nov. 29, 1972).
Poulet, Robert. "Le Narrateur à la recherche d'une histoire" *(L'Inquisitoire)*, *Rivarol* (Dec. 13, 1962).
Prasteau, J. "Prix Femina . . . Pinget est tres gentil," *Le Figaro Littéraire*, 1,024 (Dec. 2, 1965), p. 3.
Prigogine, Hélène. "Pinget, *Quelqu'un* ou l'écriture comme déjection. *Autour de Mortin* ou la parole anthropophagique," *Synthèses*, 244 (September, 1966), pp. 229–33.
Rambures, Jean-Louis de. "Comment travaillent les écrivains: Robert Pinget," (Interview) *Le Monde des livres*, 8,677 (Dec. 7, 1972), p. 32.
Ramoni, James. "*Clope au dossier* par Robert Pinget," *Tribune de Genève* (Apr. 1, 1961).
Raymond, Jean. "De Robbe-Grillet à Pinget," *Cahiers du Sud*, 369 (January, 1963), pp. 290–93. Also in *La Littérature et le réel*. Paris: 1965, pp. 243–46.
———. "*Quelqu'un* par Robert Pinget," *Cahiers du Sud*, 386.
Rhode, Eric. "Wise Babe," *New Statesman*, 73:1,876 (Feb. 24, 1967), pp. 262–63.
Ricardou, Jean. "Nouveau roman, tel quel," *Poétique*, 4 (1970), pp. 433–54.
———. *Le Nouveau Roman*. Paris: Editions du Seuil, 1973.
Robbe-Grillet, Alain. "Un roman qui s'invente lui-même" *(Mahu ou le matériau)*, *Critique* (January, 1954), pp. 82–85.
———. *Pour un nouveau roman*. Paris: Editions de Minuit, 1963.
———. *For a New Novel. Essays on Fiction*. Translated by Richard Howard. New York: Grove Press, 1966.
———. *Snapshots and Towards a New Novel*. Translated by Barbara

Wright. London: Calder & Boyars, 1965.

Rollin, Dominique. "Un rire de deux cent cinquante pages" *(L'Inquisitoire)*, *Le Nouvel Observateur* (Nov. 21, 1965).

Rohde, Hedwig. "*Passacaglia*," *Neue deutsche Hefte*, 130 (1971), pp. 162–64.

Romi, Yvette. "Pourquoi écrivez-vous?" *Le Nouvel Observateur*, 56 (Dec. 8–14, 1965), pp. 40–44.

Rose, Marilyn Gaddis. "Robert Pinget's Agapa Land," *Forum*, 8:1 (Spring, 1970), 68–70.

──────. "Robert Pinget: *Le Libera*," *The French Review*, 44:1 (October, 1970), pp. 182–83.

Roudaut, Jean. "Robert Pinget et la boussole" *(Fable, Identité)*, *Critique*, no. 303/304 (August-September, 1972), pp. 729–51.

──────. "*Baga* Par Robert Pinget," *Le Magazine Littéraire* (May 5, 1975).

Roudiez, Léon. "Pinget," in *French Fiction Today*. New Brunswick: Rutgers University Press, 1972, pp. 183–05.

Rousset, Jean. "Trois romans de la mémoire," in *Les critiques de notre temps et le nouveau roman*. Montreal: Garnier, 1972, pp. 27–35.

──────. *Narcisse romancier. Essai sur la première personne dans le roman*. Paris: José Corti, 1973.

Rubinstein, Hilde. "Fotogramme von Verdammten," *Frankfurter Hefte*, 25 (1970), pp. 750–52.

Săbik, Vincent. "Svojbytńy gazyk nového románu," *Slovenské Polh'ady*, 82:9, pp. 99–113.

Sandberg, Herni. "Robert Pinget op zoek naar een toon," *Het Vaderland* (Sept. 29, 1973).

Sandier, Gilles. "Corneille architecte du sang," *Arts et Loisirs*, 25 (Mar. 16–22, 1966), p. 17.

Saurel, Renée. "La télévision, *Autour de Mortin*," *Les Lettres Françaises*, 1,339 (June 17–23, 1970), p. 23.

Sauvage, Léo. "La lettre de Pinget . . ." (review of New York production of *Lettre Morte*), *Le Figaro* (Apr. 22, 1970).

Schlocker, Georges. "Literary Harvest in France" (account of prize controversy over *L'Inquisitoire*), *Books Abroad* (Spring, 1963).

──────. "Eingefasst von einer zone des Schweigens" *(Passacaille)*, *Die Welt der Litterautur*, 7:5 (Mar. 5, 1970), p. 12.

──────. "Metaphysisches Puzzle," *National-Zeitung*, Nov. 2, 1969.

Schmidt, Albert-Marie. "Le Prix des Critiques à Robert Pinget," *Réforme* (June 22, 1963), p. 14.

Sénart, Phillippe. "Robert Pinget, *L'Inquisitoire, La Table Ronde*," (December, 1962), p. 119.

──────. "Une littérature de discorde," *La Revue de Paris*, 4 (April, 1966), pp. 107–12.

Serreau, Geneviève. "*Graal Flibuste* par Robert Pinget," *Les Lettres Nouvelles* (April, 1957), p. 606.
Seylaz, Jean-Luc. "Pinget tel qu'en lui-même," *Ecriture I, Cahier de la Renaissance Vaudoise,* 45 (Apr. 13, 1964), pp. 115–42.
Siclier, Jacques. "*Autour de Mortin*" (review of adaptation for French television), *Le Monde* (June 11, 1970).
Simon, Pierre-Henri. "Bilan de la saison," *Le Monde,* 6,513 (Dec. 22, 1965), pp. 12–13.
Simon, Roland H. "Le Rôle de l'écriture dans *La Chute* de Camus et *Quelqu'un* de Pinget," *French Review* (February, 1974), pp. 543–56.
S. J. "Essai théâtral; *Lettre morte,*" *Le Monde des Loisirs,* 7,254 (May 10, 1968), p. v.
Skilton, David. "French experimental novelists: Robert Pinget," *Cambridge,* 89a:2,158 (Nov. 18, 1967), pp. 116–19.
―――. "State of Mind" *(Baga), The Times Literary Supplement* (London), 3,413 (July 27, 1967), p. 658.
Spacagna, Jacques. "*Architruc* et *la Manivelle,* spectacle Robert Pinget," *Paris-Théâtre,* 187, pp. 61–63.
Steisel, Marie-Georgette. "Pinget's Method in *L'Inquisitoire,*" *Books Abroad* (Summer, 1966), pp. 267–71.
―――. "Fiche Documentaire III, *Lettre Morte,*" *Théâtre de Demain,* 11 (1960), p. 32.
Sturrock, John. "Grumblings from the Graveyard" *(Cette Voix) The Times Literary Supplement* (London) (May 2, 1975).
Symons, Julian. "Creatures of the machine," *The Sunday Times* (London) (July 23, 1967), p. 45.
Tavernier, René. "Prix Femina" *(Quelqu'un), Liberté,* 7 (1965), pp. 580–82.
Thibaudeau, Jean. "Un théâtre de romanciers" *(Lettre Morte), Critique,* 16 (September, 1960), pp. 686–92.
Thomas, Johannes. "Pinget," in the book *Franzosische Literatur der Gegenwart.* Stuttgart: Alfred Kroner Verlag, 1971.
Thompson, Michael M. "Distant Reflections. A study in Pinget's Fiction." *Dissertation Abstracts* 32, 1971–72, 460A, Thesis for State University of New York at Buffalo, 1970, 264 p.
Todd, Olivier. "French Stylist" (review of *Le Fiston*), *Time and Tide,* 42:39 (Sept. 28, 1961), p. 1, 612.
Toulson, Shirley. "No escape," *The New Statesman,* 84:2,163 (Sept. 1, 1972), p. 295.
Tremois, Claude-Marie. "La silhouette entrevue . . . est-ce celle de Mortin?" (interview), *Télérama* (June 6, 1970).
Updike, John. "Grove is my Press and Avant my Garde," *The New Yorker* (Nov. 4, 1967), pp. 223–38.

Varenne, Françoise. "Vers un théâtre auditif," *Le Figaro* (Dec. 26, 1970).

Verrier, Jean. "Le Récit réfléchi" *(Passacaille), Littérature*, 5 (February, 1972), pp. 58-62.

Viatte, Auguste. *"Quelqu'un," Revue de L'Université de Laval*, 20 (1965-66), pp. 714-16.

──────. "Autour des Prix littéraires en France," *Revue de l'Université Laval*, 20:8 (April, 1966), pp. 710-19.

Villelaur, Anne. "Être ou ne pas être quelqu'un" *(Quelun'un, Autour de Mortin), Les Lettres Françaises* (Nov. 25, 1965), p. 6.

──────. "La Mort à la basse" *(Le Libera), Les Lettres Françaises*, 1,285 (May 28-June 3, 1969), p. 6.

Villemier, Jean. "*Le Libera*," *Tribune de Genève* (Feb. 21, 1969).

──────. "*Fable*," *Tribune de Genève* (Oct. 20, 1971).

Vormweg, H. "Die unüberwindliche Grenze der Zeit" *(L'Inquisitoire), Die Welt* (Oct. 14, 1965).

Walzer, P. O. "Un Hélvète affranchi" *(Baga* and *Le Fiston), Le Journal de Genève* (June 7, 1959).

──────. "Le Nouveau Pinget" *(Clope au dossier), Le Journal de Genève* (Mar. 25, 1961).

──────. "Le Degré zéro de Clope," *(Ici et Ailleurs), Le Journal de Genève* (Dec. 2, 1961).

Weightman, John. "The Paris Literary Scene," *The Observer*, 9,106 (Jan. 16, 1966), p. 26.

──────. "Gallic Experiences," *The Observer*, 9,613 (Feb. 26, 1967), p. 26.

Weinstein, Arnold. "The New Novel; Analysed," *Novel*, 5:3 (Spring, 1972), pp. 272-74.

──────. *Vision and Response in Modern Fiction*. (Utica: Cornell University Press, 1974).

Werrie, Paul. "Ha muerto el Nouveau Roman," *Estafeta Literaria*, 481 (Dec. 1, 1971), pp. 4-6.

Wohmann, Gabielle. "Literarisches Hearing" *(L'Inquisitoire), Frankfurter Hefte*, 21 (1966), pp. 502-03.

Wordsworth, Christopher. "The Lonely Furrow," *The Guardian*, 37,395 (Sept. 30, 1966), p. 7.

Zand, Nicole. "Fiche documentaire, 3, 'Lettre Morte' de Robert Pinget," *Théâtre de Demain*, 11 (October-November, 1960), p. 32.

Zbinden, L-A, "Robert Pinget: 'Je n'ai pas de vie autre que celle d'écrire,' " *La Gazette de Lausanne* (Dec. 4, 1965).

Zeltner-Neukomm, Gerda. "Die eigenmächtige Sprache," *Olten* (1965), pp. 97-108.

BIBLIOGRAPHY

———. "Moderne Literatur—eine Provokation?" *(Le Libera), Sweizer Monatshefte*, 48:6 (September, 1968), pp. 616–25.

———. "Wirklichkeit unter verhöhten Kischees," *Neue Züricher Zeitung* (Jan. 28, 1968).

———. "Der Verlorene Tatbestand" *(Le Libera), Der Monat*, 235 (April, 1968), pp. 71–74.

———. "Pinget et le roman policier," *Marche Romane*, 21:1–2 (1971), pp. 97–101.

———. "Mechanic der Traume *(Passacaille), Frankfurter Hefte*, 27 (1972), pp. 58–59.

Zilliacus, Clas. "Scoring Twice: Pinget's *La Manivelle* and Beckett's *The Old Tune*," *Moderna Språk*, 1 (1974), pp. 1–10.

Zoest, A. J. A. Van. "Pinget" *(Passacaille), Het Franse Boek*, 40 (1970), pp. 160–62.

INDEX

Abel, 136–37
Abel and Bela, 123–24, 137–38
About Mortin, 132–33
Absalom, Absalom, 76
Agapa, 56–57
Al, 124
Alice in Wonderland, 15, 37
All Those Who Fall, 123, 212
Alternation, 133, 156–57, 182, 184–85, 187–88
Anamnesis, 187
André Breton, 246
Animal Crackers, 70
Annette, 94
Aquinas, Thomas, 140
Architruc, 1, 2, 57–62, 68, 72, 83, 107, 118, 129, 134
Architruc, 124, 129–30, 228–29
Around Mortin, 48, 133–37, 217, 229
Artaud, Antonin, 207
Attempt at Indirect Criticism, 192
Auden, W. H., 213
Automatic writing, 166, 207

Bach, J., 166
Baga, 1–2, 53–62, 68, 70, 73, 117, 118, 124, 129, 182, 226–29, 233
Baga, 1, 2, 53–62, 130, 233
Bald Soprano, The, 134
Ballaison, 102
Balzac, Honoré, 14, 53, 107, 229
Bann, Stephan, 6, 221, 247
Barthes, Roland, 196, 246
Baudelaire, Charles, 209
Beckett, Samuel, 2, 7, 79; phenomena in Watt (*Monsieur Levert*), 67, 79; comparison of *Molloy* and *Clope to the Dossier*, 96; translation of Pinget's *La Manivelle*, 124, 234–35; Lucky's monologue in *Waiting for Godot*, 131; shrinking settings in *Film*, 164; words as defense against death in *The Unnameable*, 170; in group photo, 192; interior monologues, 196; parallels to Pinget, 196, 246; compared to Pinget, 212–18; in contrast to Pinget, 215
Bela, 123, 136–37
Ben, 124
Benay, Jacques, 5, 229
Béranger the First, 55, 130
Bergerac, Cyrano de, 13
Bergman, Ingmar, 11
Berrill, N. J., 230
Between Fantoine and Agapa, 3, 4, 13–20, 27, 35, 110, 124, 200, 229–31
Bianle, 151
Bible, 229
Bille, M., 85
Bille, Mme., 86, 95
Birth, theme of, 29–30, 34–35
Bjurström, Carl, 108, 236
Blanchot, Maurice, 193, 245
Blanculz, S., 232
Blank page, theme of, 119, 221
Blanès, Father, 104
Blimbraz, 149, 151
Blue Flowers, The, 209
Blue Villa, The, 243
Bohr, Niels, 230
Bois-Suspect, Duchess of, 55, 101
Bonne-Mesure, Ariane de, 81
Bonne-Mesure, Francine de, 187
Book of the Future, The, 193, 245
Bosquet, Alain, 23, 231, 233
Bourdet, Denise, 107, 236
Bouville, 62
Bovary, Emma, 129
Boyer, Philippe, 6, 234–35, 236–37
Bray, Barbara, 228–29
Brée, Germaine, 98, 194, 235
Breton, André, 13, 172, 204, 205, 207
Brindon, 41, 49, 107
Brize, Guillaume, 88–89
Brize, Simone, 71, 85–87, 89–91, 94
Butor, Michel, 198

INDEX

Cadavre Exquis, Le, 207
Calder & Boyars, iv, 68
Calvin, John, 12
Camus, Albert, 3–4
Captain Spaulding, 70
Candide, 36, 233
Carroll, Lewis, 15, 36, 51, 230
Carrouges, Michel, 210, 246
Casse-Tonnelles, 148
Castle, The, 40
Catalogs, 27, 37, 51, 53, 71, 81, 104, 118, 208, 208–09, 215
Cayrol, Jean, 197
Centre National des Lettres, 5
Cervantes, 31, 34, 36
Chanchèze, valley of, 43
Chantre, 101
Characterization, 6, 22–23, 106, 145, 204, 211, 215
Characters: Abel, 136–37; Al, 124; Annette, 94; Architruc, 1, 2, 57–62, 68, 72, 83, 107, 118, 129, 134; Bega, 1, 2, 53–61, 130, 233; Ballaison, 102; Bela, 123, 136–37; Ben, 124; Béranger the First, 55, 130; Bianle, 151; Bille, M., 85; Bille, Mme., 86, 95; Blanculz, S., 232; Blanèz, Father, 104; Blimbraz, 149, 151; Bois-Suspect, Duchess of, 55, 101; Bonne-Mesure, Ariane de, 81; Bonne-Mesure, Francine de, 187; Bovary, Emma, 129; Brindon, 47, 49, 107; Brize, Guillaume, 88–89; Brize, Simone, 71, 85–87, 89–91, 94; Chantre, 101; Cheviot, Jacques, 91; Chinze, M., 33, 78, 107–08, 225; Chinze, Mme., 75, 76, 77, 85; Chinze, Marie, 70, 73, 74, 76–77, 80–82, 85, 108, 225; Chinze, Minet, 33, 75, 79, 81, 108; Chinze, Roger, 70, 79; Claire, 94; Clope, 84–97, 107, 117, 128–29, 201, 214; Clope, Mlle., 108, Clope's mother, 93–94; Clotho, 41, 46, 107; Corcoran, Captain, 116; Cruze, 107; Cruze, Mlle., 148, 152, 157–58; Cucumber, 18–19; Curate, 14, 79; Cyrille, 105; Dame Nature, 52; David, 31, 34, 36; doctor, 134–36; Don Quixote, 31, 229; Dothiot, Anne, 95; Ducreux, children, 146–50; Ducreux, M., 51, 146–50; Erard, 139; Estragon, 182; Father Blanès, 104; Flan, Mme., 128–29; Fonfon, 113, 116; Francine, 71, 187; Françoise, 67; George, 70, 76, 79, 81; Graal Flibuste, 36, 30, 42–43, 47, 47–48, 215; Hem, Princess of, 55, 101; Humpty Dumpty, 15; Joan of Arc, 33; Jones, Tom, 46; Kiki, 85, 87, 93; King Gnar, 59; La Fleur, 51; Latirail, 22–33, 107; Lebru, Toinette, 82; Leon, 73, 75, 76, 80, 81, 88, 94, 187, 194; Levert, Gilbert, 72, 74, 76, 79, 80, 82, 125, 126, 201, 202, 209; Levert, M., 5, 69–83, 88, 94, 107, 118, 125, 127, 129, 187, 194, 215; Levert, Mme., 80, 82, 108, 118; Lorpailleur, Mlle., 24–25, 33–34, 107, 144, 146–50, 174, 177, 181; Louis, 80; Lucile, 141; Lucky, 79, 182; Mahood, 212; Mahu, 25–29, 32, 35, 107, 118, 164, 200–01, 204, 212; Mangogul, 55; Marie, 61; Martha, 79; Mathias, 202–03, 206; Maurice, 88–89; Miaille, 101, 173–86, 225; Miette, 101, 173–86; Minette, 102, 173–86; Molloy, 214–15; Monneau, Mme., 90, 152–53, 158; Mortin, Alexandre, 85, 87, 94, 107, 111, 130, 132, 135–36, 144–45, 160, 189, 201; Mortin, Mme., 90, 94; Moule Brothers, Pierre and Guillaume, 71, 85, 87, 90, 107; Naomi, 134–36; Narre, Sophie, 33, 75, 76, 82, 107, 211; Notorious Cucumber, 18–19; Novocardians, 56; Odette, 70, 79; Oedipus, 70; organist, 52; Pacot, Alice, 70, 75, 79; Pacot, Mme., 70, 75; Panza, Sancho, 31, 34, 41; Petite, Fiente, 21, 32; Phillipard, 85, 87, 107; Pierre, M., 104, 105, 109, 129; Pisson, Germaine, 88; Pommard, Judge, 85, 86, 88, 94; Pommard, Mme., 85; Porridge, J. T., 29–35, 72, 118, 201, 203; Potter, Rodolphe, 81; Pozzo, 182; Pushmi-Pullyu, 53; Queen Conegrund, 60, 233; Rara, 60; Reber, Mme., 112, 116; Renard, 31, 34; Revel, Jacques, 198; Roquentin, 19; Rousseau, Mme., 67; R. P., 61; Sampeek, W. H., 232; Serinet, 154; Sheherazade, 133; Simon, Juan, 21, 32, 40; Sinture, 21, 24, 72; Siso,

Characters (*cont'd*)
225; Sister Louise, 60–61; Songe, M., 51, 224–25; Sosie, 225; Toupin, M., 86, 88–89, 91, 94–95, 107; Ubu, 56, 130; Uncle Alfred, 140; Verveine, 86–87, 107, 146–50; Vladamir, 182; Voiret, 151; Wallas, 198, 202; wandering Jew, 30–31, woodcutter, 71, 80, 82
Charterhouse of Parma, The, 104
Château de Broy, the, 100–02, 201, 205
Chateaubriand, René, 188, 245
Chatruse, 148
Chemin des Dames, Le, 160
"Chercheurs de Poux, Les," 23
Cheviot, Jacques, 91
Chinze, M., 33, 78, 107, 108, 225
Chinze, Marie, 70, 73, 74, 76–77, 80–82, 85, 108, 225
Chinze, Minet, 73, 75, 79, 81, 108
Chinze, Mme., 75–77, 85
Chinze, Roger, 70, 79
Christ, Jesus, 174, 175, 187, 189
Christie, Agatha, 70, 197
Chronicle, definition of, 238
Chronology, 30
Churchill, Winston, 55
Claire, 94
Clope, 84–97, 107, 117, 128–29, 201, 214
Clope, Mme., 93–94, 108, 214
Clope, Mlle., 108
Clope to the Dossier, 68–69, 84–97, 98, 100, 107–10, 118, 124–27, 132, 198, 203, 209, 228–29, 234
Clotho, 41, 46, 107
Clown, theme of, 1, 55, 58, 61, 233
Coach house, 74
Cocteau, Jean, 172
Coe, Richard, 227, 233
Combray, 67
Comédie, Française, La, 124
Comédie Humaine, La, 107, 229
Conflicting hypotheses, 54, 57, 69, 80, 82, 93, 105, 118, 127, 130, 196, 201, 208, 215
Conjunctions, use of, 155, 157, 163, 184, 188
Copeau, Jacques, 227
Corcoran, Captain, 116
Corneille, Pierre, 126
Counterfeitters, The, 27, 41, 45

Crachon, 101, 107
Crazy Notion, 225
Critique, 108
Cruze, 197
Cruze, Mlle., 148, 152, 157–58
Cucumber, 18–19
Curate, 14, 79
Cycles of Pinget's Work, 7
Cyrille, 105

Dada, 205, 210
Dali, Salvador, 205
Dame Nature, 52
David, 31, 34, 36
Dead Letter, 124, 126–27, 228
De Bergerac, Cyrano, 13
De Magny Olivier, 6, 21, 44
Descartes, René, 67, 83, 172, 196, 197, 239
Death, theme of, 45, 69, 81, 82, 102, 111, 130, 133, 143, 163–64, 170–71, 174, 186, 189, 224, 234–35
Dialogue, 16, 99, 126–27, 136
Dictation, 224
Diderot, Denis, 55, 98
Discourse on Method, 67, 239
Dispossessed king, theme of, 1–2, 54–55, 57, 61, 130, 133, 172, 232
Doctor Dolittle, 53
Doctor, 134–36
Don Quixote, 31, 41, 44, 216, 229
Dort, Bernard, 196, 231
Dos Passos, John, 24
Dothiot, Anne, 95
Douves, 107
Dreyfus Affair, 160
Drunkard, theme of, 28–40, 75, 77
Duchamp, Marcel, "*objets trouvés*," 207
Ducreaux affair, 146–50
Ducreaux, children, 146–50
Ducreaux, M., 51, 146–50
Duvert, Tony, 6, 12; on mystery within mystery in *The Inquisitory*, 102; on speech and the novel, 143; on use of first person in *The Libera Me Domine*, 145–46; analysis of opening pages of *The Libera Me Domine*, 153–57, 159; general comment, 222, 230, 236, 238

Eaton, Sydney L., iv
Easter, 174

Eden, 175
Editions de Minuit, Les, iv, 4, 107, 225–29, 231
Editions de Feu, Les, 3
Egea, Esteban, iv, 180
Einstein, Albert, 13, 219
Elliptical development, 35, 85, 117, 187
Elsewhere, 38
Emory University, iv
Erard, 139
Erasers, The, 198, 200, 208
Estragon, 182
Existentialism, 11

Fable, iv, 172–86, 180, 224, 227–29, 234, 243
Fantastic voyage, 13
Fantoine and Agapa, 2, 32, 35–36, 38, 40, 53, 68–69, 83, 99, 125, 187, 189, 201, 207, 211–12
Father Blanès, 104
Faulkner, William, 53, 76
Federman, Raymond, 213, 236
Fellini, Frederico, 11
Fémina Prize, 200
Fielding, Henry, 36, 38
Film, 164
Film, Pinget's use of, 130
First person, use of, 30, 32, 144–46, 154, 174, 217
First Surrealist Manifesto, 204
Fisson, Pierre, 229
Flan, Mme., 128–29
Flaubert, Gustave, 24
Flora and Fauna, 38, 43–44, 47
Fonfon, 113, 116
For a New Novel, 193, 200, 245
For Samuel Beckett, 246
Ford Foundation, The, 5
Fournier, Alain, 36
Fox and the Compass, The, 1, 3, 4, 27–35, 68, 72, 84, 107, 124, 229, 231
Francine, 71, 187
Françoise, 67
Frost, Robert, 169
Furet woods, 71

Gallimard, 4, 200, 231
Garden, theme of, 222–24
Genesis, Book of, 51, 54
George, 70, 76, 79, 81

Gide, André, 22; writer theme, 22–23; story within a story, 27; mock voyage, 36; "Paysage moralisé" in *The Immoralist*, 41; novel within the novel, 45; fantastic voyage, 52; distinction between *"récit"* and novel, 228
Giraudoux, Jean, 37
Good Friday, 173
Graal Flibuste, 4, 36–53, 54, 59, 61–62, 68, 70, 72, 77, 100, 110, 112, 118, 124, 131, 200, 201, 204, 214, 227, 229, 231, 233
Graal Flibuste, 36, 40, 42–43, 47–48, 56, 215
Grail quest, 36–37
Grégoire, Adolphe, 237
Grenier, Roger, 233
Grove Press, iv

Haifa, 31
Happy Days, 131
Hem, Princess of, 55, 101
Here and There, 124, 127, 129
History of Surrealism, 205
Holy Communion, 173
Horizon, theme of, 50, 53, 117, 201, 232
Hottencourt, 151
House Beautiful, 219
House of fiction image, 196, 219
Howard, Richard, 193, 228, 233
Humpty Dumpty, 15
Hypothesis, The, 4, 48, 94, 124, 130–31, 162, 228

Ida's Mishaps, 232
Identity, 124, 133–36, 229
Immoralist, The, 41, 227
Impromptu of Versailles, The, 137
Indiscreet Jewels, The, 55
In The Labyrinth, 201–02
Inquisitory, The, 5, 64, 68, 98–110, 113, 124, 174, 203, 208–09, 220, 222, 227–29
Ionesco, Eugene, 33, 55, 123, 130, 134
Israel, 30–32

Jacob, Max, 61, 205, 222, 246
James, Henry, 219–20
Janvier, Ludovic, 119, 237, 246
Jarry, Alfred, 233
Jealousy, 201–02

Joan of Arc, 33
Jones, Tom, 46
Joubert, 193
Journal, theme of, 14, 27, 29, 32–33, 40, 42, 43, 45, 48, 50, 52, 58, 60, 129
Journey, 53, 54
Journey to Chaos, 213, 246
Joyce, James, 36, 200
"Jumblies, The," 232–33

Kafka, Franz, 40, 59
Keystone Cops, the, 69
Kiki, 85, 87, 93
King Gnar, 59
King is Dying, The, 130
King of Boetia, The, 61, 205, 246
King, theme of, 1–2, 54–55, 61
Kinkade, Richard P., iv
Kubrick, Stanley, 212
Kuhn, Reinhard, iv, 5, 228

Laffont, 231
La Fleur, 41
La Maison de Rendez-Vous, 201
Landon, Jerôme, iv
Last Year at Marienbad, 202
Las Vergnas, Raymond, 235
Latin, 140
Latirail, 22–33, 107
Lear, Edward, 51, 232–33
Lebru, Toinette, 82
Le Fiston, 68
L'Ecartée, 234–37
Legend, 244–45
Leon, 73, 75, 76, 80, 81, 88, 94, 187, 194
"Les Roches," 74
Lesson, The, 123
Letter, theme of, 21, 40–41, 48, 58, 69, 72–73, 75, 83, 90, 94, 100, 126–27, 187
Levert, Gilbert, 72, 74, 76, 79, 80, 82, 125, 126, 201, 202, 209
Levert, M., 5, 69–83, 88, 94, 107, 118, 125, 127, 129, 187, 194, 215
Levert, Mme., 80, 82, 108, 118
L'Hypothèse, 4
Libera Me Domine, The, 125, 135, 145–60, 160–71, 176, 184, 207, 212–14, 222; preface to, 166–67
Lieber, Claude, 6, 98, 237
L'illusion Comique, 126

Lindon, Jerôme, iv, 4, 11, 99, 192, 200
Linear progression, 11, 21, 31, 42, 46, 54, 133, 188, 197, 200, 207
Literary Youth of André Malraux, The, 232
Lorpailleur, Mlle., 22–25, 33–35, 107, 144, 146–50, 174, 177, 181
Lost notes, theme of, 110, 112, 115, 198
Louis, 80
Louis Lambert, 229
Lucile, 141
Lucky, 79, 182

McLuhan, Marshall, 11, 219
Magny, Olivier de, 6, 37, 44, 62, 100, 110, 227, 231, 233, 236
Mahood, 212
Mahu, 21–29, 32, 35, 107, 118, 164, 200–01, 204, 212
Mahu or the Material, 4, 21–28, 35, 40, 71–72, 83, 118, 124, 133, 182, 200, 202, 212–13, 227–28, 231
Maigret Gets Angry, 67–68
Malapropisms, 94, 109
Mallarmé, Stephan, 45
Malloy, 213–14
Malone, 213, 215
Malraux, André, 45
Man Who Got Away, The, 189, 225
Mangogul, 55
Man's Emerging Mind, 12, 230
Marie, 61
Martha, 79
Martin, Claude, 228
Marx, Groucho, 70
Matnias, 202–03, 206
Maupassant, Guy de, 188, 245
Mauriac, Claude, 192
Maurice, 88, 89
Meditations, 36
Melville, Herman, 42
Memoirs, theme of, 54, 56, 58, 62, 68
Miaille, 101, 173–86, 225
Michaux, Henri, 38, 211
Miette, 101, 173–86
Minette, 102, 173–86
Minuit, 224
Mock mystery story, 68, 76, 83, 97, 99, 106, 109, 111, 115, 117, 129, 130–31
Molière, play within a play in *L'Impromptu de Versailles*, 137
Molloy, 214–15

INDEX

Molloy, 96, 215, 235
Monneau, Mme., 90, 152–53, 158
Monologue, 16, 25, 28, 31, 48, 76, 111, 115, 117, 129, 133, 143, 215, 225, 239
Monsieur Levert, 48, 69–84, 85, 90, 92, 96, 107–09, 124–25, 125–27, 160–61, 182, 196, 198, 200, 209, 218, 228–29
Month of August, The, 224
Montaigne, Michel de, 52
Montesquieu voyage, 36
Morrissette, Bruce, 199, 201, 246
Mortin, Alexandre, 85, 87, 94, 107, 111, 130, 132, 135–36, 144–50, 160, 189, 201
Mortin, Mme., 90, 94
Moule Brothers, 71, 85, 87, 90, 107
Moule, Guillaume, 71
Moule, Pierre, 71, 85, 87, 90, 107
Muddled history, theme of, 159–60
Murch, Anne, 237
Murphy, 217
Mystery story, 68–69; see Mock mystery story
Nadeau, Maurice, 205
Naming as controlling, theme of, 51
Naomi, 134–46
Narcissus, 175, 186
Narrative Techniques: Alternation, (Identity), 133; (The Libera Me Domine), 156–57; (Fable), 182, 184–85; (This Voice), 187–88; Catalogs, (Mahu or the Material), 27; (Graal Flibuste), 37, 51, 53; (Monsieur Levert), 71, 81; (The Inquisitory), 104, 208–09; (Someone), 118; general use of, 208; Characterization, 6; in Mahu or the Material, 22–23; (The Inquisitory), 106, 204, 211, 215; through tone, 145, 204; through language, 211–15; Chronology, (The Fox and the Compass), 30; Conflicting hypothesis, (Baga), 54, 57; (Monsieur Levert), 69, 80, 82; (Clope to the Dossier), 93; (The Inquisitory), 105; (Someone), 118; (The Hypothesis), 130; (Dead Letter), 127; (Paralchemy), in early works generally, 196, 201; general use of, 208; compared to Beckett's monologues, 201, 215; Conjunction, use of, (The Libera Me Domine), 155; (Recurring Melody), 157, 163; (Fable), 184; (This Voice), 188; Dialogue, (Between Fantoine and Agapa), 16; (The Inquisitory), 99; (Someone), 112; (Dead Letter), 126–27; (Identity), 136; Elliptical development, (The Fox and the Compass), 35; (Clope to the Dossier), 85; (Someone), 117; (This Voice), 187; First person, use of, (The Fox and the Compass), 30, 32; (The Libera Me Domine), 144–46, 154; (Fable), 174; general, 217; Journey, centrifugal, (Graal Flibuste), 53; (Baga), 54; Journey, centripital, (Graal Flibuste), 53; (Baga), 54; Linear progression, (Between Fantoine and Agapa), 11; (Mahu or the Material), 21; (The Fox and the Compass), 31; (Graal Flibuste), 42, 46; (Baga), 54; Pinget's theatre, 133; (This Voice), 188; in mystery story, 197; parodied in The Erasers, 200, 207; Malapropisms, (Clope to the Dossier), 94; (The Inquisitory), 109; Mock mystery story, (Monsieur Levert), 68, 76, 83; (Clope to the Dossier), 97; (The Inquisitory), 99, 106, 109; (The Hypothesis), 130–31; (Someone), 111, 115, 117; (Here and There), 129; Monologue, (Between Fantoine and Agapa), 16; (Mahu or the Material), 25, 28; (The Fox and the Compass), 31; (Graal Flibuste), 48; (Monsieur Levert), 76; (Someone), 111, 115, 117; (Theatre), 133; (The Hypothesis), 133; (Here and There), 129; (The Libera Me Domine), 143; (Recurring Melody), 215; (The Month of August), 225; (Paralchemy), 239; Page numbering, (Monsieur Levert), 69; Parody, (Mahu or the Material), 28; (The Fox and the Compass), 35; (Graal Flibuste), 41, 43–45; (Baga), 55; (Monsieur Levert), 68; (Clope to the Dossier), 97, 99; (The Inquisitory), 106; (Around Mortin), 131; general use of, 204; of nineteenth century novel, 209, 217; Play within a play, (Dead Letter), 127; Punctuation, (Mahu or the Material), 28, (Clope to the Dossier), 93, 96; (Recurring Melody), 162–63; Repetition, (Clope to the Dossier), 94; (The Inquisi-

Narrative Techniques *(cont'd)*
tory), 110; *(Dead Letter)*, 126; *(Identity)*, 133; *(The Libera Me Domine)*, 153, 156; *(Fable)*, 173, 176, 179-80, 182, 184-85; *(This Voice)*, 187-88; *(Recurring Melody)*, 218, 235, 238; and alternation in *Fable*, 240-45; Sound association, general use, 6, 208, 210-11; *(Between Fantoine and Agapa)*, 14, 16, 18-19; *(Mahu or the Material)*, 23; *(The Fox and the Compass)*, 32; *(Graal Flibuste)*, 51-52; *(Monsieur Levert)*, 69, 74, 78, 80; *(Clope to the Dossier)*, 94, 96; *(The Inquisitory)*, 109; *(The Hypothesis)*, 131; *(Identity)*, 136; *(Fable)*, 181, 186; and surrealism, 207; compared to Beckett's use of, 215; Space, treatment of, *(Recurring Melody)*, 165; expressionistic landscapes in Beckett and Pinget, 215; Tense shifts, *(Monsieur Levert)*, 69; *(Clope to the Dossier)*, 93; *(Recurring Melody)*, 162, 169; *(Fable)*, 182, 184-86; Time, treatment of, *(Recurring Melody)*, 164; Tone, shifts of, *(The Libera Me Domine)*, 170; *(Recurring Melody)*, 217; Two part structure, *(Between Fantoine and Agapa)*, 13; *(Mahu or the Material)*, 21, 25-27; *(Fable)*, 182, 184; *(This Voice)*, 186; Word order, *(Fable)*, 177, 179; Wordplay, *(Between Fantoine and Agapa)*, 13-14; *(Mahu or the Material)*, 25; *(Graal Flibuste)*, 43, 48, 51; *(Baga)*, 58, 62; *(Monsieur Levert)*, 69, 83; *(Clope to the Dossier)*, 86, 94-96; *(Someone)*, 116; *(The Hypothesis)*, 131; *(Identity)*, 136; *(This Voice)*, 187; in conjunction with translations of Pinget into English, 230, 233
Narre, Sophie, 33, 75, 76, 82, 107, 211
Nausea, 19
New novel group, 192, 199, 200, 204
Night, 124
No Answer, 124, 227, 233
Notorious Cucumber, 18-19
Novels of Robbe-Grillet, The, 201
Novocardians, The, 56
Novocardian War, The, 56, 58

Odette, 70, 79
Oedipus, 70

Old and the New, The, 44, 216, 232
Old Testament, 29
Organist, 52

Panza, Sancho, 31, 34, 41
Paralchemy, 124-25, 138-42, 162, 172, 229
Parody, 7, 13, 19, 21, 28, 35, 97, 99, 106, 131, 204, 209, 217
Passing Time, 199
Paternity, theme of, 59, 73, 78, 129, 187, 200
Pauvert, Jean-Jacques, 232
Pétain, Marshal, 160
Petite Fiente, 21, 32
Peyrou, Georges, 224
Phillipard, 85, 87, 107
Pierre and Jean, 245
Pierre, M., 104, 105, 109, 129
Pingaud, Bernard, 73, 96, 215, 235, 246
Pinget, Robert: additions and deletions to work, 231-32; Antipreface, vii; autocritical comments, 15; *(Recurring Melody)*, 163, 166, 167; *(Identity)*, 197; *(This Voice)*, 218; biographical data, 3-4; difficulties of translating, 234-35; division of work into cycles, 7, 229, 237; early critical reaction to, 5, 216-17; editions of works, 230-31; English translations cited, 228-29; film, use of, 130; interior decorating, 3; Lecture: "The Mechanism of Literacy Creation," 246-47; literary prizes won, 5, 235, 237; mock chronicle, 238; projected film project, 211; theatre: Radio plays, 123-42; *About Mortin*, 132-33; *Dead Letter*, 125-27; *Architruc*, 129-30; *The Old Tune*, 127-29; *Abel and Bela*, 137-38, *The Hypothesis*, 130-31; *Paralchemy*, 138-42; *Here and There*, 127-29; *Identity*, 133-37; *The Man Who Got Away, Night*, 138; *Dictation*, 224; *The Old Tune*, 234-35; *The Month of August*, 224-25; titles, ironic use of, 237; translations, 230, 236; translations in English, 227-28. *See also* Characters; Narrative Techniques; Themes.
Pisson, Germaine, 88
Plato, 207
Play within a play, 127

INDEX

Plèiade, La, 195
Plessen, J., 237
Plumber, the, 140
Pommard, Judge, 85, 86, 88, 94
Pommard, Mme., 85
Porridge, J. T., 29–35, 72, 118, 201, 203
Portrait of a Lady, 219
Postman, Neil, 11
Potter, Rodolphe, 81
Pouillon, Jean, 198, 246
Pozzo, 182
Princess of Hem, 55, 101
Prix des Critiques, 5
Prix Fémina, 5
Procès verbal, theme of, 96, 99, 105
Project for a Revolution in New York, 243
Prometheus, 175
Proust, Marcel, 67, 116
Proust's Binoculars, 240
Psalms, the, 31
Punctuation, 28, 93, 96, 162–63
Pushmi-Pullyu, 43

Queen Conegrund, 60, 233
Queneau, Raymond, 209, 222
Quest, theme of, 2, 6–7, 20, 31–35, 45–47, 62, 111, 115, 124, 184, 188, 198, 200, 204, 213, 215, 218, 225

Rabelais, François, 12, 19, 42, 56
Rameau's Nephew, 98
Rara, 60
Raymond, Jean, 99, 235
Reber, Mme., 112, 116
"*Récit*," 228
Recurring Melody, 125, 129, 135, 144–60, 176, 201, 213–14, 218, 222, 229
Red Dust Press, iv, 228
Renard, 31, 34
Repetition, 94, 110, 126, 133, 153, 156, 173, 176, 179–80, 182, 184–85, 187–88, 218, 235, 238, 240–45
Reprieve, The, 230
Resnais, Alain, 11
Revel, Jacques, 198
Rimbaud, Arthur, 23
Robbe-Grillet, Alain, 4, 7; review of *Mahu or the Material*, 22–23, 231; search for new forms, 194; characterization, 196–97; detective theme, use of, 198; and Pinget, 198, 200–01;
preoccupation with visual perception of, 211; restoring cuts to *Graal Flibuste*, 231; repetition and alternation in *The Blue Villa*, 242–43
Robert, Marthe, 44, 216, 232, 246
Rollin, Dominique, 114, 237
Roquentin, 19
Rorschach Test, 202
Roudaut, Jean, 76, 82–83, 94, 184, 186, 229–30, 234–35, 237, 243
Roudiez, Léon, 106, 236, 238
Rousseau, Jean-Jacques, 225
Rousseau, Mme., 67
R. P., 61

Sampeek, W. H., 232
Sarraute, Nathalie, 192, 196
Sartre, Jean-Paul, 11, 12, 19, 62, 230
Saul-David story, 31
Schlocker, Georges, 235
Schmidt, Albert-Marie, 100
School of the ear, 203, 211
School of the eye, 203, 209, 210–211
Second Manifesto of Surrealism, 172
Sentimental Journey, A, 36
Seraphitus-Seraphita, 229
Serinet, 154
Série Noire, La, 197
Seylaz, Jean-Luc, 6, 196, 246
Shattuck, Roger, 205, 240, 246
Sheherazade, 133
Sheridan-Smith, Alan, 227–28
Simenon, Georges, 68–69
Simon, Claude, 196
Simon, Juan, 21, 32, 40
Simulacrum, The, 166
Sinture, 21, 24, 72
Sirancy, 74, 107, 148, 165, 225
Siso, 225
Sister Louise, 60–61
Someone, 5, 73, 106, 111–19, 125, 129, 133, 177, 198, 200, 207, 210, 213–14, 221–22, 225, 227–29
Songe, M., 51, 224–25
Sosie, 225
Sound association: general use of, 6, 208, 210, 211; *Between Fantoine and Agapa*, 14, 16, 18–19; *Mahu or the Material*, 23; *The Fox and the Compass*, 32; *Graal Flibuste*, 51–52; *Monsieur Levert*, 69, 74, 78, 80; *Clope to the Dossier*, 94, 96;

Sound association (cont'd)
  The Inquisitory, 109; *The Hypothesis,* 131; *Identity,* 136; *Abel and Bela,* 123–24, 137–38; *Fable,* 181–82, 184–86; associated with surrealism, 207; compared to Beckett's use of, 215
Space, treatment of, 165, 215
Spoken language, 13, 18, 143, 165
Squibb, F. P., iv
Stations of the cross, 173
Sterne, Laurence, 36
Stendhal, 104, 193
Stevenson, J., 227
Storytelling, theme of, 25, 33–35, 46, 215, 218, 245
Straight Is The Gate, 227
Surrealism, 12
Surrealist Revolution, The, 207
Suzanne and the Pacific, 37
Swift, Jonathan, 36

Tarot cards, 128
Teaching as a Subversive Activity, 11
Television, theme of, 112, 116
Temple to Graal Flibuste, 40
Tense changes, 69, 93, 162, 169, 182–86
Texts and Stories for Nothing, 215–17, 246
Themes: Birth, *(Baga),* 1; *(Mahu or the Material),* 1, 29–30, 34–35; Blank page, *(Someone),* 119, 221; Clown, *(Baga),* 1, 55, 58, 61, 233; Death, *(Graal Flibuste),* 45, 69; *(Monsieur Levert),* 81–82; *(Clope to the Dossier),* 102; *(The Inquisitory),* 102; *(Someone),* 111; *(Architruc),* 130; (Pinget's theatre), 133; *(The Libera Me Domine),* 143; *(Recurring Melody),* 163–64, 170–71; *(Fable),* 174; *(This Voice),* 186, 189; *(Dictation),* 224, 234–35; Dispossessed king, *(Baga),* 1–2, 54–55, 57, 61, 130, 133, 172, 232; Drunkard, *(Graal Flibuste),* 38–40; *(Monsieur Levert),* 75, 77; Garden, *(The Month of August),* 223–34; Horizon, *(Graal Flibuste),* 50, 53; *(Someone),* 117; *(Monsieur Levert),* 201, 232; Journal, *(Between Fantoine and Agapa),* 14, 27; *(Mahu or the Material),* 27, 29; *(The Fox and the Compass),* 32–33; *(Graal Flibuste),* 40, 42–43, 45, 48, 50; *(Baga),* 52, 58, 60; *(Here and There),* 129; King, *(Baga),* 1–2, 54–55, 57, 61; Letter, *(Mahu or the Material),* 21; *(Graal Flibuste),* 40–41, 48; *(Baga),* 58; *(Monsieur Levert),* 69, 72–73, 75, 83; *(Clope to the Dossier),* 90, 94; *(The Inquisitory),* 100; *(Dead Letter),* 126–27; *(This Voice),* 187; Lost notes, *(Someone),* 110, 112, 115, 198; Memoirs, *(Baga),* 54, 56, 58, 62; Muddled history, *(The Libere Me Domine),* 159–60; Naming as controlling, *(Graal Flibuste),* 51; Paternity, *(Baga),* 59, 73, 129; *(Monsieur Levert),* 78; *(Architruc),* 129; *(This Voice),* 187, 200; *(Dead Letter),* 200; Procès verbal, *(Clope to the Dossier),* 96; *(The Inquisitory),* 99, 105; Quest, (general use of), 2, 6–7, 198, 200, 204, 213; *(Between Fantoine and Agapa),* 20; *(The Fox and the Compass),* 31–35; *(Graal Flibuste),* 45–47; *(Baga),* 62; *(Someone),* 111, 115; (theatre), 124; *(Fable),* 184; *(This Voice),* 188; (in Beckett), 215, 218; (breakdown of locomotion, Beckett), 215; *(The Month of August),* 225; Storytelling, *(Mahu or the Material),* 25; *(The Fox and the Compass),* 33–35; *(Graal Flibuste),* 46; (compared to Beckett), 215; (general use of), 218, 245; Television, *(Someone),* 112, 116; Verbal madness, *(Graal Flibuste),* 16, 48, 112; *(Around Mortin),* 137, (general use of), 207; Voyage, *(The Fox and the Compass),* 30–32, 35; *(Graal Flibuste),* 35–53; *(Baga),* 53–54; *(Monsieur Levert),* 68; *(Someone),* 119; *(Here and There),* 128; (in Beckett), 215; Writing, *(Mahu or the Material),* 22–23, 27–32, 34–35; *(Baga),* 59; *(Monsieur Levert),* 81
Thibaudeau, Jean, 125
This Voice, 186–90, 222, 224, 229
Through the Looking Glass, 231
Time, treatment of, 164
Todd, Olivier, 212, 246
Tone, changes in, 170, 217
Toupin, 86, 88, 89, 91, 94, 95, 107
Tour de Feu, La, 230
Touraine, 165
Translations of Pinget, 4–5

INDEX

Travel literature, 31, 36, 40, 42–43
Travel Far, 226
Tréteau de Paris, Le, 124
Two part structure, 13–14, 21, 25–27, 182, 184, 186

Ubu, 56, 130
Uncle Alfred, 140
Unnameable, The, 170, 212, 215, 246
Unien's Voyage, 52

Verbal madness, theme of, 16, 48, 112, 131, 207
Veriville, 107
Verveine, 86–87, 107, 146–50
Vladamir, 182
Voiret, 151
Voltaire, 36
Voyage, theme of, 30–32, 35, 35–53, 53–54, 68, 119, 128, 215
Voyeur, The, 198, 200, 202, 206

Waiting for Godot, 131, 182
Wallas, 198, 202
Wandering Jew, 30–31
Watson, Donald, 228–29
Watt, 67, 186
Watt, 186
Weingartner, Charles, 11
Woodcutter, 71, 80, 82
Word order, 177, 179
Wordplay, 13–14, 25, 43, 48, 51, 58, 62, 69, 83, 86, 94–96, 116, 131, 136, 187, 230, 233
Wright, Barbara, 146, 228–29
Writing, polysemous, 12, 16
Writing, theme of, 22–23, 27–32, 34–35, 59, 81

843
P65h   331539

```
843                    331539
P65h                      8.95
Henkels
Robert Pinget.

    MAY 20 82           H11344
    DEC 26 84           H19204
    DEC 26 84           H19204
```

Johnson Free Public Library
Hackensack, New Jersey